A QUICK OVERVIEW OF THE SIGNIFICANT RULE AND GAME CHANGES IN THE 2021–2024 RACING RULES OF SAILING

BY DAVE PERRY

The following is a list of the significant changes in the 2021–2024 edition of The Racing Rules of Sailing (RRS). *These are changes from the 2017–2020 edition. NOTE: These brief summaries are not intended to be actual representations of the rules; nor is this a complete list of all the changes in the 2021–2024 RRS.*

- **Hails** The Introduction of the RRS now states that a language other than English may be used for a hail required by the rules provided that it is reasonable for it to be understood by all boats affected; however, a hail in English is always acceptable.

- **Definition Finish** The new definition Finish has eliminated the "crew or equipment in normal position" factor. Now a boat "finishes" when any part of its hull crosses the finishing line, regardless of when its crew, sails or other equipment crosses the line. Bowsprits and other pieces of equipment attached to the hull are not part of the hull. This will make it simpler for race committees to call close finishes, and anticipates the future use of electronic equipment placed on the bow of boats to assist race committees in calling starting and finishing lines, etc.

- **Definition Mark-Room** The new definition Mark-Room has some new phrases (shown below in quotation marks) but there is no change in meaning to the previous definition. Mark-room is room to round "or pass" the mark "without touching the mark." The phrase "sail the course" is now in italics because the phrase is a new definition, but it essentially means the same as the previous phrase.

- **Definition Obstruction** The new definition Obstruction permits the race committee to designate an object that is otherwise too small to be an obstruction as an "obstruction," and a "line" such as a start/finish line as an "obstruction" in the sailing instructions.

- **Definition Party** When the protest committee calls a hearing under rule 60.3(b) (Right to Protest; Right to Request Redress or Rule 69 Action) to consider redress for a boat, the new definition Party makes that boat a party. And the new definition adds these people and boats to the definition: a support person subject to a hearing under rule 69 (Misconduct), any boat that person supports, and a person appointed to present an allegation under rule 60.3(d) (see rule 63.9, Hearings under Rule 60.3(d) — Support Persons).

- **Definition Rule** The new definition Rule (b) simply states that World Sailing Regulations are "rules" only if they have been designated by World Sailing as having the status of a rule and are published on the World Sailing website. New rule 6.1 (World Sailing Regulations) lists the Regulations that are "rules" as of June 30, 2020.

- **Definition Sail the Course** This new definition Sail the Course is simply the language from previous rule 28.2 (formerly titled Sailing the Course). The intent is to provide one clear meaning of the phrase "sail the course" which appears many times throughout the RRS.

- **Definition Start** The new definition Start has eliminated the "crew or equipment" factor. Now a boat need only have its hull behind the starting line at the starting signal; the location of its crew, sails or other equipment is immaterial. This will make it simpler for race committees to call close starts, and anticipates the future use of electronic equipment placed on the bow of boats to assist race committees in calling starting and finishing lines, etc.

- **Basic Principles** In the previous rules, the Basic Principle: Sportsmanship and the Rules, stated that a fundamental principle of sportsmanship was that when a boat broke a rule it would promptly take a penalty, even if the boat was certain it would be exonerated (not penalized) because it was compelled to break a rule by another boat breaking a rule. That unintended anomaly has been corrected with two changes in the new rules. New rule 43 (Exoneration) now automatically exonerates boats that are entitled to exoneration at the time of the incident. And the new statement on sportsmanship in the Basic Principle: Sportsmanship and the Rules, about taking a penalty now excludes boats that are exonerated.

- **Rule 1.1 (Safety: Helping Those in Danger)** now includes "support persons," meaning that parents, coaches and other support persons are required to give all possible help to any person or vessel in danger; and they, and possibly even the boats they are supporting, can be penalized for failing to do so.

- **Rule 2 (Fair Sailing)** has been changed back to what it said prior to the previous rule book, which is that the only penalty for breaking rule 2 is a disqualification that is not excludable (DNE).

- **Rules 3 (Decision to Race) and 4 (Acceptance of the Rules)** have simply been reversed in order from the previous rule book because the decision to race will come before needing to accept the rules.

- **Rule 5 (Rules Governing Organizing Authorities and Officials)** is previous rule 84 (formerly titled Governing Rules). It was moved into Part 1, Fundamental Rules, because it is just as fundamental that race officials be governed by the rules as it is for the competitors (see rule 4, Acceptance of the Rules). Note that the term "event" is used in place of the term "race" in rule 5, as well as in several other places throughout the RRS, because many rules apply before and after boats are racing, including on shore.

- **Rule 6 (World Sailing Regulations)** is a combination of previous rules 5, 6 and 7. New rule 6 lists the World Sailing Regulations (or Codes) that are "rules" (see the definition Rule (b)). The text of the Regulations can be found on the World Sailing website. Note that the term "sailor classification" from the previous Regulations has been changed to "sailor categorization" to avoid confusion with the other uses of the term "classification" in the sport.

- **Part 2 preamble** In the new rules, it is the notice of race (NoR), not the sailing instructions (SI's), that is required to state if the rules of Part 2 (When Boats Meet) are replaced by the right-of-way rules of the International Regulations for Preventing Collisions at Sea (IRPCAS) or by governmental right-of-way rules. See also rule J1.2(12).

- **Rule 14 (Avoiding Contact)** The exoneration part of rule 14 (previous rule 14(b)) has been moved to new rule 43.1(c) (Exoneration). In the previous rule, in addition to a right-of-way boat, a boat entitled to room or mark-room was entitled to exoneration if the contact did not cause damage or injury. In the new rule, that boat is now exonerated only if she is actually sailing within the room or mark-room to which she is entitled.

- **Rule 16.2 (Changing Course)** There are several significant changes to rule 16.2, which is often referred to as the "anti-hunting" rule. First, it now only applies when boats are on a "beat to windward." Therefore, it does not apply before the starting signal (same as the previous rule); and it does not apply when the boats are sailing on downwind legs (different from the previous rule). Also, the rule only applies when the starboard-tack boat (S) bears away; it no longer applies when S luffs (rule 16.1 applies when S changes course to windward; i.e., luffs). And finally, the rule applies when the port-tack boat (P) is sailing to pass "to leeward" of S (the previous rule said pass "astern"), meaning that S can no longer turn this rule off by bearing away below 90 degrees to the true wind (a common move in team racing).

- **Rule 18.1 (Mark-Room) and rule 18.2(d) (Giving Mark-Room)** Previous rule 18.2(d) stated that rules 18.2(b) and 18.2(c) no longer applied when the boat entitled to mark-room had been given mark-room. That created a small unintended loophole by leaving rule 18.2(a) still in effect, meaning that a boat clear astern could become overlapped and entitled to mark-room if the boat that had been entitled to mark-room had completed her rounding but was still near the mark. That loophole has been closed by moving the phrase to a new sentence in rule 18.1 which turns all of rule 18 off when mark-room has been given.

- **Rule 18.3 (Passing Head to Wind in the Zone)** The only change to rule 18.3 is its title, which now more accurately describes when rule 18.3 applies. There is no change in meaning in the rule.

- **Rule 19.2(c) (Giving Room at an Obstruction)** The new rule 19.2(c) is now just one sentence, clarifying that the last phrase "while the boats remain overlapped" only applies while the boats are passing the continuing obstruction (no change in meaning from the previous rule).

- **Rule 20.4 (Room to Tack at an Obstruction: Additional Requirements for Hails)** New rule 20.4(a) states: "*When conditions are such that a hail may not be heard, the boat shall also make a signal that clearly indicates her need for room to tack or her response.*" This is a safety rule for when it is hard to hear hails (such as in strong winds or fast boats that are farther apart). Additional signals will commonly include arm signals, but could also include the use of lights or radios. Note that the notice of race (NoR) can specify an alternative form of communication other than a hail and require boats to use it (see new rule 20.4(b) and rule J1.2(8)).

- **Section D (Other Rules)** Previous rule 21 (Exoneration) has been moved to new rule 43 (Exoneration) in Part 4 (Other Requirements When Racing), and Section D rules have been renumbered accordingly.

- **Rule 21.1 (Starting Errors; Taking Penalties; Backing a Sail)** Now a boat sailing towards the pre-start side of the starting line to start or comply with rule 30.1 (Starting Penalties: I Flag Rule) need only keep-clear of other boats not doing so until her hull is completely on the pre-start side of the line (not her crew, sails or other equipment). This conforms the rule to the new definitions Finish and Start, which are now based on just the hull and not the crew, sails and other equipment of the boat.
- **Rule 25 (Notice of Race, Sailing Instructions and Signals)** There is a significant shift in the importance of the notice of race (NoR) in the new rules. The NoR contains rules that a boat must comply with before the event, rules that would help competitors decide whether to attend the event, and information that they will need before the sailing instructions become available. However, there was no rule in the previous RRS that stated by when the NoR had to be made available. New rule 25 states: "*The notice of race shall be made available to each boat that enters an event before she enters.*" And US Sailing adds this prescription to rule 25: "*US Sailing prescribes that the race committee shall ensure that the notice of race and sailing instructions are readily available to competitors throughout the event.*" This will include posting the documents throughout the event on the official notice board and on any online document sources for the event.

  Note that rule 25 and many other new rules now use the term "event" which includes a race or a series of races (see the preamble to Appendix J, Notice of Race and Sailing Instructions). Furthermore, the preamble to Appendix J states: "*A rule in the notice of race need not be repeated in the sailing instructions.*" Therefore, it is now even more critical that competitors read and hang onto the NoR as well as the sailing instructions for an event.
- **Rule 26 (Starting Races)** Now the notice of race (NoR) or the sailing instructions (SI's) can change the timing of the Warning signal.
- **Rule 28 (Sailing the Race)** The first sentence of new rule 28.1 states the three elements of sailing a race: "*A boat shall **start**, **sail the course** and then **finish**.*" The previous title of rule 28 was "Sailing the Course;" the new title includes all three elements. The addition of the term "then" clarifies that boats must do the elements in the order listed. Under new rule A5.1 (Scores Determined by the Race Committee), the race committee can essentially disqualify a boat without a hearing for not sailing the course (see the new "NSC" in rule A10). Deleted from new rule 28.1 is reference to "the course described in the sailing instructions" because there are times the course is not described in the sailing instructions (see rule 27.1, Other Race Committee Actions Before the Starting Signal). The "string rule" in previous rule 28.2 is now the new definition Sail the Course.
- **Rule 29.1 (Individual Recalls) and Rule 30 (Starting Penalties)** To conform to the new definition Start, for the purposes of rules 30.1 (I Flag Rule), 30.2 (Z flag Rule), 30.3 (U Flag Rule) and 30.4 (Black Flag Rule), a boat is on the course side of the starting line (OCS) or in the triangle formed by the ends of the starting line and the first mark if any part of her hull is across the starting line (her crew, sails and other equipment is immaterial).

SIGNIFICANT CHANGES TO THE RULES 5

- **Rule 32 (Shortening or Abandoning After the Start) and rule 35 (Race Time Limit and Scores)** adds the term" race" before "time limit" to clarify the rule is referring to the race time limit.

- **Rule 33 (Changing the Next Leg of the Course) and rule 34 (Mark Missing)** adds the phrase "while boats are racing" to clarify the race committee must make the required actions only when acting while boats are racing.

- **Rule 37 (Search and Rescue Instructions)** New rule 37 states: "*When the race committee displays flag V with one sound, all boats and official and support vessels shall, if possible, monitor the race committee communication channel for search and rescue instructions.*" Flag V has been added to Race Signals.

- **Part 4 (Other Requirements When Racing)** This section has been reorganized into two distinct sections: Section A, General Requirements (rules 40–47), and Section B, Equipment-Related Requirements (rule 48 – 55), with an attempt to consolidate all the racing rules pertaining to a boat's equipment in Section B.

- **Rule 40 (Personal Flotation Devices)** New rule 40 has been significantly reorganized, with some minor changes in its meaning. Note that rule 40.1, which, when in effect, requires each competitor to wear a personal flotation device (PFD), can be put in effect by the notice of race or the sailing instructions. And if flag Y is displayed ashore, it must be accompanied by a sound signal (see rule 40.2(b)).

- **The previous US Sailing prescription to rule 40** requiring every boat to carry life-saving equipment conforming to government regulations that apply in the racing area while racing has been deleted. That does not change any legal requirement a boat may have under laws that pertain in the sailing area. It just means that boats cannot be penalized under the racing rules for the failure to do so. US Sailing continues to support compliance with the applicable laws, including laws on carrying required life-saving equipment, adding this statement to the beginning of the US Sailing edition of the rule book: "*As the national authority for the sport, US Sailing is committed to promoting compliance with applicable government regulations regarding life-saving equipment.*"

The racing rule which creates the standard for the PFDs that boats are required to carry onboard is rule 1.2 (Life-Saving Equipment and Personal Flotation Devices) which states: "*A boat shall carry adequate life-saving equipment for all persons on board, including one item ready for immediate use, unless her class rules make some other provision.*" If a boat is protested, it is up to the protest committee to determine whether its life-saving equipment is "adequate." It is generally accepted that approximately 50 Newtons of floating capability is "adequate." Boats carrying "life-saving equipment" that is clearly not adequate, with no other adequate device onboard, are breaking rule 1.2 and can be penalized.

Note that a class, or the notice of race or sailing instructions for an event, can require competitors to wear U.S. Coast Guard Approved lifejackets (PFDs) as US Sailing does for its championships. See rule J2.2(5) (Notice of Race and Sailing Instructions).

- **Rule 41 (Outside Help)** Rule 41(a) permits a boat to receive help for a crew member who is ill, injured or in danger (which can include being in the water). The previous rule 41 said that if a boat gained a significant advantage from help received under rule 41(a) it could be protested and penalized. This has been deleted in new rule 41 to remove any motivation for competitors not to avail themselves of help when they are in danger.

- **Rule 42.3(c) (Propulsion: Exceptions)** Rule 42.3(c) contains some new exceptions for when boats can pump. Boats may now pump on a beat to windward if they are able to surf down the front of a wave (for instance a large powerboat wake moving to windward), and they may pump as much as they like to initiate foiling (lifting up on hydrofoils).

- **Rule 43 (Exoneration)** "Exoneration" means "freed from penalty." Several rules in the previous rule book contained exoneration provisions (specifically rule 14(b) involving contact, rule 21 involving room and mark-room, and rule 64.1(a) involving being compelled to break a rule). Those rules have now been consolidated into the new rule 43. In the previous rules, the protest committee "exonerated" boats as part of its decision. New rule 43 exonerates boats entitled to exoneration at the time of the incident, and says they cannot be penalized. This works with the new Basic Principle: Sportsmanship and the Rules, which says that boats which have broken a rule do not need to take a penalty if they are exonerated. Note that if a boat is protested, the protest committee will decide if the boat is indeed entitled to exoneration or not based on the facts it finds. Rule 43 has been added to rule 86.1(a) (Changes to the Racing Rules) meaning that the notice of race and the sailing instructions cannot change rule 43.

- **Rule 44.1 (Penalties at the Time of an Incident: Taking a Penalty)** now allows for the notice of race or the sailing instructions to specify the use of the Scoring Penalty (rule 44.3, Scoring Penalty) or some other penalty.

- **Rule 44.2 (One-Turn and Two-Turns Penalties)** In order to finish after completing a penalty turn, a boat need only have her hull on the course side of the finishing line (her crew, sails and other equipment is immaterial).

- **Rule 47 (Trash Disposal)** "Support persons" have been added to rule 47 (previously rule 55), clarifying that the term "participants" in the Basic Principle: Environmental Responsibility, includes support people. This means that support people (parents, coaches, etc.) who intentionally put trash in the water, and the boat(s) they are supporting, can be penalized (see rule 64.5, Decisions Concerning Support Persons). Rule 47 has been added to rule 86.1(a) (Changes to the Racing Rules) meaning that the notice of race and the sailing instructions cannot change rule 47.

- **Rule 48.2 (Limitations on Equipment and Crew)** Rule 48.2 (previously rule 47.2) now clarifies that if a boat is capsized and drifts towards the next mark or across the finishing line without all the sailors on board or in contact with the boat, that is OK. Furthermore, when the crew begins sailing the boat again, anyone in the water simply needs to be in physical contact with the boat, not onboard.

- **Rule 49.2 (Crew Position; Lifelines)** The phrase "on the deck" has been removed from this rule. The reasons include: (1) it is not unusual for crew sitting on the rail to be supported only at their upper legs when hiking facing outboard, (2) the term "sitting on the deck" was unclear regarding which part of the competitor's body needs to be in contact, and (3) it is often difficult to define where the sheerline and hull becomes the deck.

- **Rule 50.1 (Competitor Clothing and Equipment)** Under rule 50.1(b) (previously rule 43.1(b)) it is the class rules or the notice of race (not the sailing instructions) that can specify a lower or higher weight limit for competitor clothing and equipment. Rule 50.1(c) is a rule regarding quick releases for trapeze harnesses which goes into effect January 1, 2023.

- **Rule 55.3 (Setting and Sheeting Sails: Sheeting Sails)** is previous rule 50.3. There is no change in meaning. Note that rule 55.3(a) says that a headsail clew can be "connected" to a whisker pole. "Connected" is a new definition in *The Equipment Rules of Sailing* (C.6.3, Boat Control Definitions) which means: "*to bring together or into contact so that a real link is established by which one item affects the function of the other.*" Therefore, as in the previous rule, the headsail may be sheeted at its clew to a pole, provided a spinnaker is not set.

- **Part 5 (Protests, Redress, Hearings, Misconduct and Appeals)** The previous standard protest form has been replaced with two forms: a hearing request form and a hearing decision form.

- **Rule 60 (Right to Protest; Right to Request Redress or Rule 69 Action)** now clarifies that a boat, or the race or technical committee, can give a report alleging inappropriate behavior by a support person to the protest committee requesting its action under rule 60.3(d) or by any person requesting action under rule 69.2(b) regarding misconduct. Rule 60.4(a) now only requires the technical committee to protest if it decides that a boat or personal equipment does not comply with the class rules or with rule 50 (Competitor Clothing and Equipment).

- **Rule 61.1 (Protest Requirements: Informing the Protestee)** The phrases "intending to protest" and "that she was involved in or saw" have been removed from rule 61.1(a). There is no change in meaning. If a boat wants to protest, it must inform the other boat of its intention at the first reasonable opportunity; and if the incident occurred in the racing area, it shall hail "Protest," and fly a flag if required. Note that a boat can protest an alleged breach of a rule of Part 2 (When Boats Meet) or rule 31 (Touching a Mark) only if it was involved in or saw the incident (see rule 60.1(a), Right to Protest; Right to Request Redress or Rule 69 Action).

- **Rule 61.1(a)(4)**, which says that a boat does not need to hail or fly a protest flag when it is obvious there has been injury or serious damage, now only applies when it is obvious to the protesting boat at the time of the incident.

- **Rule 61.1(b)**, regarding protests by the race, protest or technical committees, clarifies that a notice posted on the official notice board within the appropriate time limit satisfies the rule's notification requirement.

- **Rule 62 (Redress)** Rule 62.1(b) has been changed so that now, in order to be entitled to redress based on injury or physical damage caused by another boat that was racing, the offending boat needs to have taken a penalty or be penalized by the protest committee first. This will require boats to protest in order to become entitled to redress under rule 62.1(b) if the offending boat does not take a penalty.

  Rule 62.1(d) has added "support persons" to the list of offenders that may entitle a boat to redress.

  Rule 62.2(a) now states that on the last scheduled day of racing a request for redress based on a protest committee decision shall be delivered no later than 30 minutes after the decision was posted.

- **Rule 63.6 (Taking Evidence and Finding Facts)** Rule 63.6(a) now requires protest committees to take "hearsay evidence." "Hearsay evidence" is the testimony or information of a person not present at the hearing, presented to the protest committee by another person. "Hearsay evidence" includes oral reports, written statements and photographic evidence. Reasons for this change include (a) protest committees often do not know the evidence is "hearsay" until after they have heard it, (b) often "hearsay evidence" can be useful, such as a list of mark roundings from a member of the race committee, and (c) often it is impractical to bring the videographer into the hearing. Rule 63.6(a) now also gives the protest committee the right to exclude evidence which it considers to be irrelevant or unduly repetitive.

  Rule 63.6(c) still gives each party the right to question any person giving evidence. In the case of "hearsay evidence," the person "giving" the evidence includes the originator of the evidence (the person who wrote the written testimony or told the party their account of the incident). The protest committee must protect the party's right by allowing the party to call the person giving the evidence as a witness, and to reconvene or reopen the hearing if needed.

  New rule 63.6(d) states that the protest committee must consider the credibility of any evidence and assign "weight" to it before deciding the facts and making its decision. The World Sailing *Judges Manual* advises that hearsay evidence of the description of a racing incident should be given little or no weight.

  Finally, Appendix M, which is advisory, contains one bullet point that likely should have been deleted. It is in rule M3.2, bullet 9, which advises the protest committee to not accept written evidence from a witness who is not available to be questioned unless all the parties agree. This of course would violate the protest committee's obligation to accept all the parties' evidence in rule 63.6(a), so should be ignored.

- **Rule 63.9 (Hearings under Rule 60.3(d) — Support Persons)** provides the due process rules for hearings involving support people.

- **Rule 64.1 (Decisions: Standard of Proof, Majority Decisions and Reclassifying Requests)** provides a basic standard of proof for protest committees. It says "*A protest committee shall make its decision based on a balance of probabilities, unless provided for otherwise in the rule alleged to have been broken.*" The rule goes on to state some other procedural actions for protest committees.

SIGNIFICANT CHANGES TO THE RULES 9

- **Rule 64.5 (Decisions Concerning Support Persons)** clarifies that a support person or a boat that person supports can only be penalized if they are a party to a hearing held under rule 60.3(d) (Right to Protest; Right to Request Redress or Rule 69 Action) or rule 69 (Misconduct).

- **Rule 64.6 (Discretionary Penalties)** New rule 64.6 states *"When a boat reports within the protest time limit that she has broken a rule subject to a discretionary penalty, the protest committee shall decide the appropriate penalty after taking evidence from the boat and any witnesses it decides are appropriate."*

- **Rule 66.3 (Reopening a Hearing)** This new rule requires the protest committee to at least consider all requests it receives from parties to reopen a hearing (note, rule 66.2 permits parties to make written requests within the time limit in rule 66.2); and to add at least one new member, if practicable, when it is considering a request to reopen a hearing based on a claim that the protest committee made a significant error.

- **Rule 69.1(b)(2) (Misconduct: Obligation not to Commit Misconduct: Resolution)** "Misconduct" is now conduct that may bring, or has brought, the sport into disrepute.

- **Rule 70 (Appeals and Requests to a National Authority)** Rule 70.3 now states: *"However, if boats will pass through the waters of more than one national authority while racing, an appeal or request shall be sent to the national authority where the finishing line is located, unless the sailing instructions identify another national authority."* Rule 70.5 now provides that the notice of race or (not "and") the sailing instructions can state that an appeal is denied (provided it meets the criteria in the rule).

- **Rule 78.2 (Compliance with Class Rules: Certificates)** Rule 78.2 now reinserts the deadline for complying with rule 78.2 which was inadvertently omitted in the 2017-2020 RRS.

- **Rule 87 (Changes to Class Rules)** has been changed such that now only the notice of race (not the sailing instructions) may change a class rule (see rule J1.2(3)).

- **Rule 88.1 (National Prescriptions: Prescriptions that Apply)** If boats will pass through the waters of more than one national authority while racing, rule 88.1 has been changed such that now the notice of race (not the sailing instructions) must identify the prescriptions that will apply and when they will apply.

- **Rule 90.3 (Race Committee; Sailing Instructions; Scoring: Scoring)** New rule 90.3(e) allows the notice of race to put a time limit on making changes to race or series results, including the correction of errors; and it provides a default time limit of 24 hours after the protest time limit for the last race, being informed of the protest committee decision after the last race, or the results are published. This allows race organizers to state an "end" to the event. The rule of course makes an exception to certain scoring change actions such as appeals and rule 69 hearings, etc.

- **Appendix A5 (Scores Determined by the Race Committee)** Rule A5.1 now requires the race committee to basically disqualify boats without a hearing that do not sail the course correctly (score them "NSC", meaning "Did not sail the course"; see rule A10, Scoring Abbreviations). In the previous rules, the race committee was required to protest boats that failed to sail the course correctly. Under the new rules, boats scored NSC will have to request redress under rule 62.1(a) (Redress) if they dispute the race committee's judgment.

  Note, new rule A5.3, about alternative scoring for boats that come to the starting line but do not start, etc., or do not come to the starting line at all, is previous rule A9, and it now requires the notice of race or sailing instructions to put it into effect.

- **Appendix J (Notice of Race and Sailing Instructions)** The new rules remove all requirements that a rule included in the notice of race (NoR) be repeated in the sailing instructions, and require the NoR to contain rules a reasonable competitor would want to know when deciding whether to enter an event or when preparing for the event in the weeks before the event begins. Note, the preamble to Appendix J states: "*A rule in the notice of race need not be repeated in the sailing instructions.*" And rule J2.1 (Sailing Instruction Contents) states: "*Unless included in the notice of race, the sailing instructions shall include the following…*". This significantly increases the importance of the NoR, and competitors are well advised to not only read the NoR carefully, but have a copy available to them at the event (see the changes to rule 25 discussed above).

- **Notice of Race and Sailing Instructions Guides (formerly Appendices K and L)** These guides, which were formerly Appendix K and Appendix L, have been removed from the RRS. They are available, in various formats, at the World Sailing website at sailing.org/racingrules/documents.

- **Race Signals** A new flag V has been added to Race Signals. It means "monitor communication channel for safety instructions" (see rule 37, Search and Rescue Instructions). Race Signals now includes an orange and a blue flag. The staff displaying the orange flag is one end of the starting line, and the staff displaying the blue flag is one end of the finishing line (see Appendix S, Standard Sailing Instructions, rules S9.2, The Start, and S11.1, The Finish). New to Race Signals is this statement: "*When a visual signal is displayed over a class flag, fleet flag, event flag or race area flag, the signal applies only to that class, fleet, event or race area.*"

DAVE PERRY

Understanding the Racing Rules of Sailing
through 2024

Illustrations by Brad Dellenbaugh

TENTH EDITION

AN OVERVIEW OF THE RULES...

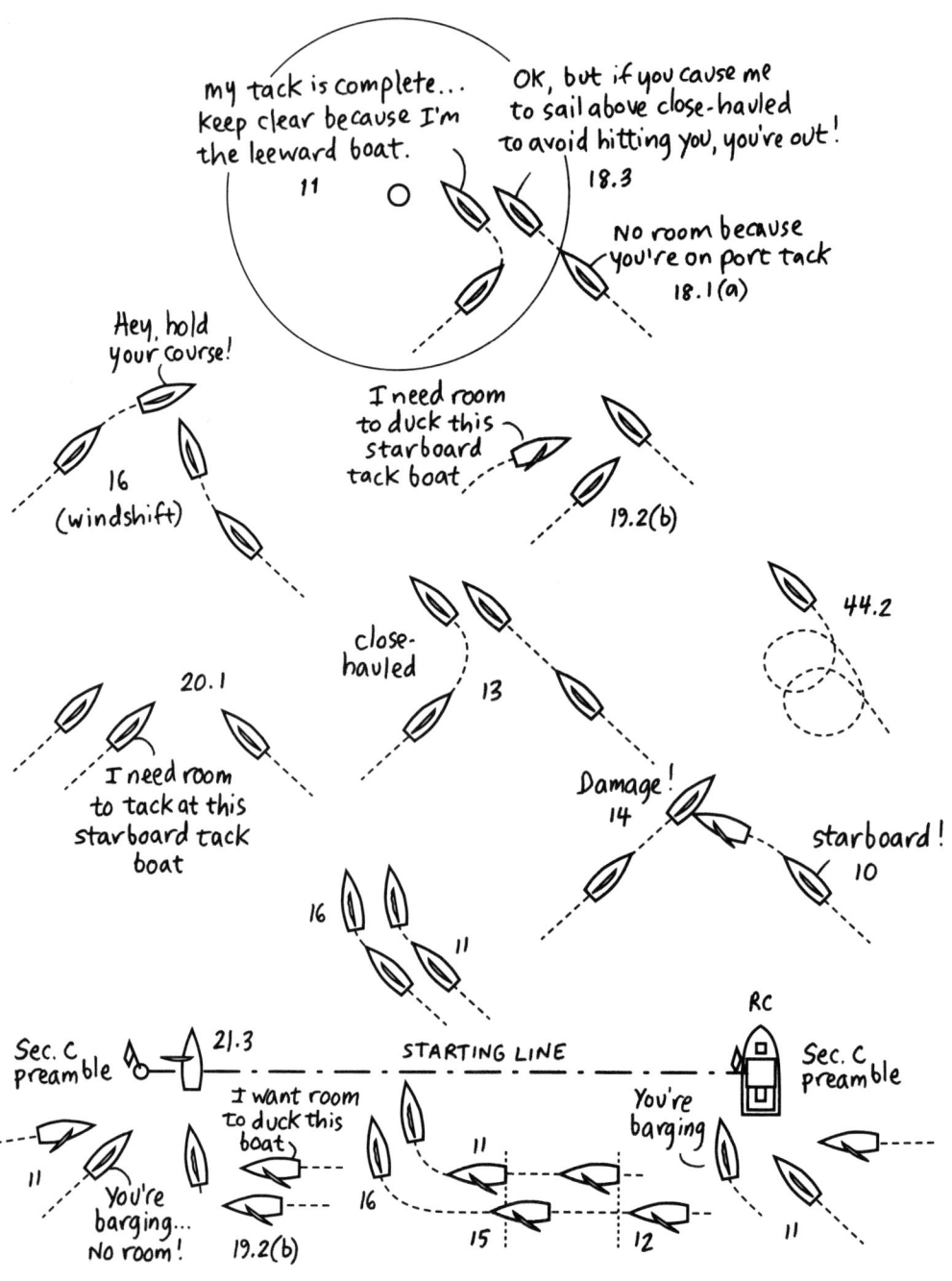

...FROM START TO FINISH

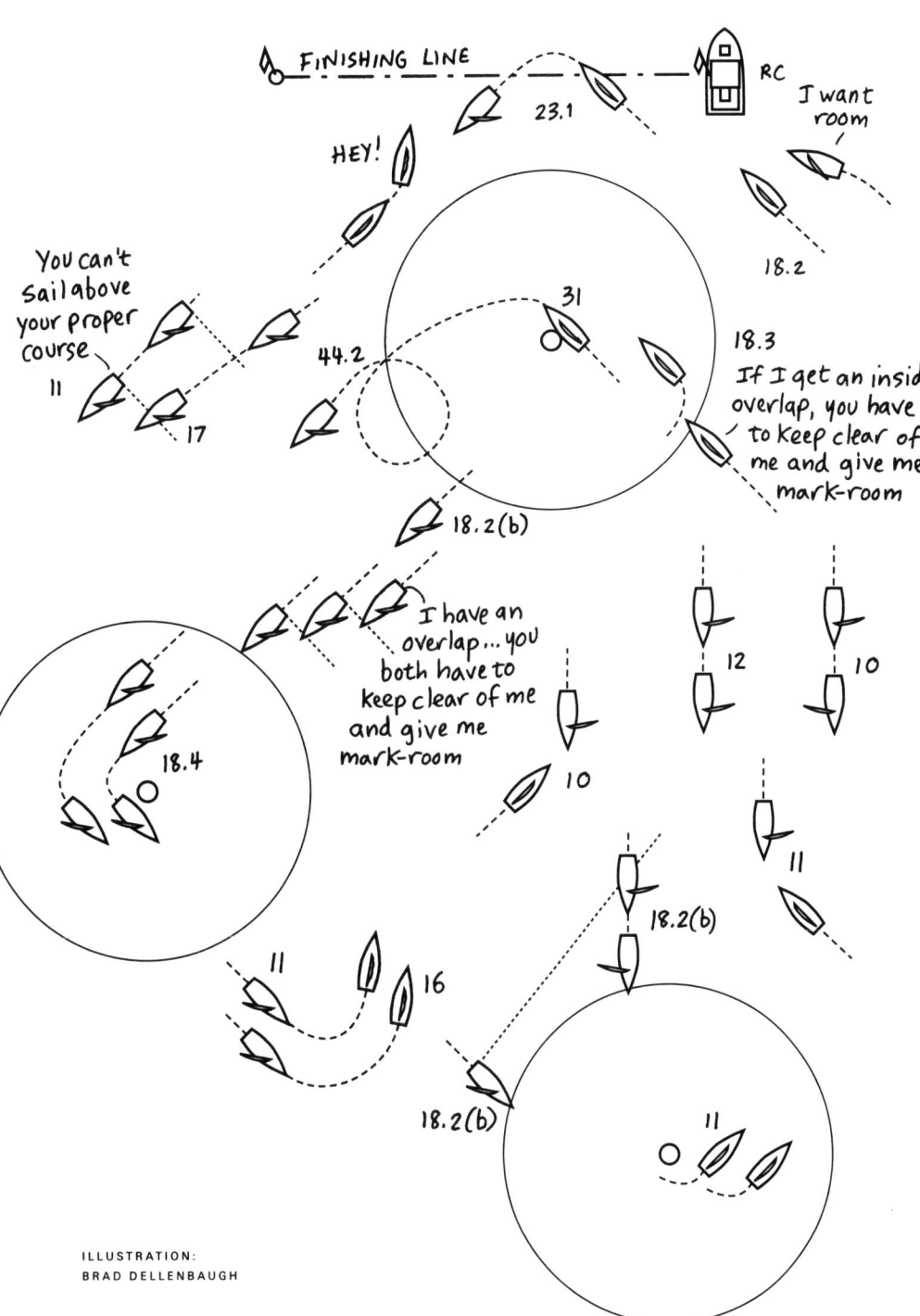

ILLUSTRATION:
BRAD DELLENBAUGH

OTHER BOOKS BY DAVE PERRY

Dave Perry's 100 Best Racing Rules Quizzes

Winning in One-Designs

To order rulebooks, *US Sailing Appeals and World Sailing Cases*, books by Dave Perry and other US Sailing publications, please call (800) US SAIL-1 or go to ussailing.org

TO CONTACT US SAILING

Phone: (401) 342-7900
Fax: (401) 342-7940

info@ussailing.org
ussailing.org

ISBN: 978-1-938915-41-3

Published by the United States Sailing Association

© 2020 by the United States Sailing Association and Dave Perry

Illustrations © 2020 by Brad Dellenbaugh

The Racing Rules of Sailing for 2021–2024
© 2020 by World Sailing

Permission to reprint *The Racing Rules of Sailing for 2021–2024* has been granted to the United States Sailing Association (US Sailing) by World Sailing. All rights reserved.

No part of this book may be reproduced in any form without permission from the author, illustrator or publisher.

November 2020

Previous editions published in 1985, 1989, 1993, 1997, 2001, 2004, 2008, 2012 and 2016

Cover photo · © Felipe Juncadella / UP TOP Media
M32 photo courtesy of the Marstrom 32 Class
Cover design · Bradley Schoch

Foreword

My hope is that each sailor who reads this book will be able to say honestly that they do finally know and understand the rules. I realize that a rules book doesn't often make for the best bedtime reading, but I've made a conscious effort to write in an easy to follow, conversational style. In addition, I've taken the time to go into each rule in enough depth so that you can feel confident that you actually do understand what the rule means and how it applies to your racing. And Brad Dellenbaugh has provided his usual clear and humorous diagrams that make understanding the rules even easier.

IN LEARNING THESE RULES and their tactical implications I strongly recommend an attitude that is positive about accepting that challenge, realistic about letting go of some of what was previously known about the rules, and willing to make the effort to fully study and understand them.

If you're new to sailboat racing, Chapter 2 covers the basic terms you'll hear throughout the book and around the race course; and it lists the basic rules which you will need to know so you can get out there and start having fun without feeling that you're lost and in everyone's way. But, after reading Chapter 2, I encourage you to take the extra time to read through the rest of the book. Obviously you won't be able to visualize all the situations discussed, but at least you will have been exposed to the big picture right off the bat; and I can promise that your understanding of the rules will happen much faster because you will know how to answer most of your own rule questions as they arise, which they will!

If you are already an experienced racer, I'm confident that you will find this book an informative and useful reference. Wherever possible, I have quoted from the US Sailing appeals and World Sailing cases so that you will know their authoritative interpretation and explanation of the rules. I have also gone into depth in areas which commonly cause the most problems or raise the most questions. As a result, this reference will also be extremely useful to sailors serving as judges on a protest committee. The most useful appeals and cases are quoted or referenced with the discussion of each rule; and each discussion goes into sufficient depth to provide the answers or at least the guidelines to resolve most protests or questions which come up. Both competitors and judges will find the extensive use and reference to the appeals and cases very useful and timesaving when they are either lodging a protest or trying to resolve one in the hearing.

NOTE: At the time this book was published, World Sailing had not yet completed their revisions of their Case Book; therefore the quotes from the cases may not be 100% accurate. I expect that the substance of the interpretations are accurate, but encourage you to double-check the actual cases. You can find both the Appeals and the Case books at: ussailing.org/competition/rules-officiating/appeals/

I wish to point out that my opinions expressed in this book are my personal opinions, and not those of the US Sailing Appeals Committee of which I am a member.

It is nearly impossible to race sailboats without getting involved in some rules-related situations, whether it's in a crowded mark rounding, a protest hearing, a measurement problem, or an appeal. It is my hope that this book, which blends the rules and the appeals and cases together, will answer most of your rules questions and expand your knowledge and awareness of what is in the US Sailing appeals and World Sailing cases so that you can continue to satisfy your own rules curiosity into the future, and feel confident that you in fact do understand the rules yourself.

This book will be published every four years with the revisions of *The Racing Rules of Sailing*. As it is my goal to provide a useful and accurate reference for all sailors, I welcome your comments and suggestions concerning improvements and inaccuracies. Please send them to my attention by May 1, 2024, or sooner at: 239 Barberry Road, Southport, CT 06890.

And now, enjoy your understanding of the rules!

Good Sailing,
Dave Perry

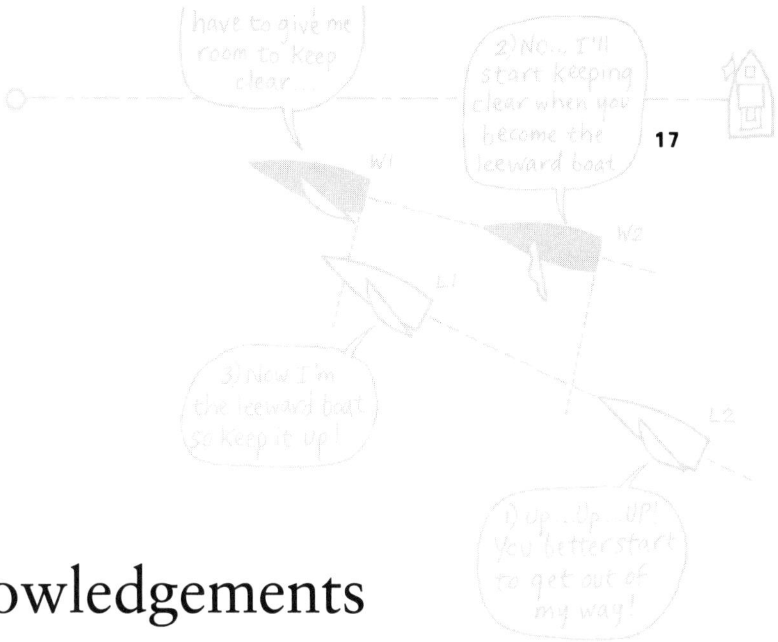

Acknowledgements

I'D LIKE TO THANK the following people, and for the reasons given:

My father, Hop Perry, who began my rules interest and taught me the first rules I knew; my mother, Jan Perry, who, along with her father Northrop Dawson, stimulated and encouraged my desire to write; and my wife Betsy, who has enhanced this book (and my life) with her contributions and her support.

Bill Bentsen and Dick Rose, members of both the US Sailing and World Sailing Racing Rules Committees over the years, who have generously given me tremendous amounts of their time and insight as I have learned more about the rules; and who have inspired me to become a strict analyst of the exact word in each rule so as to learn and interpret only what the rule writers wrote.

Harry Anderson, who patiently tolerated my endless rule questions during his every visit to Yale from '73 to '77, and who answered each with the same high care and interest to explain exactly why he gave the answer he did. Gregg Bemis, whose countless hours of conversation on the rules I will always cherish. David and Brad Dellenbaugh, who have helped me gain tremendous insights into the rules by their high-minded approach to analyzing and interpreting the rules. Tom Ehman, who shares my insatiable curiosity to understand the rules. Andy Kostanecki with whom (along with Dick Rose) I shared my first experience at writing a rule and who was wonderful to work with. Goran Petersson, whose sincere dedication to listening to sailors and welcoming their input on the racing rules I admire and appreciate so much. And my fellow members on the US Sailing Appeals Committee past and present for their high level of rules interpretation and interest in the rules.

I also acknowledge the many ideas the legendary Paul Elvström included in his classic book, *Paul Elvström Explains...the Yacht Racing Rules*, which include the waterproof cover, bird's-eye view of the race course, use of simple diagrams, focus on the rules sailors needed to know, and of course the famous small plastic boats! Many of his ideas are used in this book.

I would also like to thank the many friends with whom I've enjoyed much open-minded and friendly, thoughtful debate on the rules, completely devoid of any self-righteousness or the ill effects of taking debate personally; and all the sailors I've met while sitting on protest committees, who have given clear and honest testimonies so that the facts of what happened were clear, enabling everyone involved to learn from and enjoy the more intellectual challenge of applying the rules to the seemingly endless variety of situations we find ourselves in while racing.

I can't say enough about the talent and energy of my friend Brad Dellenbaugh, whose illustrations are an equal half of making this book fun and effective. I also thank Joy Shipman and the staff at US Sailing for all their efforts towards the publication of this book. Finally, I want to acknowledge all those sailors who took the time to write to me with their critical comments and suggestions for the improvement of this book, and in particular my friend Peter Haynes.

As individual words form together to create a rule, so have all these people formed together to become my teacher in a subject that never ceases to give me pleasure each time I feel I know and understand a rule a little more clearly.

To all of you: Thank you!

Table of Contents

Significant Changes to the Rules	1–10
An Overview of the Rules	12–13
Contacting US Sailing	14
Foreword	15
Acknowledgements	17
Table of Contents of *The Racing Rules of Sailing* Where to find the RRS discussed in this book	21–33
Introduction How to learn the most from this book	35–37
Glossary of Terms An explanation of terms not defined in the racing rules	38
Code	39
Speed, Distance and Time Table	41

1 **An Overview of the Rules System** 43–50
A brief history of the development of the rules,
an explanation of where the rules are located and
a discussion of the protest and appeals process

2 **A Simplified Version of *The Racing Rules of Sailing*** 51–55
An explanation of the basic terms and rules useful
to know if new to sailboat racing

3 **Sportsmanship and the Rules** 57–59
A discussion of the Basic Principles:
Sportsmanship and the Rules

4 **The Fundamental Rules (Part 1)** 61–73
A discussion of rules 1–6, the Fundamental Rules: Safety;
Fair Sailing; Decision to Race; Acceptance of the Rules;
Rules Governing Organizing Authorities and Officials;
World Sailing Regulations

5 **The Definitions** 75–107
An explanation of the defined terms used in
The Racing Rules of Sailing

6	When Boats Meet – Right of Way (Part 2 – Section A) A discussion of the Part 2 preamble and rules 10–13	109–122
7	When Boats Meet – General Limitations (Part 2 – Section B) A discussion of rules 14–17	123–168
8	When Boats Meet – At Marks and Obstructions (Part 2 – Section C) A discussion of rules 18.1, 18.2 and 43.1(b)	169–199
9	When Boats Meet – At Marks and Obstructions Tacking, Gybing and Other Exceptions to Rule 18 (Part 2 – Section C) A discussion of rules 18.1, 18.3 and 18.4	201–219
10	When Boats Meet – Room to Pass and Tack at an Obstruction (Part 2 – Section C) A discussion of rules 19–20	221–242
11	When Boats Meet – Other Rules (Part 2 – Section D) A discussion of rules 21–23	243–248
12	Conduct of a Race (Part 3) and Other Requirements When Racing (Part 4) A discussion of rule 31, Touching a Mark; rule 42, Propulsion; rule 44, Penalties at the Time of an Incident; rule 47, Trash Disposal; and rule 55, Setting and Sheeting Sails	249–274
13	Protests, Redress, Hearings, Misconduct and Appeals (Part 5) A discussion of rules 60, 61, 62, 64 and A9	275–292
14	The Finishing Line How to continue to grow your rules knowledge, including links and addresses to useful rules resources	293–297
About the Author		299
About the Illustrator		301
Race Signals		inside back cover

The Racing Rules of Sailing Contents

Page numbers in **bold** indicate where the text of each rule is quoted. All other numbers indicate where a discussion of each rule is located. "RRS" by a rule indicates there is no specific discussion of that rule in this book; you can find the text of the rule in *The Racing Rules of Sailing for 2021–2024* (online at ussailing.org/competition/rules-officiating/racing-rules).

RACE SIGNALS	inside back cover
Online Rules Documents	RRS
Introduction	
Terminology	**84, 252**
	38, 75, 100, 253, 267
Hails	RRS
Notation	RRS
Revision	RRS
Appendices	RRS
World Sailing Regulations	72-73, 103
Interpretations	47, 254, 258
DEFINITIONS	
Abandon	75-76
Clear Astern and *Clear Ahead; Overlap*	76
Conflict of Interest	78
Fetching	79
Finish	80
Keep Clear	82
Leeward and *Windward*	84
Mark	86
Mark-Room	87, 180
Obstruction	89

22 UNDERSTANDING THE RACING RULES OF SAILING THROUGH 2024

Overlap (See *Clear Astern* and *Clear Ahead; Overlap*)	91
Party	91
Postpone	93
Proper Course	94
Protest	97, 275
Racing	98
Room	99, 180
Rule	100
Sail the Course	101, 171
Start	101
Support Person	103
Tack, Starboard or *Port*	105
Windward (See *Leeward* and *Windward*)	105
Zone	105

BASIC PRINCIPLES

Sportsmanship and the Rules	57, **63-64**, 275-276
	57-59, 63-67, 112, 266
Environmental Responsibility	271

PART 1 · FUNDAMENTAL RULES

1	Safety	61
	1.1: Helping Those in Danger	61, 103, 290
		61-63, 256, 287
	1.2: Life-Saving Equipment and Personal Flotation Devices	63
2	Fair Sailing	58, 63
		58-59, 63-67, 111, 117,
		135, 138, 235, 287, 290
3	Decision to Race	69
		63, 69
4	Acceptance of the Rules	69-70, 103
		70-71, 103-104
5	Rules Governing Organizing Authorities and Officials	71
6	World Sailing Regulations	72
		103

PART 2 · WHEN BOATS MEET

Preamble to Part 2	109-110, 248
	98, 109-110, 112

SECTION A · RIGHT OF WAY

Preamble to Part 2, Section A **83, 113**
186

10 On Opposite Tacks **113, 114**
52, 64, 84, 112-117, 120-121, 124,
128, 130, 134, 136-138, 141, 143, 165,
184, 187-188, 193-194, 198, 217,
229-231, 233, 238, 240, 270

11 On the Same Tack, Overlapped **118**
52, 54, 84, 96, 113-114,
118-121, 130, 132-134, 136, 146-147, 149,
151, 155-157, 159-160, 164-165, 167,
184, 186-188, 193, 196, 205-206,
213, 215, 225-229, 231

12 On the Same Tack, Not Overlapped **119**
52, 84, 113-114, 118-121, 132,
134, 148, 159, 205, 217, 225-226, 230

13 While Tacking **120**
54, 105, 113, 120-121, 128,
133-134, 151-152, 156, 165, 182-183,
195, 197-198, 203-204, 217, 233

SECTION B · GENERAL LIMITATIONS

14 Avoiding Contact **123**
54, 98, 109-112, 115, 123-130, 142,
149-150, 161, 165, 167, 183, 186,
190, 205, 207, 228, 266, 270

15 Acquiring Right of Way **130**
99, 105, 122, 128-136, 146-148,
157, 164-168, 170, 178, 184, 189-190,
196, 198, 202, 205-207, 227-228,
233, 238, 244-246, 250, 269

16 Changing Course **136**
54, 83, 99, 142, 149, 170, 184, 186,
190, 196, 202, 207, 218, 224, 237

    16.1 **136**
83, 99, 123, 127, 136-152,
155-157, 161-162, 164-165,
167-168, 185-186, 195-196,
205-208, 215, 224, 228

    16.2 **139**
139-142, 144-145

17 On the Same Tack; Proper Course **151, 158**
94-97, 122, 151-168, 191-192,
207, 212, 223-224, 228

SECTION C · AT MARKS AND OBSTRUCTIONS

Preamble to Section C		**213**
		159, 186, 201, 213, 240
18	Mark-Room	**170**
		54, 76, 78, 84, 87-88, 99, 105,
		149, 153, 169-199, 201-219
	18.1: When Mark-Room Applies	**170, 183, 188, 217**
		88, 170-171, 183, 188, 190,
		195-196, 213
	18.1(a)	**217**
		175-180, 176, 182, 203, 217-218
	18.1(b)	**217**
		217-218
	18.1(c)	**217**
		149, 186, 195, 201, 218
	18.1(d)	**217**
		214, 219
	18.2: Giving Mark-Room	**175**
		170, 175-184, 189, 201-203,
		205, 207, 214, 218, 240
	18.2(a)	**175**
		175-180, 182, 187,
		190-191, 203, 205, 208
	18.2(b)	**175, 178, 193-194**
		88, 173-178, 182-183, 185,
		187, 190-191, 193-198, 210
	18.2(c)	177, 197-198
	18.2(c)(1)	**190, 195**
		190, 194-195
	18.2(c)(2)	**195**
		88, 187, 195-196
	18.2(d)	**197, 198**
		190, 197-198
	18.2(e)	174
	18.2(f)	178
		177-179, 202, 206-207
	18.3: Passing Head to Wind in the Zone	**201**
		169-170, 179-180,
		192, 201-209
	18.4: Gybing	**209**
		169-170, 191, 201, 210-212

19	Room to Pass an Obstruction	**222**
		54, 99, 169-171, 186, 213-214, 217, 219, 221-223, 228, 230, 247
	19.1: When Rule 19 Applies	**222**
		222-223
	19.1(a)	**222**
	19.1(b)	**222**
	19.2: Giving Room at an Obstruction	**223**
	19.2(a)	**223, 224**
		215, 224, 236
	19.2(b)	**224**
		157, 214-215, 222-228, 230-231, 236
	19.2(c)	**229**
		91, 214, 227, 229-231, 240
20	Room to Tack at an Obstruction	**232**
		99, 169-170, 213, 221-222, 233-235, 240
	20.1: Hailing	**232, 240**
		233-234, 236-238, 240-241
	20.1(a)	**232, 235**
		234-235
	20.1(b)	**232**
		234
	20.2: Responding	**232**
		233, 236
	20.2(a)	**232**
		235
	20.2(b)	**232**
		234, 236, 241
	20.2(c)	**232**
		235-240, 242
	20.2(d)	**232**
		237, 239
	20.2(e)	**232**
		240
	20.3: Passing On a Hail to an Additional Boat	**233**
		235
	20.4: Additional Requirements for Hails	**233, 242**
		242

SECTION D · OTHER RULES

	Preamble to Section D	**243**
21	Starting Errors; Taking Penalties; Backing a Sail	**244** 35, 54, 136, 138, 243-244
	21.1	**244** 103, 243-246, 248
	21.2	**244** 244-246, 250, 268-269
	21.3	**244** 244-246
22	Capsized, Anchored or Aground; Rescuing	**61, 246** 89, 221, 243, 246-247
23	Interfering with Another Boat	**247** 246-248
	23.1	**247** 98, 109-111, 247-248
	23.2	**248** 246, 248

PART 3 · CONDUCT OF A RACE

25	Notice of Race, Sailing Instructions and Signals	RRS
26	Starting Races	54, 98
27	Other Race Committee Actions before the Starting Signal	75
28	Sailing the Race	**80, 98, 171, 244** 35, 80, 82, 98-99, 101-102, 111, 171, 190, 212, 214, 244-245, 288, 290
29	Recalls	102
30	Starting Penalties	102-103, 244-246, 278
31	Touching a Mark	**249** 54, 78, 81, 99, 111, 125, 170, 180, 184-185, 189-190, 215, 249-253, 265-266, 270, 276-277
32	Shortening or Abandoning After the Start	75-76
	32.1	**76**
	32.2	**82**
33	Changing the Next Leg of the Course	RRS
34	Mark Missing; *Race Committee Absent*	RRS
35	Race Time Limit and Scores	RRS
36	Races Restarted or Resailed	RRS
37	Search and Rescue Instructions	RRS

PART 4 • OTHER REQUIREMENTS WHEN RACING

Preamble to Part 4   255

SECTION A • GENERAL REQUIREMENTS

40	Personal Flotation Devices	63
41	Outside Help	**62**
		66
42	Propulsion	**253**
		100-101, 254-255, 258, 262-264
	42.1: Basic Rule	**253, 254**
		254-257
	42.2: Prohibited Actions	**257**
		255-259, 261-262
	42.3: Exceptions	**62, 256, 260**
		253, 255, 258-262
43	Exoneration	**184**
		58, 196, 202, 205
	43.1	252
	43.1(a)	190, 238-240, 245
	43.1(b)	**184**
		133, 135, 142-143, 146, 149, 170, 182, 184-196, 205-208, 215, 218, 228, 237
	43.1(c)	124, 190, 196
	43.2	**184**
		124, 185
44	Penalties at the Time of an Incident	265
		54, 58, 110, 125, 135, 215, 250, 253
	44.1: Taking a Penalty	**111, 125, 248, 251, 253, 265, 270**
		111, 125-126, 248, 252-253, 265-270, 279
	44.2: One-Turn and Two-Turns Penalties	268
		58, 80, 125-126, 129, 245, 248, 250-253, 265-266, 268-270
	44.3: Scoring Penalty	58, 125, 252-253, 265-266, 268-270, 278
45	Hauling Out; Making Fast; Anchoring	256
		253, 256
46	Person in Charge	RRS
47	Trash Disposal	**271**
		271-272

SECTION B · EQUIPMENT-RELATED REQUIREMENTS

48	Limitations on Equipment and Crew	**62**
49	Crew Position; Lifelines	**101, 273**
50	Competitor Clothing and Equipment	**RRS**
51	Movable Ballast	**65, 101**
52	Manual Power	**101**
53	Skin Friction	**101**
54	Forestays and Headsail Tacks	**101, 273**
55	Setting and Sheeting Sails	**272-273**
		101, 273
	55.1: Changing Sails	**272**
	55.2: Spinnaker Poles; Whisker Poles	**273**
		273-274
	55.3: Sheeting Sails	**273-274**
	55.3(a)	**273**
	55.3(b)	**273**
	55.3(c)	**273**
	55.3(d)	**273**
	55.4: Headsails and Spinnakers	**273**
56	Fog Signals and Lights; Traffic Separation Schemes	**RRS**

PART 5 · PROTESTS, REDRESS, HEARINGS, MISCONDUCT AND APPEALS

Preamble to Part 5 — 276

SECTION A · PROTESTS; REDRESS; RULE 69 ACTION

60	Right to Protest; Right to Request Redress or Rule 69 Action	**276** 67, 97, 110, 264, 276, 292
	60.1	**276** 276, 290
	60.2	**277** 81, 91-92, 277
	60.3	**92, 278, 292** 91-92, 103, 105, 276-277, 279, 292
	60.4	91-92, 280
	60.5	73, 280
61	Protest Requirements	**280** 81, 97
	61.1: Protest Requirements: Informing the Protestee	**280**
	61.1(a)	**280** 49, 280-285
	61.1(a)(1)	**280** 280, 282
	61.1(a)(2)	**280** 281
	61.1(a)(3)	**280-281** 281
	61.1(a)(4)	**280** 281
	61.1(b)	**280** 286
	61.1(c)	**92, 279**
	61.2: Protest Requirements: Protest Contents	**286** 92, 97, 279, 286
	61.3: Protest Requirements: Protest Time Limit	**287** 280, 286, 287

62	Redress	**287**
		59, 69, 92, 97, 190, 291
	62.1	**287**
		287-288
	62.1(a)	**287**
		47, 49, 71, 80-81,
		91-93, 102, 278, 289
	62.1(b)	**129, 287**
		112, 129, 290
	62.1(c)	**287**
		62, 290
	62.1(d)	**287**
		67, 290,
	62.2	**288-289**
		49, 98, 289-290, 292

SECTION B · HEARINGS AND DECISIONS

63	Hearings	92, 279
	63.1: Requirement for a Hearing	**79**
		49, 72, 112, 264, 277
	63.2: Time and Place of the Hearing; Time for Parties to Prepare	**292**
		279, 292
	63.3: Right to Be Present	79, 264
	63.4: Conflict of Interest	78-79
	63.5: Validity of the Protest or Request for Redress	**281**
		281-282, 284
	63.6: Taking Evidence and Finding Facts	**264**
		47, 79, 264
	63.7: Conflict between Rules	RRS
	63.8: Protests between Boats in Different Races	110
	63.9: Hearings under Rule 60.3(d) — Support Persons	92

64	Decisions	93
	64.1: Standard of Proof, Majority Decisions and Reclassifying Requests	RRS
	64.2: Penalties	**111, 248, 272** 110-112, 125, 186, 248, 252, 262, 270, 272
	64.3: Decisions on Redress	**291** 49, 59, 62, 75, 291
	64.4: Decisions on Protests Concerning Class Rules	RRS
	64.5: Decisions Concerning Support Persons	**105** 103, 279
	64.6: Discretionary Penalties	RRS
65	Informing the Parties and Others	112
66	Reopening a Hearing	47, 289
67	Damages	**70-71, 270** 111-112, 270

SECTION C · MISCONDUCT

69	Misconduct	59, 64, 67-69, 73, 91-92, 105, 111, 277, 279, 287, 290
	69.1: Obligation not to Commit Misconduct; Resolution	**103-104** 66-67, 91, 93, 98, 279
	69.2: Action by a Protest Committee	67, 68, 91, 98, 277-279, 290
	69.3: Action by a National Authority and World Sailing	RRS

SECTION D · APPEALS

70	Appeals and Requests to a National Authority	**50** 47-49, 69, 71, 92, 289
71	National Authority Decisions	**48** 47

PART 6 · ENTRY AND QUALIFICATION

75	Entering an Event	111
76	Exclusion of Boats or Competitors	RRS
77	Identification on Sails	RRS
78	Compliance with Class Rules; Certificates	111-112
79	Categorization	RRS
80	Rescheduled Event	RRS
81	*Indemnification or Hold Harmless Agreements*	RRS

PART 7 · RACE ORGANIZATION

85	Changes to Rules	100-101
86	Changes to the Racing Rules	44-45
	86.1	45, 100-101, 258, 262, 274
	86.2: Prescriptions that Apply	RRS
	86.3: Changes to Prescriptions	45
87	Changes to Class Rules	RRS
88	National Prescriptions	292
89	Organizing Authority; Notice of Race; Appointment of Race Officials	RRS
90	Race Committee; Sailing Instructions; Scoring	
	90.1: Race Committee	69
	90.2: Sailing Instructions	46
	90.3: Scoring	48, 278 58, 64
91	Protest Committee	RRS
92	Technical Committee	RRS

APPENDICES

A	Scoring	RRS
	A5.1: Scores Determined by the Race Committee	80-81, 101-102, 278
	A9: Guidance on Redress	**291, 292**
B	Windsurfing Fleet Competition Rules	RRS
	Changes to the Definitions	107, 172
C	Match Racing Rules	RRS
	C2.4	107, 172
	C2.6	122
	C9.1	71
D	Team Racing Rules	189
	D1.1(a)	107, 172
	D2.6(b)(2)	71
E	Radio Sailing Racing Rules	RRS
	E1.1	107, 172
F	Keyboarding Racing Rules	RRS
	Changes to the Definitions	107, 172
G	Identification on Sails	273
H	Weighing Clothing and Equipment	RRS
J	Notice of Race and Sailing Instructions	45, 70
	J1.1(3)	46
	J1.2(11)	70
	J1.2(12)	110
	J1.3(1)	100
	J2.1(1)	100
	J2.1(4)	171
M	Recommendations for Protest Committees	RRS
	Preamble to Appendix M	**46**
	M2.3	79
N	International Juries	50
P	Special Procedures for Rule 42	262-263
	P5, Flags O and R	262
R	*Procedures for Appeals and Requests*	47, 289
S	Standard Sailing Instructions	RRS
T	Arbitration	266
U	*Audible-Signal Starting System*	98
V	*Alternative Procedures for Dispute Resolution*	58, 266

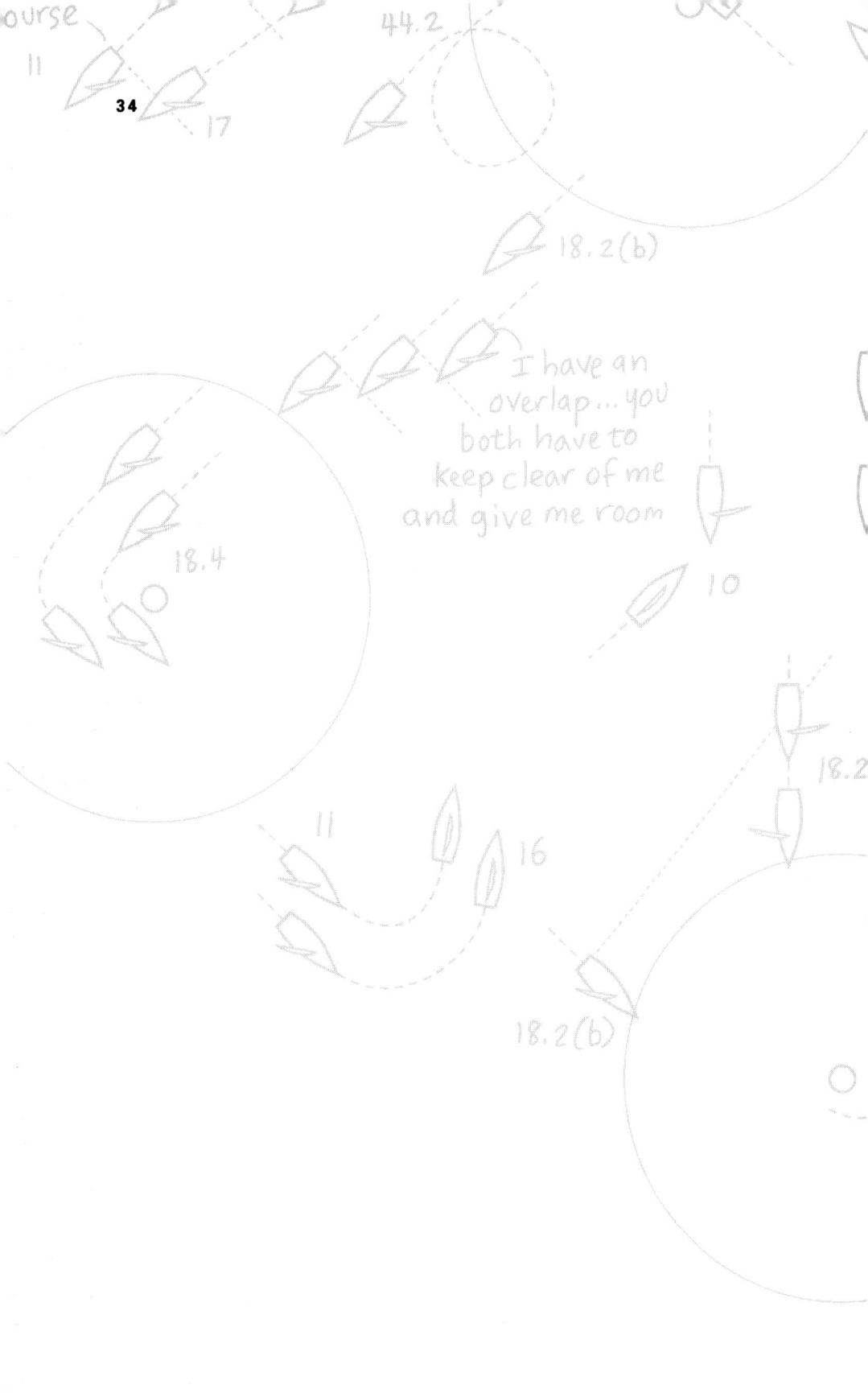

Introduction

How to Learn the Most from This Book

Give a man a fish and you feed him for a day.
Teach him how to fish and you feed him for a lifetime.
Lao Tzu, founder of Taoism

It is one goal of this book to help you learn and understand the rules and the appeals/cases better. It is an equal goal to help you see how you can continue to answer your own rules questions as they arise, whether in the position of a competitor, a race committee member or a judge. Here are some suggestions that will make it much easier for you to accomplish both.

DON'T TRY TO MEMORIZE THE RULES

It is the wrong approach to try to memorize the four situations where a *port-tack* boat has right of way over a *starboard-tack* boat, just as it's confusing to try to simply memorize the entire text of rule 18.2 (Giving Mark-Room). Each rule has a clear purpose, which I have tried to explain thoroughly. You'll learn and remember the rules faster and more clearly if you take a step back and try to see exactly what actions each rule is trying to produce or eliminate. For example, when you are over the starting line at the gun you have taken an unfair head start on your competitors. You can remedy your mistake simply by returning behind the line and starting properly; and it makes complete sense that while you are returning you have to stay out of the way of boats that have started correctly. This is the purpose of rule 28.1 (Sailing the Race) and rule 21 (Starting Errors; Penalty Turns; Backing a Sail), which you can easily understand and apply in your racing without knowing the exact wording of each rule.

LET GO OF PREVIOUS INTERPRETATIONS OF THE RULES

My advice is: Read this book with an open mind. Be careful not to hurry through sections that you feel you already know. Read each word and discussion carefully. It's very common and easy to superimpose what you "think" a rule says or should say; and in many cases this causes you to miss a subtle difference in what the rule is actually saying. Sailors seriously interested in understanding the rules will find real pleasure and benefit in learning a rule correctly.

WHEN ALL ELSE FAILS, READ THE DIRECTIONS

It is usually not difficult to answer your own rules questions if you follow this route. When you have a question, first look in the Contents of *The Racing Rules of Sailing* (RRS) in the front of this book to see which rule(s) may apply. Look at the titles of the Parts, then the Sections and finally the rules themselves to find the one(s) that might pertain to your situation. For example, if it involves two or more boats, the appropriate rule(s) are probably in Part 2, When Boats Meet. To find the rule(s), first determine what the relationships of the boats are just before, during and just after the incident. For instance, have they been converging for some time or does one of the boats suddenly change course and cause the convergence; are they on the same or opposite *tacks*; are they *overlapped* or not, and so forth. Also determine where they are on the course; i.e., are they behind the starting line, near a *mark* or halfway down a reaching leg? Then look through the titles of the rules in Part 2 for the description most similar to the situation.

When you have found the rule you feel applies, read it out loud. As Bill Bentsen, member of the US Sailing and World Sailing Racing Rules Committees for many years, says, "Before answering a rules question I always read the rule first." Then read the discussion of the rule in this book, along with each appeal and case referenced in the discussion. It is also good advice to read the definition of each italicized word in the rule. If you have access to the US Sailing appeals and World Sailing cases (on-line at: ussailing.org/competition/rules-officiating/appeals), check the helpful index and read any appeals/cases that may pertain to your situation. If you are still not confident in the answer, write down your question in the back of your rule book and discuss it with the local rules expert or one of the US Sailing Certified Judges in your area.

USEFUL FEATURES OF THIS BOOK

Brad and I have included the following features in the book with the hope that they will be useful to you:

1) **A "blimp's eye" chart** in the front of the book which shows an entire race course with the rule numbers for the situations that commonly arise in each location. This feature should be very useful when you're involved in a *protest* but you're not sure what rule number applies.

2) **A "question and answer" format,** indicated by the sailor's head or fish in the margin, in which I ask and answer the most commonly asked rules questions. Perhaps you'll recognize some as questions you may have.

3) When a term defined in the Definitions is used in its defined sense, I have printed it in *italic* type. To emphasize words or phrases throughout my explanations and discussions of the rules, I have used **bold** type.

4) **A Glossary of Terms** explaining the meaning of terms commonly used in discussing the *rules* but not defined in *The Racing Rules of Sailing*. (Located after this Introduction.)

5) **A table for calculating** boat speed, distance and time that will be useful when preparing for a *protest* or hearing one. (Located after this Introduction.)

6) **An index** listing each 2021–2024 rule number and where the primary discussion of that rule is located in this book. (Located after the Table of Contents in this book.)

7) **A summary** of the significant changes in the rules. (First few pages of this book.)

8) Extensive quotes from **US Sailing Appeals** and **Questions** (referred to as "Appeals" or "Questions") and **World Sailing Cases** (referred to as "Cases").

Veteran readers of the book will notice that we have not included the complete *Racing Rules of Sailing* book. It has grown to be quite large, and it is readily available in electronic or printed form from the US Sailing Store, at: shop.us-sailing.org.

Glossary of Terms

To keep the rules short and simple, the rule writers use common terms when possible. When a term is not defined in *The Racing Rules of Sailing* (RRS), it is intended to be interpreted in its common, everyday dictionary meaning (see RRS Introduction, Terminology). The following is a glossary of some of the terms you will find in *The Racing Rules of Sailing* and their discussion in this book that are not defined in the RRS themselves:

Approaching a *Mark*   getting closer to the time a boat will arrive at the *mark*

Bearing Away   turning away from the direction of the wind

Beat to Windward   a boat is on a "beat to windward" whenever she is racing upwind; i.e., when her fastest course to the next *mark* is close-hauled or above.

Close-hauled Course   the course a boat will sail when racing upwind; i.e., when sailing as close to the wind as she can and not lose too much speed

Heading Up   another term for "luffing" (see below)

Inside Boat   when two *overlapped* boats are near a *mark* or *obstruction*, the boat that is between the other boat and the *mark* or *obstruction*

Gybing   the maneuver involving changing *tacks* with the boat's bow away from the wind; when sailing directly downwind, a boat changes *tacks* when her mainsail crosses her centerline

Leaving a *Mark*   sailing past the *mark* in the final phase of the rounding or passing maneuver

Luffing   turning toward the direction of the wind

May or Can   means permissive; have option of doing it

Outside Boat   when two *overlapped* boats are near a *mark* or *obstruction*, the boat that is not between the other boat and the *mark* or *obstruction*

Shall   means mandatory; must do it

Tacking   the maneuver involving changing *tacks* with the boat's bow toward the wind; when sailing upwind, a boat changes *tacks* the moment her bow passes head to wind

Code

Throughout this book, in order to consolidate space and to conform to the appeals, I have used the following code:

- **S**   *starboard-tack* boat
- **P**   *port-tack* boat
- **L**   *leeward* boat
- **W**   *windward* boat
- **A**   boat *clear ahead*
- **B**   boat *clear astern* (behind)
- **M**   middle or intervening boat
- **I**   inside boat (at a *mark* or *obstruction*)
- **O**   outside boat (at a *mark* or *obstruction*)

When combined, the codes work like this:

- **SL**   the boat is on *starboard-tack* and *overlapped* to *leeward* of the other boat.
- **PI**   the boat is on *port-tack* and *overlapped* on the inside of the other boat.

Speed, Distance & Time Table

(based on the formula: distance = rate x time)
(1 knot = 6076 feet per hour)

Boat speed	Feet per second	Meters per second
1 knot	1.69	0.51
2 knots	3.38	1.01
3 knots	5.06	1.52
4 knots	6.75	2.03
5 knots	8.44	2.53
6 knots	10.13	3.04
7 knots	11.81	3.54
8 knots	13.50	4.05
9 knots	15.19	4.56
10 knots	16.88	5.06

In other words, if your boat is going 4 knots, you will travel 6.75 feet per second. One way to determine your boat's speed is to sail by a buoy or other fixed object and count how many seconds it takes for the buoy to go from your bow to your stern. If in a 24-foot boat it takes 3 seconds to go by the buoy, you are going 8 feet per second, or just under 5 knots.

It's very useful to know your boat's approximate speed on all points of sail in all wind and wave conditions, particularly in a protest hearing. For instance, in the above example you know that a *zone* that is three lengths wide is about 9 seconds' worth of sailing before the *mark*. You also know that if you tack in front of another boat and she claims to have hit you only 3 seconds after you became close-hauled, you can point out that, by her own testimony, she held her course for a full boat-length after you were close-hauled.

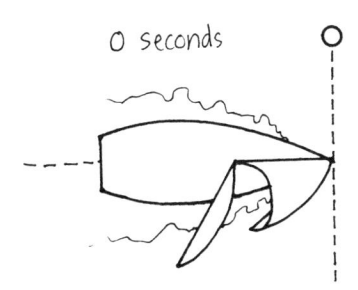

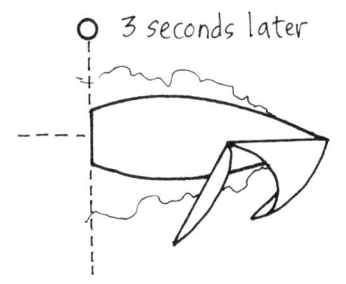

1

An Overview of the Rules System

Here is an overview of how the rules system works, and where the *rules* and their interpretations are located.

BRIEF HISTORY

Up through the early 1920s, different parts of the world had their own versions of racing rules. Then, as more sailors started traveling to other countries for international regattas, the European and United States yacht racing associations agreed on a common set of right-of-way rules in 1929. However, as racing grew in popularity and the boats were getting smaller, the existing rules were not clear and precise enough to make them easily enforceable.

In the mid-1930s Mike Vanderbilt, defender of the America's Cup in the J-boats *Enterprise* (1930), *Rainbow* (1934) and *Ranger* (1937) began work on a new draft of the rules based on the three basic relative positions boats can be in: on the same tack, on different tacks, and in the act of changing tacks. In 1948 the North American Yacht Racing Union (NAYRU), predecessor to the United States Sailing Association (US Sailing) and the Canadian Yachting Association (CYA), adopted Vanderbilt's draft as their official rules.

In 1949 the International Yacht Racing Union (IYRU), predecessor to the International Sailing Federation (ISAF), which became the World Sailing Association in 2016, created a Racing Rules Committee to study the various racing rules that were being used throughout the world. From 1950 to 1959, Mike

Vanderbilt and Gregg Bemis of the United States, Gerald Sambrooke-Sturgess of Great Britain and others worked hard to draft one set of rules under which the entire world would race. In 1960 the IYRU adopted a draft, largely based on the "Vanderbilt draft," and these rules came into effect in 1961. Since then, racing throughout the world has been done under the same code of rules.

Beginning in 1961, the IYRU's policy became that these rules would be locked in place for four-year periods lasting through the Olympic Games. During these four-year periods, sailors would communicate their ideas for improvements to their Racing Rules Committees, which would also study the rules for areas of improvement. After each Olympics, the IYRU would adopt a revised set of rules for the next four-year period.

Over the years since 1961, in the process of being revised to clarify their meaning and to meet changes in the sport, the rules became longer and more filled with exceptions. As newcomers joined the sport, they (and those who taught them) found learning the rules to be a formidable task. In 1991, ISAF took formal action to simplify the rules. A draft of "experimental rules" was offered to sailors each year from 1993–1996 for their review, trial and input. This "world-wide" research project resulted in a highly refined and simpler set of rules that went into effect in 1997. The rules at *marks* and *obstructions* remained long and confusing to some, so a similar effort was made to simplify and clarify those rules in the 2009–2012 rules. It is World Sailing's intention to minimize the changes to the racing rules as much as possible to enhance their understanding.

THE RULES AND HOW THEY ARE UPDATED

The rules are *The Racing Rules of Sailing*. They are published by World Sailing. Each national authority (US Sailing in the United States) adopts these rules for racing in its own country. Some rules permit each national authority to make some additions or modifications, called "prescriptions." So when racing in a different country, a sailor need only learn what prescriptions, if any, that national authority has made. But notice that there are no modifications permitted to the Definitions and "right of way" rules in Part 2 (see rule 86, Changes to the Racing Rules), thus ensuring that these remain identical throughout the world.

Though rule 86 restricts which rules the sailing instructions can change, rule

86.3 says, *"If a national authority so prescribes, the restrictions in rule 86.1 do not apply if rules are changed to develop or test proposed rules."* US Sailing prescribes to rule 86.3:

> (a) *In exception to rule 86.1, an organizing authority may request, and US Sailing may authorize, proposed changes to the racing rules for a specific event. The authorization shall be stated in a letter of approval to the organizing authority, and the letter shall be posted on the official notice board.*
>
> (b) *The proposed rules shall be stated in the notice of race and sailing instructions, and the organizing authority shall promptly report the results of the test to US Sailing."*

World Sailing and the national authorities are very interested in having sailors study the rules for improvements and give their input. In the United States, suggestions or comments should be sent to the Racing Rules Committee at rules@ussailing.org.

WHERE THE RULES ARE LOCATED

*The **rules** are located in the following places.*
*(See the definition **Rule**.)*

1. **The World Sailing rule book (*The Racing Rules of Sailing*) and any prescriptions of the national authority.** US Sailing creates one "rule book" that includes the World Sailing rules, appendices and US Sailing prescriptions. See its Contents for an overview of where each rule is located and what each appendix covers. Notice that rule titles are not part of the *rules*.

2. **Class rules.** Each class publishes rules specific for that class, which are available from the class secretary, and generally on the class website.

3. **Club or "local" rules.**

4. **The Notice of Race & Sailing Instructions.** Appendix J (Notice of Race and Sailing Instructions) lists the information that must be contained in the notice of race (NoR) and sailing instructions (SI). The NoR or SI are required to tell you when class and "local" rules apply, as well as when parts or the whole of an appendix apply. They may even change some of *The Racing Rules of Sailing* (see rule 86, Changes to the Racing Rules).

Notice that rule 90.2 (Sailing Instructions) prohibits any oral instructions unless there is a procedure specifically set out in the SI; and even then, they can be given only on the water. This is obviously to avoid confusion and potential prejudice to sailors not hearing about a change.

Every sailor should take a few minutes to read the NoR and SI for a race or event. Normally, a race committee will not answer oral questions concerning any rule, NoR or SI for the above stated reason. You should give them your question(s) in writing in ample time for them to consider their answer, seek the judges' opinions (when necessary), and post each question with its answer in writing on the official notice board.

5. **Any other conditions or documents that might apply to a particular race or series.** Note, Case 98 states "Any other documents that will govern the event must be listed in the notice of race (see rule J1.1(3))."

PROTEST SYSTEM

A "*protest*" is merely the means of bringing an incident in which a boat may have broken a *rule* to a hearing after the race where the sailors involved and the members of the protest committee can review the incident and decide how the *rules* apply.

The rules for how to file a *protest* are clearly stated in Part 5, Section A (Protests; Redress; Rule 69 Action). Rules concerning how the protest hearing must be run, including a listing of all the sailor's rights, are in Part 5, Section B (Hearings and Decisions).

Appendix M (Recommendations for Protest Committees) contains detailed recommendations for how protest committees should conduct the hearing. The preamble to the Appendix clearly states the fundamental principle of "innocent until the jury is satisfied of guilt:" "*In a protest or redress hearing, the protest committee should weigh all testimony with equal care; should recognize that honest testimony can vary, and even be in conflict, as a result of different observations and recollections; should resolve such differences as best it can; should recognize that no boat or competitor is guilty until a breach of a rule has been established to the satisfaction of the protest committee; and should keep an open mind until all the evidence has been heard as to whether a boat or competitor has broken a rule.*"

APPEALS SYSTEM

If you are penalized in a protest hearing and you feel that the protest committee applied the *rules* incorrectly to the facts it found or failed to follow the correct procedures in hearing the *protest*, you can "appeal" its decision to a "higher court." All the rules and procedures for submitting an appeal are located in rule 70 (Appeals and Requests to a National Authority) and Appendix R (Procedures for Appeals and Requests).

Note that you cannot appeal the "facts" that were found by the protest committee. You can only appeal its interpretation and application of the *rules* to those facts, or its procedures (rule 63.6, Taking Evidence and Finding Facts; rule 70.1, Appeals and Requests to a National Authority; and rule 71.3, National Authority Decisions). If after a hearing you, as a *party* to the hearing, feel the protest committee found the wrong facts, you can ask it to reopen the hearing under rule 66 (Reopening a Hearing); and if you feel it used improper procedures (as opposed to disagreeing with its decision), you may request redress under rule 62.1(a) (Redress).

In the United States the "highest court" is the US Sailing Appeals Committee. When it decides a case that in its opinion is a clear and useful interpretation of a *rule*, it publishes that decision. It can also submit the appeal and its decision to the World Sailing Racing Rules Committee, which in turn can publish the appeal in its *Case Book*. US Sailing's *Appeals Book* and World Sailing's *Case Book* are available on-line at: ussailing.org/competition/rules-officiating/appeals, or available for purchase from US Sailing's on-line Store: store.ussailing.org.

"What is the status of US Sailing's appeals and World Sailing's cases?"

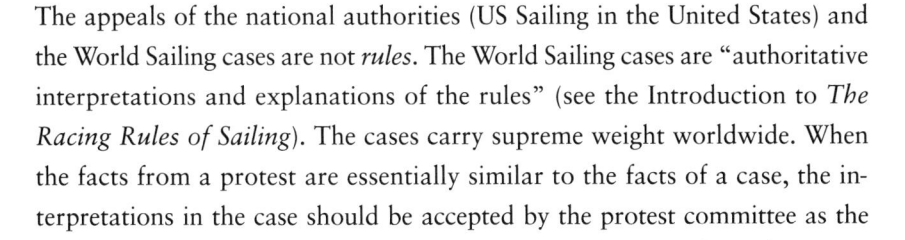

The appeals of the national authorities (US Sailing in the United States) and the World Sailing cases are not *rules*. The World Sailing cases are "authoritative interpretations and explanations of the rules" (see the Introduction to *The Racing Rules of Sailing*). The cases carry supreme weight worldwide. When the facts from a protest are essentially similar to the facts of a case, the interpretations in the case should be accepted by the protest committee as the correct interpretation of the *rules* for that protest or request for redress. (See Appeal 99.)

The decisions of national authority appeals committees are "final" (see rule 71.4). Therefore, when the facts from a protest are essentially similar to the facts of a US Sailing appeal, and no World Sailing case conflicts with the interpretations in the appeal, a protest committee in the United States is well advised to follow the appeal in making its decision (Appeal 99). Sailors and protest committees can and should refer to the appeals for guidance.

"What's the best way to use the appeals and case books?"

Both the US Sailing *Appeals Book* and World Sailing *Case Book* are designed for easy, quick reference. Each has an index which lists each rule, and then each appeal or case that interprets that rule with a short description of each appeal or case. Instead of reading the *Appeals* or *Case Books* from front to back, you should read each appeal or case pertaining to a particular rule. The appeals and cases themselves are each very short. You are given the facts, a diagram when relevant, and then the decision. I like to read the facts, close the book, think out what my decision would be, then compare it with the actual decision.

"Can the decision on an appeal change the results of a race or series?"

Absolutely yes. Rule 71.4 (National Authority Decisions) states, *"The decision of the national authority shall be final…all parties to the hearing and the protest committee…shall be bound by the decision."* And rule 90.3(d) (Scoring) says, *"The race committee shall implement scoring changes directed by the protest committee or national authority as a result of decisions made in accordance with the* **rules.** *"*

In Case 61 it was asked, "May the notice of race or sailing instructions state that, while the right of appeal is not denied, final regatta standings and awards will not be affected by any appeal decision? ANSWER: No…An appeal involves not only the adjudication of a dispute on the meaning of a rule but also, in the event of a change or reversal of the decision of the protest committee, an adjustment of the results of the race and the final standings of the regatta on which the awards are based."

"Can anyone appeal the decision of a protest committee?"

No. Only a *party* to the hearing can appeal the decision in that hearing (rule 70.1, Appeals and Requests to a National Authority). (For more explanation on who qualifies as a *party*, see the discussion of the definition *Party*.) In particular, if you weren't a *party* to a hearing, but the decision in that hearing affected you and you believe that the protest committee acted improperly, your recourse is to request redress under rule 62.1(a) (Redress). (See Appeal 64 and Case 55.)

"If I'm a party to the hearing and I feel the protest committee is prejudicing, or has prejudiced, the outcome of the hearing by denying me any of my procedural rights under Part 5, Section B (Hearings and Decisions), do I have to 'object' at the time if I want to retain my right to appeal?"

You are not required to, but I strongly encourage you to do so. Remember that an appeals committee can only base its decision on the facts as presented to it by the protest committee. When a competitor appeals on the grounds that the protest committee made a prejudicial procedural error, generally there is little or no record of it in the protest committee's "facts found." As a result it becomes very difficult for the appeals committee to ever learn enough facts to uphold the appeal.

Therefore, if you are in a situation where the protest committee is denying you your procedural rights, you should state your "objection" right then, so that the hearing can continue properly. If, after the hearing, you feel the protest committee has prejudiced the outcome of the hearing by denying you any of your procedural rights, you should request redress under rule 62.1(a) (Redress). The reason for this is that a protest committee must give you a hearing and, more importantly, must find facts and give you a decision (rule 63.1, Hearings; rule 64.3, Decisions on Redress). Otherwise, you may never get any facts regarding the alleged improprieties on which to base an appeal. Note that the time limit for requesting redress for a protest committee action/omission is the protest time limit or two hours after the "incident," whichever is later (rule 62.2). The "incident" will be the improper action/omission of the protest committee (see Appeal 90).

Note that, when seeking redress from the protest committee in a hearing in which you were a *party*, you are not allowed to base your claim on the committee's decision. Your claim must be based on an alleged procedural error (see rule 62.1(a)).

"Are there ever times when I am not allowed to appeal?"

Yes. Rule 70.5 (Appeals and Requests to a National Authority) is very clear on this:

There shall be no appeal from the decisions of an international jury constituted in compliance with Appendix N. Furthermore, if the notice of race or the sailing instructions so state, the right of appeal may be denied provided that

(a) it is essential to determine promptly the result of a race that will qualify a boat to compete in a later stage of an event or a subsequent event (a national authority may prescribe that its approval is required for such a procedure);

US Sailing prescribes that its approval is required. Go to rules.ussailing.org and click on 'No Appeal' for more information or to obtain approval.

(b) a national authority so approves for a particular event open only to boats entered by an organization affiliated to that national authority, a member of an organization affiliated to that national authority, or a personal member of that national authority; or

(c) a national authority after consultation with World Sailing so approves for a particular event, provided the protest committee is constituted as required by Appendix N, except that only two members of the protest committee need be International Judges.

2

A Simplified Version of *The Racing Rules of Sailing*

There's no disagreeing that there are a lot of rules to know when racing sailboats. But just as in every other sport, you don't need to know and completely understand them all before you go racing. I love to play soccer, and I've got the basic rules down: keep my hands off the ball, try to kick the ball into the goal to score, try not to kick the other guys in the shins and stop when the referee blows the whistle. I'm still a bit hazy on what "offsides" means, what the difference between an "indirect" and a "direct" kick is, and just how many elbows in the ribs I'm supposed to peacefully accept as part of the game. But I still have a great time playing, and I learn a bit more about the rules each time I go out.

Here then are a few basic rules you should know so that you can get into racing without feeling like you're just in everyone's way. At first, take the racing easy just to get the feel of how it works; and never be worried about asking too many questions; that's exactly how we all learned what was up. Of course, the one danger in learning just the basic rules is that there will be places on the course where there are exceptions or where the actual rule has more detail. So you should really take the time to read through this book. It's written in language that is easy to understand. The more you race, the more situations you'll run into that are exactly as covered and described here, and the sooner you'll be comfortable enough to get in there and mix it up out on the course.

52 UNDERSTANDING THE RACING RULES OF SAILING THROUGH 2024

Now, if you are just getting into sailing and racing, you've probably noticed that there are a few different words and phrases used around the track. Clearly the rules wouldn't be using them if they didn't make things easier; so we've included some illustrations to help you understand what some of these terms mean.

BASIC RULES

These are simplified summaries of the basic rules that apply when you and another boat are about to hit. When one boat has the "right of way," that means that the other boat is required to "keep clear;" in other words to stay out of the way of the right-of-way boat.

1) If you are on **opposite** *tacks* (booms on different sides), the boat on *starboard tack* has the right of way over the boat on *port tack* (just as at a four-way stop, the car on the right gets to go first). (Rule 10)

2) If you are on the **same** *tack* (booms on the same sides), the *leeward* boat has the right of way over the *windward* boat; and a boat coming up from behind can't hit the boat ahead (just as on the road). (Rules 11 and 12)

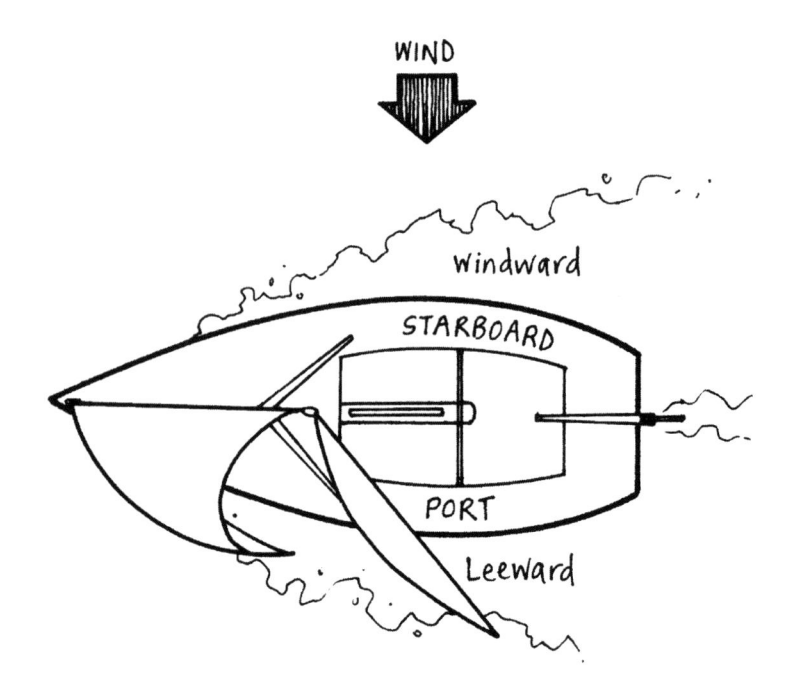

A SIMPLIFIED VERSION OF THE RULES   53

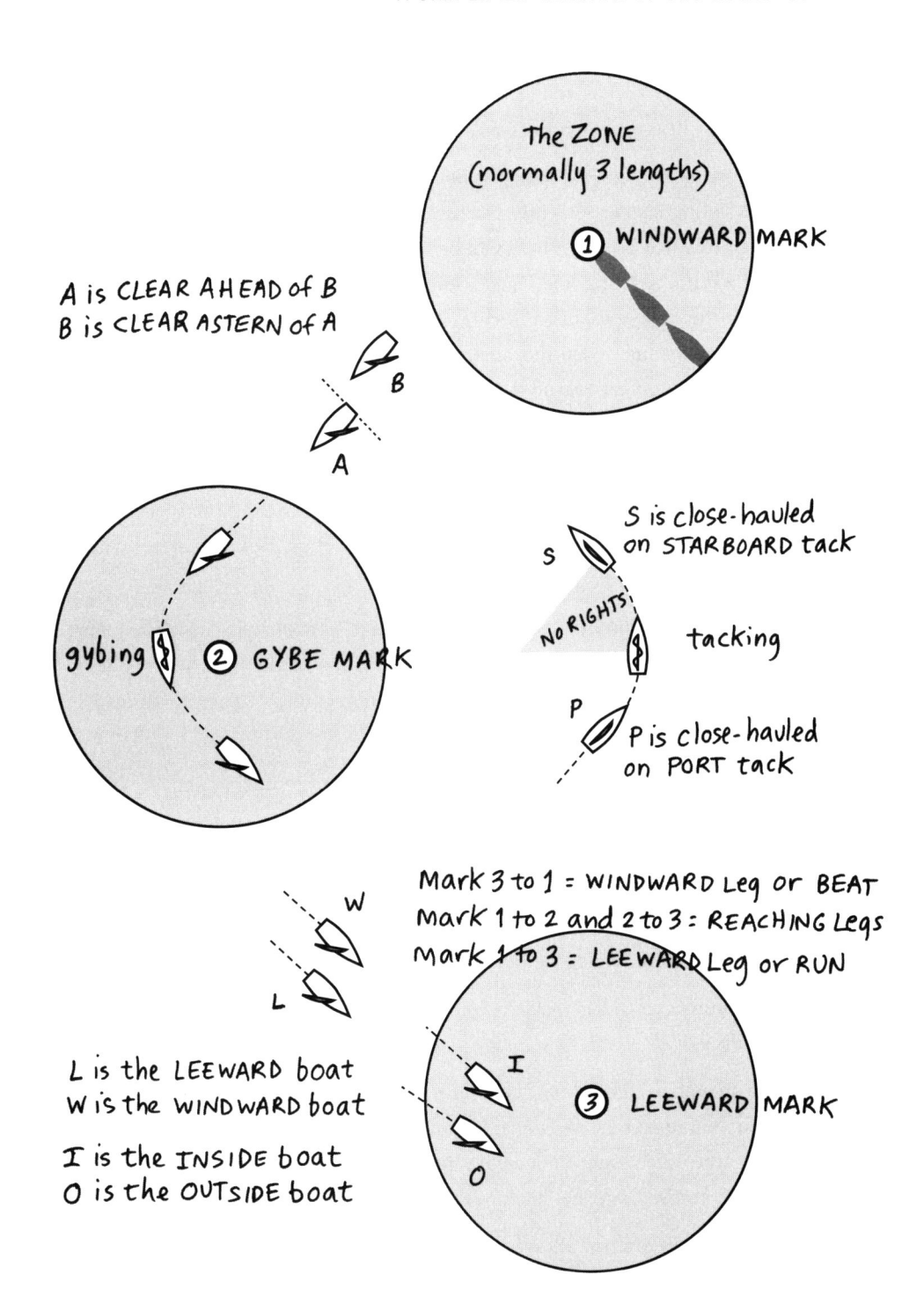

The ZONE (normally 3 lengths)

① WINDWARD MARK

A is CLEAR AHEAD of B
B is CLEAR ASTERN of A

gybing ② GYBE MARK

S is close-hauled on STARBOARD tack

NO RIGHTS

tacking

P is close-hauled on PORT tack

Mark 3 to 1 = WINDWARD Leg or BEAT
Mark 1 to 2 and 2 to 3 = REACHING Legs
Mark 1 to 3 = LEEWARD Leg or RUN

③ LEEWARD MARK

L is the LEEWARD boat
W is the WINDWARD boat

I is the INSIDE boat
O is the OUTSIDE boat

3) If you are **tacking**, you have to stay out of the way of a boat sailing in a straight line (just as you cannot pull out onto a road immediately in front of a car driving down the road). (Rule 13)

4) Before most races, the race committee will give each competitor a copy of the sailing instructions (SIs) that contain the specific information on how the races will be run. There will be an imaginary line between two marks called the "starting line," and a timing system to tell you when you can *start* the race (explained in rule 26 or the SIs). You must be completely behind this line when the starting signal is made. If you are not, simply turn back and get behind the line. However, while you are returning, you must stay clear of all boats that *started* correctly. (Rule 21)

5) Anytime you have the right of way you may turn toward another boat, but you must be sure that the other boat has enough time and space to get out of your way. That's why *windward* boats must be very careful when they pass close by to *leeward* boats. (Rule 16)

6) When you are three boat-lengths from a *mark*, or are passing an *obstruction* on the same side as another boat, you have to give any boat between you and the *mark* or *obstruction* enough *room* to round or pass it. (Rules 18 and 19)

7) One large exception to number 6 (above) is at the starting *marks*, where you do **not** have to give *windward*/inside boats *room* to pass between you and the starting *mark* when you are about to *start*. If a *windward*/inside boat tries to squeeze in between you and the starting *mark* (like a race committee boat), they are "barging," which is definitely illegal but unfortunately very common. (Rules 18 and 11)

8) You must avoid all collisions if possible, even if you have the right-of-way. (Rule 14)

9) If you make a right-of-way boat have to **change their course** to avoid hitting you, you must take a penalty. Normally the penalty is to simply get away from the other boats immediately and sail two circles in the same direction. When you're done, get back in the race. (Rule 44)

10) Finally, you are not allowed to touch the racing *marks* (rule 31). If you **touch a racing *mark***, the penalty is just one circle. (Rule 44)

If you have the right-of-way and another boat makes you change course to avoid hitting her, she has broken a *rule*. You can tell her this by "protesting" her. To do this, immediately hail the word "Protest." If you are racing on a boat 20 feet or longer you must **also** put up a red flag as quickly as possible (usually immediately) after the incident. Then at the finish tell the race committee which boat you are protesting, and onshore fill out the hearing request form the race committee will give you. Soon afterward, the protest committee (usually three knowledgeable sailors) will hold a hearing at which both boats have the opportunity to tell their story. The committee will then make its decision. (Rules 60 to 67)

Hike hard, sail fast and enjoy!

3

Sportsmanship and the Rules

"You haven't won the race if in winning the race you have lost the respect of your competitors."

Four-time Olympic Gold Medalist, Paul Elvström

BASIC PRINCIPLES — SPORTSMANSHIP AND THE RULES

Competitors in the sport of sailing are governed by a body of *rules* that they are expected to follow and enforce. A fundamental principle of sportsmanship is that when a boat breaks a *rule* and is not exonerated she will promptly take an appropriate penalty or action, which may be to retire.

This statement of principle is located in the rule book just before Part 1 (Fundamental Rules). It is no coincidence that the subject of "sportsmanship" is given a status above all the rules in our sport. The history of sailboat racing is filled with the tradition of exciting competition played out with respect among the competitors and officials. In keeping with that tradition, when we race we agree to be fair and honest, to be good sports and to attempt to win using our own superior boat speed and racing skills.

At the heart of what makes our sport so fulfilling is the principle that we have a competitor-enforced, "no-referee" rules system; that is we have the responsibility to follow the *rules* on our own, to self-penalize ourselves when we break a *rule*, and to protest ("enforce" the *rules*) when we believe another boat has broken a *rule*. In this regard, our sport is unique compared with most other sports. I am constantly amused watching a pro tennis singles match (two players) when I count at least ten referees: One calling each of the four lines on each side, one calling the net, and an umpire to settle disputes. Even at the highest levels of racing we "call our own lines."

The *rules* are intended to provide for safe, fair and equitable racing worldwide; and to make competitor enforcement as easy as possible by clearly defining which boat has the right of way and which boat the requirement to *keep clear* when boats meet. When competitors know they have broken a *rule* and it's their fault, they are expected to promptly take a penalty (One- or Two-Turns Penalty or 20% Scoring Penalty or retire). Competitors who "never drop out," even when they know they are in the wrong, because they think the other boat won't go through with a protest or they think they have a chance to "win" the *protest* in the hearing, just waste the time of all the people involved in the *protest* and diminish the quality of the racing for all. Furthermore, they break rule 2 (Fair Sailing) which says, "*A boat and her owner shall compete in compliance with recognized principles of sportsmanship and fair play.*" And if they are disqualified under rule 2, they are not allowed to drop the DSQ from their series score (see rules 2 and 90.3(b), Scoring).

Rule 44 (Penalties at the Time of an Incident) provides that the One- (for touching a *mark*) or Two- (for fouling a boat) Turns Penalty or other voluntary penalty will almost always be available to a boat. Given that often a boat does not realize she has broken a rule until returning ashore and consulting with a rules expert, etc., US Sailing has instituted an experimental system where a boat can take a Scoring Penalty on shore before a protest hearing begins, as well as providing for a lesser penalty on the water. These options are in a US Sailing prescription to the racing rules, under Appendix V (Alternative Penalties).

When a competitor believes that another boat may have broken a *rule*, she can protest. A *protest* is merely the means of bringing an incident in which a boat may have broken a *rule* to a hearing after the race where the sailors involved and the members of the protest committee can review the incident and decide how the *rules* apply. *Protests* that are the result of honest differences of opinions on the *rules* or observations of the incident should never have a negative taint to them. Quite the contrary, *protests* are an essential part of our competitor-enforced rule system and are expected, particularly in situations where a boat has gained an advantage in the race or series by breaking a *rule*.

When a boat is forced to break a *rule* through no fault of her own, she is known as the "innocent victim," and in many cases is "exonerated" (meaning freed from having to take a penalty) by rule 43, Exoneration. If a boat feels her score has been made significantly worse through no fault of her own by the organizing authority, race committee, protest committee or technical committee, or another competitor in certain circumstances, she can request redress under rule 62 (Redress); in this case, rule 64.3 (Decisions on Redress) reminds the protest committee to make as fair an arrangement as possible for all boats affected.

Finally, note that you are responsible for ensuring that your crew, boat owner and *support persons* are aware of the *rules*, and that they know that by your participation in the race, they have agreed to accept the *rules*, and that **you** can be penalized if they break any of the *rules* (see the discussion in the definition *Support Person*).

The rule writers have taken some excellent measures to amplify the message that sailboat racing should be synonymous with good sportsmanship and integrity with regard to fair play. However, in the end of the day it is up to us, the sailors, to use the *rules* as they are written and intended. One problem is that some feel that the rewards from winning justify cheating, such as the "good feeling" of winning, the attention and hype, the benefit to business and sponsors and so on. Obviously, this is a personal decision that all sailors must make for themselves. The hope is that the temptations to cheat can't possibly overpower the realization that once people start bending or ignoring the *rules*, or develop their own "common law," the whole exercise of playing the game becomes meaningless for everyone involved.

Rule 2 (Fair Sailing) and rule 69 (Misconduct) provide the external "weight" to encourage strict and voluntary rule observance. However, people who race should want to know that everyone whom they've spent the time, money and energy to race against is sailing within the *rules*; and when they know or suspect that someone isn't, then rather than joining in, they should take action under the *rules* to encourage the others to stop.

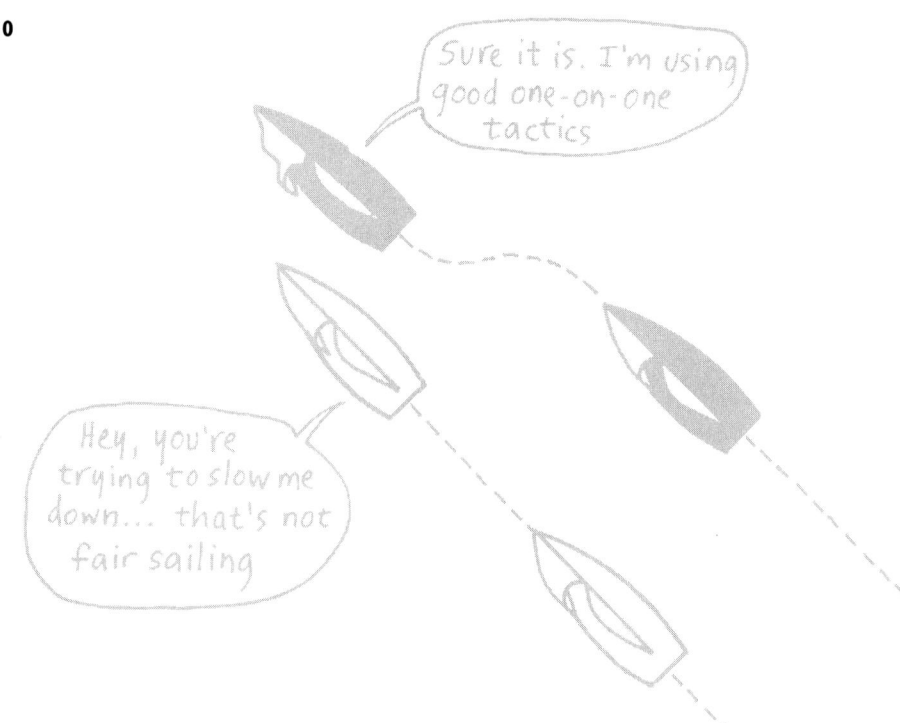

4

Part 1
Fundamental Rules

The first rules in the rule book are appropriately called the "Fundamental Rules" and they address six very important issues in our sport: safety and helping others when in a position to do so, fairness while racing, responsibility for one's own safety, acceptance of the rules under which we race, responsibility for organizing authorities and race officials to follow the rules, and World Sailing Regulations regarding advertising, drug use (primarily an issue of caution for Olympic-bound racers), betting, discipline and eligibility.

RULE 1 — SAFETY

RULE 1.1 — HELPING THOSE IN DANGER

A boat, competitor or *support person* shall give all possible help to any person or vessel in danger.

This rule is the first fundamental rule, reaffirming that this principle must be the one to which all sailors and those supporting sailors hold above all others. Remember that the word "shall" is mandatory. If it were proved that a sailor or *support person* was in a position to help, but did not do so, he or she would be liable for disqualification or other penalty. Note that the rule requires the giving of all "possible" help; this is to leave no question about the extent to which sailors and their *support persons* should help each other when in danger.

The rule book is very supportive of this principle.

- Rule 22 (Capsized, Anchored or Aground; Rescuing) reads in part, "…*a boat shall avoid a boat that is…trying to help a person or vessel in danger.*"

62 UNDERSTANDING THE RACING RULES OF SAILING THROUGH 2024

- Rule 41 (Outside Help) reads, *"A boat shall not receive help from any outside source, except (a) help for a crew member who is ill, injured or in danger; (b) after a collision, help from the crew of the other vessel to get clear..."*.

- Rule 42.3(g) (Propulsion, Exceptions) reads, *"Any means of propulsion may be used to help a person or another vessel in danger."*

- Rule 48 (Limitations on Equipment and Crew) reads in part, *"No person on board shall intentionally leave, except...to help a person or vessel in danger..."*.

"If I do stop and help a boat or person in danger, can I get some compensation for the places and/or time I may have lost?"

You bet! When you have lost places and/or time as a result of a rescue, you are permitted to request redress under rule 62.1(c) (Redress), and the protest committee, acting under rule 64.3 (Decisions on Redress), can give you appropriate compensation for the places and/or time lost. In the event you go to a rescue, try, if possible, to accurately note the time and your position when you began sailing to the rescue and when you got back in the race. On boats in offshore races it is common to keep a log, supported by GPS data, of times and positions to help the protest committee provide the fairest compensation.

A now famous instance of these rules at work is the rescue made by Canadian Finn sailor Larry Lemieux in the 1988 Summer Olympic Games held in the rough seas off Pusan, South Korea. While in second place midway through a race, Larry noticed a 470 sailor in the water separated from his boat and having great difficulty. Larry went to the sailor's rescue, succeeded in getting him safely back to his boat, and after the race requested redress. The Olympic Jury awarded Larry points equal to finishing second in that race!

Case 20 reads: "SUMMARY OF THE FACTS: Dinghy A capsized during a race and seeing this dinghy B sailed over to her and offered help. A accepted help and B came alongside, taking the crew of two aboard. Then all hands worked for several minutes to right A, whose mast was stuck in mud. Upon reaching shore, B requested redress under rule 62.1(c). The protest committee considered several factors in its decision. First, A's helmsman was a highly experienced sailor. Secondly, the wind was light, and the tide was rising and would shortly have lifted the mast free. Thirdly, she did not ask for help; it was offered. Therefore, since neither boat nor crew was in danger, redress was refused. B appealed, stating that rule 1.1 does not place any onus on a boat giving help to decide, or to defend, a decision that danger was involved.

"DECISION: B's appeal is upheld. A boat in a position to help another that may be in danger is bound to do so. It is not relevant that a protest committee later decides that there was, in fact, no danger or that help was not requested."

RULE 1.2 — LIFE-SAVING EQUIPMENT AND PERSONAL FLOTATION DEVICES

A boat shall carry adequate life-saving equipment for all persons on board, including one item ready for immediate use, unless her class rules make some other provision. Each competitor is individually responsible for wearing a personal flotation device adequate for the conditions.

Rule 1.2 gives the highest prominence to these safety issues. Note that it is **each sailor's** responsibility to decide when to wear his or her life-jacket (often referred to as a "personal flotation device" or "PFD"). Often class rules and/or sailing instructions will require you to wear your life-jacket any time you go afloat. Be sure to check those rules.

Also, the race committee can require you to wear your life-jacket by displaying flag Y (rule 40, Personal Flotation Devices). Note, however, that though the race committee has the option to use this signal, it does not shift away from you any of your responsibility for your own safety (see rule 3, Decision to Race). Rule 40 also clarifies that wet suits and dry suits are not adequate personal flotation devices.

RULE 2 — FAIR SAILING

A boat and her owner shall compete in compliance with recognized principles of sportsmanship and fair play. A boat may be penalized under this rule only if it is clearly established that these principles have been violated. The penalty shall be a disqualification that is not excludable.

As was discussed in Chapter 3, Sportsmanship and the Rules, when we race we should all agree to hold ourselves to the highest principles of fairness and good sportsmanship. This is clearly stated in the Basic Principles: Sportsmanship and the Rules: "*Competitors in the sport of sailing are governed by a body of rules that they are expected to follow and enforce. A fundamental principle of sportsmanship is that when a boat breaks a rule and is not exonerated she will promptly take an appropriate penalty or action, which may be to retire.*"

Rule 2 gives these principles their teeth. When a boat or competitor clearly violates these principles, he or she breaks rule 2 and is liable to penalty.

Note that a penalty for breaking this rule is more severe than for most other rules. Rule 2 clearly states that if you are in a series that allows you to discard your worst race, a disqualification for breaking rule 2 cannot be discarded (see rule 90.3(b), Scoring). Notice also that a boat can be penalized under rule 2, even when another rule applies to the situation. Therefore, in any incident or situation where the principles in rule 2 have been clearly violated, regardless of what other *rules* may also have been broken, a boat is liable to disqualification under rule 2. This becomes very significant given that a boat has to count that disqualification in her final score.

"*Could you give some examples of when you would consider the principles in rule 2 have been violated?*"

Sure, recognizing that each protest committee is given the discretion to judge what they deem to be "recognized principles of sportsmanship and fair play." In deciding whether a competitor has competed in compliance with the principles in rule 2, I feel it is important to consider the motive for their actions; i.e., was it an intentional violation of one of the principles?

In Case 47, "An experienced helmsman of a port-tack boat hails 'Starboard!' to a beginner who, although on starboard tack, not being sure of himself and probably being scared of having his boat holed, tacks to port to avoid a collision. No protest is lodged. One school of thought argues that it is fair game, because if a helmsman does not know the rules, that is his own hard luck. The other school rejects this argument, on the grounds that it is quite contrary to the spirit of the rules to deceive a competitor in that way. It is known that such a trick is often played, particularly where novices are involved. Question: In such as case, in addition to breaking rule 10, has the port-tack boat broken rule 2? Answer: A boat that deliberately hails 'Starboard' when she knows she is on port tack has not acted fairly and has broken rule 2. The protest committee might also consider taking action under rule 69."

PART 1 — FUNDAMENTAL RULES **65**

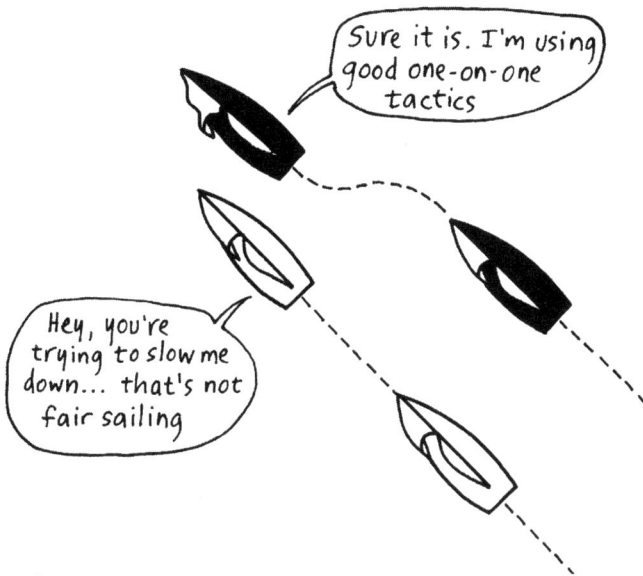

Other examples:

- A *port-tack* boat is reaching by to *leeward* of a *starboard-tack* boat before the start. The *starboard-tack* boat does not change her course, but just as the boats are passing her boom suddenly flies out and hits the *port-tacker*'s shroud. Clearly there is no way for port to *keep clear* at that moment. If it is determined that S's skipper let the boom out **intentionally to hit the boat on port,** I would penalize S under rule 2. If it is determined that S was simply sailing her boat, perhaps responding to a gust of wind, etc., I would penalize P for not *keeping clear*.

- Two boats come off the starting line side by side in very light air. Suddenly, the *leeward* boat rocks hard to windward, the tip of her mast hitting the tip of the *windward* boat's mast. The *leeward* boat does not change course. Again, if it is determined that the action was done solely to try to touch the *windward* boat, I would penalize the *leeward* boat under rule 2. I would apply the same reasoning to a *leeward* boat whose crew goes out on the trapeze in light air or otherwise reaches out and touches the *windward* boat for the sole purpose of "fouling the other boat out." (See Case 73.)

- A boat is on a heavy-air overnight race. Each time the boat tacks, the crew down-below move the sails back and forth to the windward side to increase the boat's stability. Not only would I penalize this boat for breaking rule 51 (Movable Ballast), I would penalize her under rule 2 as well.

One common practice that is not a violation of rule 2 is the tactic whereby one boat tries to make it harder for another boat to do well in a race or series, including by trying to put boats between herself and the other boat at the finish, provided the boat tries to sail within the *rules* and provided her motive is to benefit her own series score. Case 78 says, "In a fleet race for one-design boats, boat A uses tactics that clearly interfere with and hinder boat B's progress in the race. While using those tactics, A does not break any rule, except possibly rule 2 or 69.1(a). Question: In which of the following circumstances would A's tactics be considered unsportsmanlike and a breach of rule 2 or of rule 69.1(a)?

(a) The protest committee finds that there was a reasonable chance that A's tactics would benefit her final ranking in the event.

(b) The protest committee finds that there was a reasonable chance that A's tactics would increase her chances of gaining selection for another event, but would not benefit her final ranking in the event.

(c) The protest committee finds that there was a reasonable chance that A's tactics would increase her chances of gaining selection to her national team, but would not benefit her final ranking in the event.

(d) The protest committee finds that A and a third boat, boat C, had agreed that they would both adopt tactics that benefited C and that there was a reasonable chance that A's tactics would benefit C's final ranking in the event.

(e) The protest committee finds that A was attempting to worsen B's race or series score for reasons unconnected with sport.

Answer: In circumstance (a), A would be in compliance with recognized principles of sportsmanship and fair play. In circumstances (b) and (c), A would break rule 2, and possibly rule 69.1(a). In circumstance (d), both A and C would break rule 2, and possibly rule 69.1(a). In addition, by receiving help prohibited by rule 41 from A, C would also break rule 41. In circumstance (e), A would break rule 2, and possibly rule 69.1(a) because, with no good sporting reason, her actions would clearly break recognized principles of sportsmanship and fair play."

Though some may shiver at the notion that it is okay for one boat to actively try to hinder another boat's race, the racing rules themselves are in no way constructed to discourage, inhibit or prevent this. In fact, it is quite common for one boat to try to start close to leeward of another for the purpose of hindering the other's start, to intentionally tack on someone's wind on a beat, or to luff a boat downwind. In addition, it is quite common for sailors to be aware of "who their competition is" from the outset of a race or series and to actively seek opportunities to hinder them early on. As long as it's done within the racing rules, it breaks no rules including rule 2.

"What happens if a boat hinders my race and causes me to finish worse than I would have otherwise finished, and is found to have broken the Fair Sailing rule (rule 2) in the process?"

Then you are entitled to redress under rule 62.1(d) (Redress)! You can request this yourself, or the race or protest committee can do it on your behalf (rule 60, Right to Protest; Right to Request Redress or Rule 69 Action).

RULE 69 — MISCONDUCT

When a protest committee decides that an individual competitor may have acted in a way that is contrary to the sport, it can conduct a hearing under rule 69 (Misconduct). Rule 69.2(b) permits a protest committee to call a hearing when it believes that a competitor may have committed an act of misconduct which is conduct that is a breach of good manners or sportsmanship, unethical behavior, or conduct that may bring, or has brought, the sport into disrepute (see rule 69.1(b)). The protest committee may have first-hand knowledge of the situation, or it may have received a report from someone else — anyone else. Notice that a boat does not "protest" under rule 69; however, she can suggest in a *protest* or a letter to the protest committee that a hearing under rule 69 be considered.

If the protest committee decides that the competitor has acted improperly, it can warn him, change his boat's score in one or more races including a disqualification that may not be excluded, exclude him from the event or venue, or take other action available to it (see rule 69.2(h)). Notice that when it imposes a penalty greater than one DNE (disqualification that is not excludable) it must also report its action to the national authorities involved.

Rule 69 is to be used when the competitor's conduct is clearly a breach of rule 69.1(a). Generally the misconduct will be conspicuously obvious, flagrant and/or deliberate, offenses or errors so bad they cannot escape notice or be condoned, or actions exceeding reasonable or excusable limits.

In my opinion, any **deliberate infringement** of the *rules* is misconduct. For example: S deliberately rams P causing damage (perhaps because the skipper of S had been disqualified based on a protest by the skipper of P in a protest hearing the night before). Another example is when a competitor deliberately cuts a *mark* or *starts* ahead of the starting line for the purpose of hindering another competitor's race. (See Case 34.)

Further examples of a breach of good manners or sportsmanship include: **proven lying** in a protest hearing (as opposed to honest differences in recollection of the incident); **intentional cheating** (for instance, racing with an unmeasured sail or removing mandatory ballast, as opposed to class or racing rule violations caused by ignorance); **intentional damage to another boat** afloat or on shore, (for instance, cutting someone's shrouds in the night); **fighting**, particularly where there is injury or damage; **stealing** from another boat or from private property at a club or elsewhere; and **foul or threatening language**, particularly if it is continued after receiving a clear warning.

Obviously rule 69 is an important rule, but its effectiveness relies on the integrity of the protest committee that chooses to invoke it. Each case must be carefully examined to determine, as accurately as possible, exactly what happened, what events led up to the incident, and what the probable motives of the individuals involved were. The hearing and deliberations should be conducted as objectively as possible with an effort to keep emotions out, and must follow rule 69.2's due process rules strictly. A competitor's previous actions should not be weighed in the case unless germane and accurately represented. Appeals and cases that are cited as precedent must be closely examined to be sure that they are truly nearly identical in all ways. And before imposing a penalty under rule 69.2(h), the protest committee must thoroughly consider if the weight of the punishment is justified by the competitor's action. See the World Sailing and US Sailing Judges manuals for guidance on holding rule 69 hearings.

Disqualification from a series for misconduct is a strong penalty by itself, due to the effect it generally has on the individual(s) and from the adverse publicity it can create. But in addition, depending on the severity of the penalty, this penalty must also be reported to US Sailing or the appropriate national authorit(ies). In turn they can conduct an investigation and exclude the competitor(s) or boat(s) from the sport for a period of time. This is extremely strong as it will have an impact on the sailor's life beyond just their sailing, in ways that may extend beyond just the time period of their penalty.

Note that a sailor against whom an allegation of a breach of rule 69 is made, and a person bringing an allegation under rule 69, is a *party* to a hearing (see the definition *Party*), and as such has the right to appeal the decision of the protest committee under rule 70.1(a) (Appeals and Requests to a National Authority). U.S. sailors may also file a grievance under Regulation 15 of the US Sailing Regulations when they feel actions have been taken against them that are not in accordance with the *rules*.

RULE 3 — DECISION TO RACE

The responsibility for a boat's decision to participate in a race or to continue *racing* is hers alone.

There have been attempted lawsuits brought unsuccessfully against race committees by sailors who have had accidents during races in strong winds. Their contentions have been, in part, that the race committee has jeopardized their safety by holding races in severe conditions. The decision to start, postpone or abandon a race is within the jurisdiction of the race committee (see rule 90.1, Race Committee; Sailing Instructions; Scoring). Rule 62 (Redress) should not be interpreted to restrict or interfere with its authority and responsibilities in matters of race management. Under rule 3, each boat has the sole responsibility to decide whether or not to race. And if a boat decides not to race, she cannot claim her score was made worse through no fault of her own. (See Appeal 39.)

Notice that it is the **boat's** responsibility to decide. Every sailor on a boat has the responsibility to voice his or her opinion as to whether or not to *start* or to continue to *race*. Nothing in this rule protects an owner, skipper or helmsman from a liability suit by their crew.

RULE 4 — ACCEPTANCE OF THE RULES

RULE 4.1

(a) By participating or intending to participate in an event conducted under the *rules*, each competitor and boat owner agrees to accept the *rules*.

(b) A *support person* by providing support, or a parent or guardian by permitting their child to enter an event, agrees to accept the *rules*.

RULE 4.2

Each competitor and boat owner agrees, on behalf of their *support persons*, that such *support persons* are bound by the *rules*.

RULE 4.3

Acceptance of the *rules* includes agreement

(a) to be governed by the *rules*;

(b) to accept the penalties imposed and other action taken under the *rules*, subject to the appeal and review procedures provided in them, as the final determination of any matter arising under the *rules*;

(c) with respect to any such determination, not to resort to any court of law or tribunal not provided for in the *rules*; and

(d) by each competitor and boat owner to ensure that their *support persons* are aware of the *rules*.

RULE 4.4

The person in charge of each boat shall ensure that all competitors in the crew and the boat's owner are aware of their responsibilities under this rule.

RULE 4.5

This rule may be changed by a prescription of the national authority of the venue.

Rule 4 states that when you decide to race under the World Sailing *Racing Rules of Sailing*, you agree to be governed by those *rules*, and to keep actions made in accordance with the *rules* within the rules system of the sport; i.e., not to take them to any outside court. Note that Appendix J (Notice of Race and Sailing Instructions) requires that the Notice of Race include, when applicable, an entry form to be signed by the boat's owner or owner's representative, containing words such as: "'I agree to be bound by *The Racing Rules of Sailing* and by all other *rules* that govern this event'." (See rule J1.2(11).)

    This agreement becomes especially important when an incident results in a high cost of repair or replacement. Rule 67 (Damages) states, "*The question of damages arising from a breach of any* **rule** *shall be governed by the prescriptions, if any, of the national authority.*"

In the United States, US Sailing prescribes "...*that responsibility for damages arising from any breach of the* **rules** *shall be based on fault as determined by application of the* **rules**, *and that she shall not be governed by the legal doctrine of 'assumption of risk' for monetary damages resulting from contact with other boats.*" Furthermore, the prescription states, "*A protest committee shall find facts and make decisions only in compliance with the* **rules**. *No protest committee or US Sailing appeal authority shall adjudicate any claim for damages. Such a claim is subject to the jurisdiction of the courts.*"

In other words, a protest committee can find only the facts; and a protest committee, or appeals committee acting on an appeal, can decide only which boat was at fault under the *rules*. They cannot decide issues of claims for damages.

When you disagree with a protest committee's application or interpretation of the *rules*, you may appeal under rule 70.1 (Appeals and Requests to a National Authority), unless the right of appeal has been denied under rule 70.5, rule C9.1 (match racing) or rule D2.6(b)(2) (team racing). If you feel that any of your rights as a competitor have been denied by the organizing authority, race committee, protest committee or technical committee, and it hurt, or may hurt, your score or place in a race or series through no fault of your own, you can request redress under rule 62.1(a) (Redress) and you can appeal that decision as well.

If ever you feel you've been aggrieved by an action not under the jurisdiction of the *rules*, you can take your grievance to the organizing authority for the race or series, or to US Sailing through Regulation 15 of the US Sailing Regulations.

Finally, note that you are responsible for ensuring that your crew, boat owner and *support persons* are aware of the *rules*, and that they know that by your participation in the race, they have agreed to accept the *rules*, and that **you** can be penalized if they break any of the *rules* (see the discussion in the definition *Support Person*).

RULE 5 — RULES GOVERNING ORGANIZING AUTHORITIES AND OFFICIALS

The organizing authority, race committee, technical committee, protest committee and other race officials shall be governed by the *rules* in the conduct and judging of the event.

In previous editions of the rule book this was rule 84. Note the use of the term "event." This reminds organizers and race officials that they must comply with all the *rules* for organizing and officiating the event (not just the racing), including any appropriate World Sailing Codes (see the definition *Rule (b)*).

RULE 6 — WORLD SAILING REGULATIONS

RULE 6.1

Each competitor, boat owner and support person shall comply with the World Sailing Regulations that have been designated by World Sailing as having the status of a rule. These regulations as of 30 June 2020 are the World Sailing:

- Advertising Code
- Anti-Doping Code
- Betting and Anti-Corruption Code
- Disciplinary Code
- Eligibility Code
- Sailor Categorization Code

RULE 6.2

Rule 63.1 does not apply unless protests are permitted in the Regulation alleged to have been broken.

From the Introduction to *The Racing Rules of Sailing*, "*…the World Sailing Regulations are referred to in the definition Rule and in rule 6, but they are not included in the book because they can be changed at any time. The most recent versions of the Regulations are published on the World Sailing website; new versions will be announced through national authorities.*"

World Sailing Regulations can be found at: sailing.org/documents/regulations/regulations.

Note, the World Sailing Regulations that have the status of "rules" rank as a *rule* (see the definition *Rule*), and sailors, *support persons* or race organizers and race officials who break those *rules* are subject to appropriate penalty or discipline. For instance, all competitors whether Olympic-bound or not, are prudent to recognize that the use of banned drugs is prohibited in sailing, as is betting.

Also note, rule 60.5 (Right to Protest; Right to Request Redress or Rule 69 Action) states, *"However, neither a boat nor a committee may protest for an alleged breach of rule 69 or a Regulation referred to in rule 6, unless permitted by the Regulation concerned."*

gybing no rights tacking

PORT TACK

close-hauled

5

The Definitions

The Definitions are the "dictionary" of the rule book. Words and terms like "racing," "obstruction" and "proper course" are specifically defined so that there is no question or debate as to their meaning. When a defined word or term is used in a *rule*, it is printed in *italic* type. The meaning of several other terms such as "boat" and "technical committee" is given in the Terminology section in the Introduction to the rule book. Before studying the *rules*, be sure to study the Definitions and Terminology and then actively check back to them as you go through each *rule*; you'll find that in a short time you will be confident of each *rule's* full meaning.

ABANDON

A race that a race committee or protest committee *abandons* is void but may be resailed.

A race committee can *abandon* a race before it starts (rule 27.3, Other Race Committee Actions Before the Starting Signal), while it is under way (rule 32, Shortening or Abandoning After the Start) or even after one or more boats have finished (rule 32.1). To signal an *abandonment* on the water, the race committee will make three consecutive sound signals and display flag N (meaning return to the starting area for a new start), flag N over H (meaning return to the harbor and await further instructions) or flag N over A (meaning no more races that day). (See Race Signals.) A protest committee, acting on a request for redress, can *abandon* a race (rule 64.3, Decisions on Redress). A race that has been properly *abandoned* may be resailed.

N

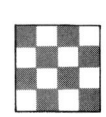

N over H

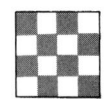

N over A

Notice that once the race has started, the race committee is governed by rule 32 when deciding whether to *abandon* a race. Rule 32.1 lists the five scenarios in which the race committee may *abandon* a race:

(a) because of foul weather,
(b) because of insufficient wind making it unlikely that any boat will *finish* within the time limit,
(c) because a *mark* is missing or out of position, or
(d) for any other reason directly affecting the safety or fairness of the competition.

Rule 32.1 also states that the race committee may *abandon* a race because of an error in the starting procedure.

"Does rule 32.1(d) mean that the race committee can abandon a race in progress when a large wind shift occurs?"

Yes, when in its judgment the wind shift has made the race an unsatisfactory test of skill and therefore "unfair." However, in my opinion it is desirable to reduce the number of subjective decisions a race committee can make once the race has started and it can see who is or isn't doing well. Therefore, once a race has been started, race committees should make every attempt to anticipate and react to wind shifts and to reposition *marks* in order to keep the race "fair" before deciding to *abandon*, particularly after the first boat has rounded the first *mark*.

After at least one boat has *started*, *sailed the course* and *finished* within the race time limit, if any, the race committee and protest committee are required, before *abandoning* the race, to consider the consequences for all boats in the race or series (see rule 32 and Appeal 100).

CLEAR ASTERN AND CLEAR AHEAD; OVERLAP

One boat is *clear astern* of another when her hull and equipment in normal position are behind a line abeam from the aftermost point of the other boat's hull and equipment in normal position. The other boat is *clear ahead*. They *overlap* when neither is *clear astern*. However, they also *overlap* when a boat between them *overlaps* both. These terms always apply to boats on the same *tack*. They apply to boats on opposite *tacks* only when rule 18 applies between them or when both boats are sailing more than ninety degrees from the true wind.

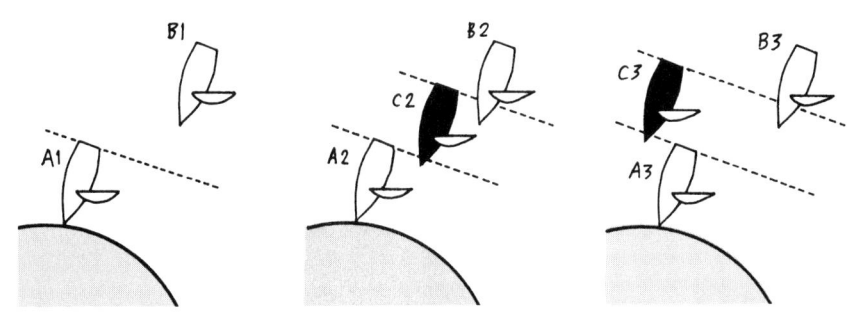

In position 1, A and B are not overlapped; A is clear ahead and B is clear astern.

In position 2, C is in between A and B and overlapped with both of them; therefore B is overlapped with A.

In position 3, C is not in between A and B; therefore B is overlapped with C, C is overlapped with A, and A and B are not overlapped.

Putting aside for a moment what *tack* the boats are on, let's look at two boats sailing near each other. To figure out if they are *overlapped*, take one of the boats and draw a line down her centerline. Then find the aftermost point of her hull or equipment in **normal position**. Draw another line perpendicular to the centerline and through the aftermost point. If the other boat's hull and equipment in **normal position** are completely behind that line, she is *"clear astern"* and the other boat is *"clear ahead."* If she is across that line at all, then neither boat is *clear astern* of the other; therefore they are *"overlapped."*

Now let's say one of the boats was *clear ahead* of the other boat by five feet. Put a third boat in between the two. If the boat that was *clear astern* now *overlaps* this middle boat and the middle boat *overlaps* the boat that was *clear ahead*, the definition says that now each boat is *overlapped* with each other including the boats that were originally *clear astern* and *clear ahead* of each other.

One point worth discussing is determining the aftermost point of the hull and equipment in normal position. It literally means the point on the boat that is the farthest aft; i.e., the point that would hit a wall first if the boat were backed into one. Notice also the term "normal position." "Normal position" is generally interpreted as the position where your equipment is normally located in the existing wind and sea conditions. If your auxiliary engine is tilted up, then in all likelihood the propeller is the aftermost point; and if you've been sailing the race with it up, you can't come into a *mark* and quickly swing the engine down just to break an *overlap* by making your boat shorter.

Finally, notice that the terms "clear astern," "clear ahead" and "overlap" do not apply to boats on opposite *tacks* unless either rule 18 (Mark-Room) applies between them (which is when one of the boats is in the *zone* at a *mark*), or unless both of the boats are sailing below a beam reach (90 degrees to the true wind), as they would be doing on a downwind leg. So two boats side by side on opposite *tacks* inside the *zone* at a leeward *mark* are considered to be *overlapped*.

CONFLICT OF INTEREST

A person has a *conflict of interest* if he
(a) may gain or lose as a result of a decision to which he contributes,
(b) may reasonably appear to have a personal or financial interest which could affect his ability to be impartial, or
(c) has a close personal interest in a decision.

Rule 63.4 (Conflict of Interest) reads, "*(b) A member of a protest committee with a **conflict of interest** shall not be a member of the committee for the hearing, unless (1) all **parties** consent, or (2) the protest committee decides that the **conflict of interest** is not significant.*" The purpose of this rule is clearly to provide competitors with the fairest possible hearing without any taint of prejudice or self-interest among the protest committee members.

Persons who, in my opinion, **could** be considered to have a *conflict of interest* are parents (or offspring), instructors or coaches, employers or employees, and sponsors or financial contributors. Normally, members of the same yacht club or association or a fellow sailor with the same nationality are not considered to have a "conflict of interest." However, in the right set of circumstances, any of these persons could be judged to have a *conflict of interest*.

"Can a person with a conflict of interest be on a protest committee?"

Yes, if all the *parties* are OK with the person being on the committee, or if the protest committee itself decides that the conflict is not significant. See the discussion of rule 63.4 (Conflict of Interest). This reflects the fact that often it is difficult to find qualified or willing people to be on the protest committee.

There are times when protest committee members will have witnessed an incident or will have initiated a *protest* against a boat; for example, under rule 31 (Touching a Mark) if they see a boat touch a *mark*. In this context they do not have a *conflict of interest*. However the US Sailing prescription to rule 63.1 states: "*US Sailing prescribes that: (a) No person who brings an incident to the attention of the protest committee or who will give evidence regarding an incident shall, when practicable, be a member of the protest committee for a hearing involving that incident.*" Therefore that person is not allowed to be **both** a member of the protest committee as well as the protestor or even a witness. However, if the sailing instructions specifically state that that prescription does not apply, the person **can** be a member of the protest committee and be the protestor or a witness. Note that rule 63.6 (Taking Evidence and Finding Facts) requires them to state that they saw the incident, and to give all their evidence and testimony in front of the *parties* to the hearing. (See also rule 63.3(a), Right to Be Present, and Appeal 39.)

"What can I do if I honestly feel a member of the protest committee might have a conflict of interest?"

If you feel any member of a protest committee has a *conflict of interest*, you may object. Rule 63.4(a) reads, "*A **party** to the hearing who believes a member of the protest committee has a **conflict of interest** shall object as soon as possible.*" The protest committee should then consider your objection before proceeding (Appendix M2.3, Recommendations for Protest Committees; Before the Hearing). In evaluating members of a protest committee as potentially having a *conflict of interest*, the important criterion is: will their hearing of the evidence, their finding of the facts and/or their application and interpretation of the *rules* be hindered by any prejudice or favoritism toward or against any of the *parties* to the hearing? If members of the protest committee honestly feel that any predisposition on their part will affect their decision in the hearing, they should respectfully decline to serve. Furthermore, rule 63.4(a) requires them to "*declare any possible **conflict of interest** as soon as* [they are] *aware of it.*"

FETCHING

A boat is *fetching* a *mark* when she is in a position to pass to windward of it and leave it on the required side without changing *tack*.

Assume you are on *starboard tack* approaching the windward *mark* to be left to port. You are sailing a close-hauled course and it is close whether you are going to make it around the *mark*. You luff up to head to wind, coast around the *mark*, and then bear away onto the next leg of the course. You "fetched" the *mark* because you never went past head to wind during your rounding maneuver. If you had gone past head to wind, you would have instantly changed *tack* from *starboard tack* to *port tack* and you would have failed to "fetch" the *mark*. Anytime you are in a position where you can "fetch" the *mark*, you are *fetching*.

Note, if a boat is approaching a port-hand windward *mark* on *port tack*, and has to tack to round the *mark* (i.e., change *tack*), she is not *fetching* the *mark*.

FINISH

A boat *finishes* when, after *starting*, any part of her hull crosses the finishing line from the course side. However, she has not *finished* if after crossing the finishing line she

(a) takes a penalty under rule 44.2,
(b) corrects an error in *sailing the course* made at the line, or
(c) continues to *sail the course*.

You *finish* when any part of your hull (not your crew or equipment) crosses the finishing line. Therefore, in a strong adverse current for example, all you need to do is get your bow across the finishing line to get your finishing place or time. Rule 28.1 (Sailing the Race) states, "*After **finishing** she need not cross the finishing line completely.*"

The "hull" is the boat's main body or shell. Things attached to the hull like racks, or things protruding from the hull like prods for the spinnaker, are not part of the "hull" (see the World Sailing *Equipment Rules of Sailing* and a dictionary.)

If you foul a boat at the finishing line or touch a finishing *mark*, it's possible that you will have crossed the finishing line before doing your penalty turns (see rule 44.2, Penalties at the Time of an Incident). That is not a problem. Simply get clear of other boats, do your penalty turn(s) and then cross the finishing line again. You *finish* when you cross the finishing line after taking your penalty; i.e., the first time you crossed the line will be disregarded.

If you do not *finish* correctly, the race committee is required to score you DNF (Did not *finish*) without needing to protest you (rule A5.1, Scores Determined by the Race Committee). If you feel it has incorrectly scored you DNF, you can request redress under rule 62.1(a) (Redress). However, if you *finish*, but the race committee thinks it saw you touch a finishing *mark* or foul

THE DEFINITIONS **81**

White wins because her hull crosses the finishing line before Gray's hull. The position of the sails and equipment are no longer relevant for determining when a boat finishes.

another boat and you do not take a penalty, it must score you as having *finished* and then it can protest you for breaking rule 31 (Touching a Mark) or the appropriate racing rule in accordance with rules 60.2 (Right to Protest; Right to Request Redress or Rule 69 Action) and 61 (Protest Requirements).

Note, if the race committee thinks you skipped a *mark* or otherwise failed to *sail the course* correctly, it is required to score you NSC (Did not *sail the course*) without needing to protest you (rule A5.1, Scores Determined by the Race Committee). Again, if you feel it has incorrectly scored you NSC, you can request redress under rule 62.1(a).

Sometimes, when coming up to a finishing line, it is not always clear which way to go across it. The definition says that a boat *finishes* when she crosses the finishing line from the course side. The "course side" is the side the last *mark* of the course prior to the finishing line is on. Therefore, simply cross the line in the natural direction from the last *mark* you rounded or passed, regardless of any required sides either of the finishing *marks* may have had at other times during the race (see Cases 45 and 129).

"If the race committee shortens the course at a leeward mark that was supposed to be left to port, but anchors the committee boat to the left of the mark looking downwind, do I cross the finishing line leaving the mark to starboard, or do I hook around the mark and leave it to port?

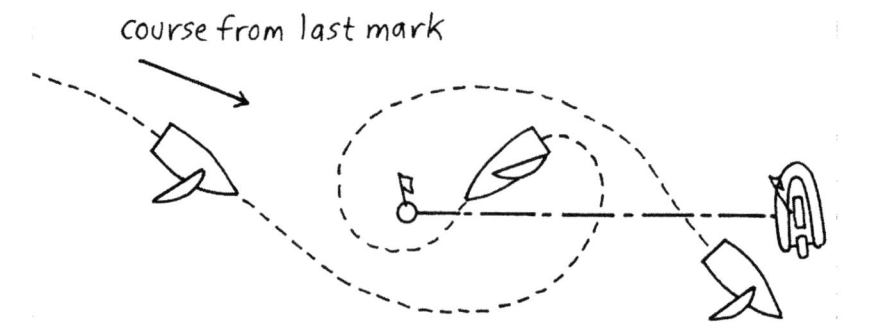

82 UNDERSTANDING THE RACING RULES OF SAILING THROUGH 2024

course from last mark

Boat X finishes when she crosses the finishing line the third time.

You cross the finishing line from the "course side," which means leaving the mark to starboard. Case 129 says, "After the race committee shortens the course, the mark is no longer a rounding mark. It becomes a finishing mark (see rule 32.2). To comply with rule 28, boats must finish in accordance with the definition Finish. Therefore they must cross the finishing line from its course side." And if you realize you have crossed the finishing line in the wrong direction, you can correct your error so that your course complies with rule 28.1 (Sailing the Race). Remember that this may require that you "unwind your string" first before crossing the line in the correct direction (see the definition *Sail the Course*).

Finally, there are times when the course requires boats to sail through a gate after each lap, or the course is windward/leeward twice around with the start/finish line in the middle of the beat. If boats cross the line on their way to the windward mark, they are continuing to *sail the course*, and therefore they have not "finished."

KEEP CLEAR

A boat *keeps clear* of a right-of-way boat

(a) if the right-of-way boat can sail her course with no need to take avoiding action and,
(b) when the boats are *overlapped*, if the right-of-way boat can also change course in both directions without immediately making contact.

The *rules* are structured so that when two boats converge on the race course, one has the right-of-way and the other must stay out of her way; i.e., *keep clear*. The preamble to Part 2, Section A reads, "*A boat has right of way over another boat when the other boat is required to **keep clear** of her.*" I call the boat that is required to *keep clear* the "keep-clear" boat.

The principle in the definition is clear: right-of-way boats should be able to sail their race without keep-clear boats getting in their way. That means that not only must a keep-clear boat not hit a right-of-way boat, she must also not get so close that the right-of-way boat can no longer sail her straight-ahead course because she has to take action to avoid contact with the keep-clear boat. Though this avoiding "action" will normally be a change of course, it could also be a change of speed or some other action.

On the issue of "need," I believe that when the right-of-way boat has a reasonable apprehension that contact will occur without action on her part, she is justified in saying she "needed" to take action, even if subsequent analysis of the situation shows that the keep-clear boat would have actually cleared her by inches (see Case 50).

The second part of the definition (part (b)) closes a possible loophole caused by rule 16 (Changing Course). Rule 16.1 requires that when right-of-way boats change course, they give other boats *room* to *keep clear*. The loophole is that a *windward* boat (W) or a *port-tack* boat (P) could position herself so close to a *leeward* boat (L) or a *starboard-tack* boat (S) such that the moment L or S changed course she would hit W or P. W or P could then claim that L or S had broken rule 16.1 by not giving her *room* to *keep clear*. The definition closes that loophole by addressing **overlapped** boats and telling W or P that she is not *keeping clear* if she allows herself to get so close to L or S that L or S couldn't change course in **both** directions at that moment without "immediately" making contact with her. Keep in mind that boats on opposite tacks are considered "overlapped" when rule 18 applies between them, or when both of them are sailing more than 90 degrees from the true wind.

Note that the word "if" in part (b) of the definition suggests that L or S does not need to actually hit W or P to prove she couldn't change course without making immediate contact. If the protest committee decides that L or S could not have changed course in both directions without immediately hitting W or P, then W or P has broken rule 11 (On the Same Tack, Overlapped) or rule 10 (On Opposite Tacks) simply by their extreme close proximity to the right-of-way boats.

"Do I have to keep clear of the right-of-way boat's crew, sails, equipment, spars, etc. even when they are clearly out of their 'normal position'?"

Yes. In the "Introduction" to *The Racing Rules of Sailing*, under "Terminology," it says, "*'Boat' means a sailboat and the crew on board.*" And the definition makes no distinction regarding whether or not a boat is carrying her crew, sails, equipment, spars, etc. in "normal position" (see Case 91). The only exception is in the rare instance where a boat is *keeping clear* and suddenly something from the right-of-way boat flies out unexpectedly and immediately makes contact with the keep-clear boat. Case 77 describes such a case where just after rounding a leeward *mark*, the head of the spinnaker of the boat *clear ahead* (A) came loose and flew back and touched the headstay of the boat *clear astern* (B). The decision concludes, "[Rule 12] requires B to keep clear of A, which she is doing because nothing B did or failed to do required A 'to take avoiding action' (see the definition Keep Clear). This is shown by the fact that the contact between them results exclusively from A's equipment moving unexpectedly out of normal position."

LEEWARD AND WINDWARD

A boat's *leeward* side is the side that is or, when she is head to wind, was away from the wind. However, when sailing by the lee or directly downwind, her *leeward* side is the side on which her mainsail lies. The other side is her *windward* side. When two boats on the same *tack overlap*, the one on the *leeward* side of the other is the *leeward* boat. The other is the *windward* boat.

The definition *Tack, Starboard* or *Port* tells us that we are always on a *tack*,

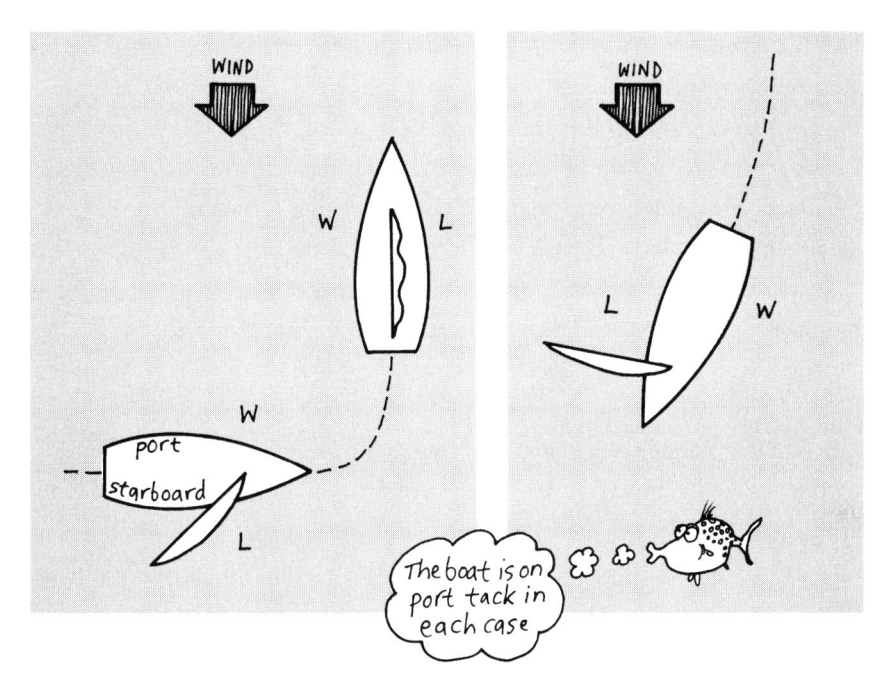

THE DEFINITIONS **85**

The boat on the left is reaching with her port side toward the wind; therefore her port side is her windward side and she is on port tack. When she luffs up to head to wind she remains on port tack. The boat on the right is sailing by the lee with her mainsail lying naturally on her starboard side. Therefore her port side is her windward side by definition and she is also on port tack.

and that whether we are on *port* or *starboard tack* is determined by our *windward* side; i.e., if our *windward* side is our port side, we are on *port tack*.

This definition tells us that our *windward* side is the side closest to the wind, and that our *leeward* side is the opposite side. If the boat is heading directly into the wind, then whichever side **was** the *windward* side before the boat was head to wind is still considered the *windward* side.

The only exception is when the boat is heading directly downwind or "by the lee" (which means the boat has continued to turn past directly downwind without the boom changing sides). In that case, the *windward* side is the side opposite the side the boom is on.

"If I'm sailing close-hauled on port-tack in light air and heel the boat sharply to windward such that the boom falls to the port side of the boat, am I now on starboard tack; or if I'm sailing by the lee and forcibly holding the mainsail over the port side with my arm, am I still on starboard tack?"

No. Remember that when you are not sailing directly downwind or by the lee, your *tack* is determined by the side of the boat the wind is blowing over. In your first case, when you are sailing close-hauled, the wind is blowing over your port side regardless of where your boom is located; therefore you are on *port tack*. The same would be true if you are sailing along on *port tack*, and then go head to wind and push your boom out on the port side to back down. You are still on *port tack* as long as your bow doesn't **pass** head to wind. The moment it **passes** head to wind, you are now on *starboard tack*.

When you are sailing directly downwind or by the lee, your *leeward* side is the side on which your mainsail "lies." "Lies" is used intentionally to indicate that it is the side where your mainsail would **naturally** lie; i.e., be pushed by the wind, as opposed to by the control of some other force such as your arm, the mainsheet or gravity. Therefore, in your second case, you are now on *port tack* because if you released the mainsail, it would lie on your starboard side. The same would be true if, while sailing directly downwind, you trimmed the mainsail in amidships. Your *tack* will be determined by where the mainsail would lie naturally; in this case, most likely it will want to go back out to the side it was on before you trimmed it in.

Finally, there is the definition of *windward* and *leeward* boat. If the boats are **on the same** *tack* and they are **overlapped**, the one on the *leeward* side of the other is the *leeward* boat. The other is the *windward* boat. Notice that if they are not *overlapped*, they are not *"windward"* and *"leeward"* boats; they are *"clear ahead"* and *"clear astern."*

MARK

An object the sailing instructions require a boat to leave on a specified side, a race committee vessel surrounded by navigable water from which the starting or finishing line extends, and an object intentionally attached to the object or vessel. However, an anchor line is not part of the *mark*.

A *mark* can be an inflatable ball, a bell buoy, a large power boat, an island or any object the sailing instructions so indicate. Notice that often the sailing instructions require that government marks be passed on their required side as you sail from one turning *mark* to the next. These government marks are *marks* of the course as well. Also note that the entire object is the *mark*, not just the above-water part.

THE DEFINITIONS 87

10 seconds to start...

I hope W knows that the keep-off buoy and its line are part of the committee boat and he's not allowed to hit them or get room between them and L!

I'm sure W has read the definition of a mark and knows that... Right?!

On a starting line between a race committee boat and a buoy, the **entire** race committee boat is a *mark* even though the actual end of the line is marked by a flag or some other specific point on the boat. Note that anything that is **intentionally** attached to the object is also part of the *mark*; for instance, a flag, a long antenna or a swimming platform. This also includes something temporarily attached such as a Whaler tied up to the race committee boat, or a "keep-off buoy" hung off the transom of the race committee boat to keep boats farther away. However, the race committee's anchor line is not part of the *mark*.

MARK-ROOM

Room for a boat to leave a *mark* on the required side. Also,

(a) *room* to sail to the *mark* when her *proper course* is to sail close to it, and
(b) *room* to round or pass the *mark* as necessary to *sail the course* without touching the *mark*.

However, *mark-room* for a boat does not include *room* to tack unless she is *overlapped* inside and to *windward* of the boat required to give *mark-room* and she would be *fetching* the *mark* after her tack.

This definition is central to applying rule 18 (Mark-Room). It describes the "space" (see definition *Room*) a boat needs to give another boat when one of them is in the *zone*. The definition describes two different points in time: first, while the inside boat is sailing "to" the *mark*; and then while the inside boat is rounding or passing the *mark*.

Let's look at the first part of the definition first. Rule 18 begins to apply when the first of the boats involved reaches the *zone* (rule 18.1), which is normally when she is three of her hull lengths from the *mark*. From that point, the outside boat or the boat *clear astern* must give the other boat *mark-room*. *Mark-room* is the space the inside or *clear ahead* boat needs to leave the *mark* on the required side. (See Case 118.)

Furthermore, if the *proper course* of the inside or *clear ahead* boat is to sail close to the *mark* (within a couple of feet or so), which will certainly be the case when the boat is rounding the *mark*, then *mark-room* includes the *room* (i.e., the space) needed to sail to the *mark* in a "seamanlike way," which means handling her boat in a normal way without risk of touching the boat giving her *mark-room* or the *mark*. Allowing her this space is to prevent an outside boat with luffing rights from luffing an inside boat inside the *zone* before she gets to the *mark*. Note, however, the use of the term "*proper course*" in the definition is purely a test for whether the boat is entitled to *room* to sail to the *mark*; it does not mean that the boat is entitled to space to actually sail her "*proper course*" to the *mark*.

Say, for instance, the inside boat was leaving the *mark* to port. Clearly, it would not be "seamanlike" to sail a course that will result in touching the *mark* or leaving the *mark* to starboard. Therefore, to sail "to" the *mark*, P will sail a course that will bring her slightly to the right of the mark in anticipation of her rounding or passing maneuver at the *mark*. See the discussion of the definition *Room* for a discussion on how far from the mark it is "seamanlike" to sail.

An example of a boat in the *zone* whose *proper course* is **not** to sail close to the *mark*, is a boat approaching the finishing line a couple lengths from one of the finishing *marks*. Clearly the boat is in the *zone* of the finishing *mark*, but her *proper course* will be to cross the finishing line as soon as possible, which may mean she will get no closer than two lengths to the actual *mark*. In that case, *mark-room* does not include space for her to sail "to" the *mark* (see the discussion of rules 18.2(b) and 18.2(c)(2) in Chapter 8 to understand why this is important).

"OK, I understand that when I'm a keep-clear boat and I'm approaching a rounding mark, I get room to sail "to" the mark in a seamanlike way. But how much room do I get when I am rounding or passing the mark; and when have I taken all the room I am entitled to?"

You are entitled to *room* to round or pass the *mark* as necessary to *sail the course*, which means just enough space to allow you to round the *mark* in a "seamanlike way" (see the definition *Room*). "Seamanlike way" means the space needed to handle your boat in a competent but not expert way, and not be at risk of touching the *mark* or the outside right-of-way boat during your rounding. Note, *mark-room* does not include the space you might want to sail your *proper course*; i.e., the course you might want to sail for tactical reasons such as a wide and tight rounding. (See Case 21 for more discussion of *mark-room*.)

Once you have rounded the *mark* and are on a course needed to begin sailing the next leg, and you can *keep clear* of an outside right-of-way boat without risk of touching the *mark* or fouling another boat, you have been given *mark-room* and you must thereafter *keep clear* of right-of-way boats. This might occur before you have left the *mark* astern, or even after you've left the *mark* astern if there's a strong adverse current.

Note that when an inside boat needs to tack in order to *sail the course*, she is entitled to the space she needs to tack to round or pass the *mark*, but only when she is *overlapped* to *windward* of a boat that is required to give her *mark-room*, and she would be *fetching* the *mark* after her tack. This occurs most commonly at the windward *mark*; it is rare a boat needs to tack around a leeward *mark* in order to *sail the course*.

OBSTRUCTION

An object that a boat could not pass without changing course substantially, if she were sailing directly towards it and one of her hull lengths from it. An object that can be safely passed on only one side and an object, area or line so designated by the sailing instructions are also *obstructions*. However, a boat *racing* is not an *obstruction* to other boats unless they are required to *keep clear* of her or, if rule 22 applies, avoid her. A vessel under way, including a boat *racing*, is never a continuing *obstruction*.

An *obstruction* can be **anything** on the race course including a moored boat, dock, breakwater, cruising boat, iceberg in the racing area or another boat in your race, large enough to qualify it as an *obstruction*. In determining whether the object can be considered an *obstruction,* the definition offers three criteria:

1) The object must be large enough to require you to change course substantially **if** you were aiming right at the largest part of it, regardless of whether you **actually** are or not. In other words, it is a hypothetical test. An object does not become an *obstruction* or cease to be an *obstruction* based on where you are actually aiming at the time in the race. (See Cases 11 and 125.)

2) The amount of course change required is determined from a point one of your boat's overall lengths away from the object. This strongly suggests that you keep a lookout for anything ahead of you, as opposed to suddenly finding yourself about to hit something right in front of you and needing to slam your tiller over to miss it.

3) The size of the course change must be "substantial;" i.e., a large course change. In a twenty-foot boat, a course change of 10 degrees moves the bow about three and a half feet. Done when one boat-length away, a 10-degree alteration will clear a seven-foot object on either side. **As my general rule** I would say that a course change less than 10 degrees is not "substantial;" i.e., a stationary object clearly less than one-third your boat's length would not be an *obstruction*, though a moving object will require a larger alteration to get around it. Obviously, a lobster pot or an average-size channel marker is not going to require you to change your course "substantially," but a race committee boat, a breakwater or another sailboat in a race will.

A powerboat can be an *obstruction* if it's large enough. When a race committee decides to use a powerboat as one end of the starting line, the powerboat becomes a *mark* also. Notice that it doesn't cease to be an *obstruction*. It is always an *obstruction,* but now it also happens to be a *mark.*

The sailing instructions can make other objects (i.e., objects that do not otherwise qualify to be an *obstruction*), areas (e.g., an area marked by keep-out buoys) or lines (e.g., a starting or finishing line) an *obstruction*, but they need to specifically state that the item is an *obstruction.*

If the sailing instructions merely say something like "boats cannot cross the starting line when sailing to the leeward mark," that does not make the starting line an *obstruction*.

"Can you clarify the times when a boat in a race can be considered an 'obstruction'?"

Sure. A boat in a race, either your race or another race, is an "obstruction" when either:

1) it has the right of way over at least two boats in the situation; or
2) it is capsized or has not regained control after capsizing; or
3) it is anchored or aground; or
4) it is trying to help a person or vessel in danger.

Otherwise, boats in a race are not considered *obstructions*.

Furthermore, when *obstructions* are boats under way, including boats that are *racing*, they are never considered "continuing" *obstructions*. This pertains to the application of rule 19.2(c) (Giving Room at an Obstruction).

OVERLAP

See *Clear Astern and Clear Ahead; Overlap*

PARTY

A *party* to a hearing is

(a) for a protest hearing: a protestor, a protestee;
(b) for a redress hearing: a boat requesting redress or for which redress is requested; a boat for which a hearing is called to consider redress under rule 60.3(b); a race committee acting under rule 60.2(b); a technical committee acting under rule 60.4(b);
(c) for a request for redress under rule 62.1(a): the body alleged to have made an improper action or omission;
(d) a person against whom an allegation of a breach of rule 69.1(a) is made; a person presenting an allegation under rule 69.2(e)(1);
(e) a *support person* subject to a hearing under rule 60.3(d) or 69; any boat that person supports; a person appointed to present an allegation under rule 60.3(d).

However, the protest committee is never a *party*.

It is important to understand exactly who is, and is not, a *party* to a hearing. The primary reason is that the rules in Part 5, Protests, Redress, Hearings, Misconduct and Appeals, provide many specific rights and obligations for *parties* to a hearing and many requirements of a protest committee regarding *parties* to a hearing. Furthermore, only a *party* to a hearing may appeal a decision of a protest committee under rule 70.1 (Appeals and Requests to a National Authority).

When boats lodge a *protest* they automatically become a *party* to the hearing (protestor), as do the boats they are protesting (protestee). The same is true when they request redress under rule 62 (Redress), or when redress is being requested or considered for them by the race, technical or protest committee under rules 60.2(b), 60.3(b) or 60.4(b) (Right to Protest; Right to Request Redress or Rule 69 Action).

When boats request redress under rule 62.1(a), claiming that an improper action or omission of the race committee, organizing authority or technical committee made their score or place significantly worse, those bodies also become a *party* to the hearing. Note that the protest committee holding the hearing is never a *party*, even when it is the subject of a request for redress under rule 62.1(a).

Often, in the course of a hearing, a third boat will become a "suspect." The protest committee has the right to protest that third boat. Rule 60.3(a)(2) (Right to Protest; Right to Request Redress or Rule 69 Action) says, "*[The protest committee] may protest a boat if during the hearing of a valid **protest** it learns that the boat, although not a **party** to the hearing, was involved in the incident and may have broken a **rule**.*" And rule 61.1(c) (Protest Requirements; Informing the Protestee) says, "*If the protest committee decides to protest a boat under rule 60.3(a)(2), it shall inform her as soon as reasonably possible, close the current hearing, proceed as required by rules 61.2 and 63, and hear the original and the new **protests** together.*" Once the protest committee protests the third boat, that boat (now a "protestee") becomes a *party* to the hearing.

A *support person* subject to a hearing called under rule 60.3(d) (Right to Protest; Right to Request Redress or Rule 69 Action) or rule 69 (Misconduct) is a *party*, as is any boat that person supports, and any person appointed to present an allegation under rule 60.3(b). (See rule 63.9, Hearings under Rule 60.3(d) — Support Persons.)

THE DEFINITIONS **93**

"If, after acting on another boat's request for redress, the protest committee abandons the race in which I was first, can I consider myself a 'party to the hearing' because I was 'penalized,' and as such appeal the decision?"

Absolutely not. Rule 64 (Decisions) discusses "penalties," using disqualification as the usual penalty. You were not given a specific "penalty" when the race was *abandoned*. Obviously *abandoning* the race changes series results, moving some competitors up and some down. You may have been disappointed by the *abandonment*, but you were not "penalized" by it.

A "penalty" results from a rule breach either accepted voluntarily or imposed by a protest committee decision. Because you were not liable to be penalized in the incident, you are not a *party* to the hearing and are not entitled to appeal (see Appeal 64).

On the other hand, you certainly can request redress under rule 62.1(a) (Redress), making you a *party* to your redress hearing. You must be prepared to demonstrate what "improper action or omission" the protest committee made in reaching its decision to *abandon* the race, and how the action/omission made your finishing score or place significantly worse through no fault of your own. Then, once the protest committee has made a decision on your redress request, you may appeal **that** decision. Note, however, that a boat is not entitled to redress if the claim is simply that the protest committee's decision made her score or place worse (see rule 62.1(a)).

Finally, persons against whom an allegation of a breach of rule 69.1(a) (Misconduct) has been made, and the person presenting such an allegation, are a *party* to a hearing, thereby giving them standing to appeal the protest committee's decision should they want to do so.

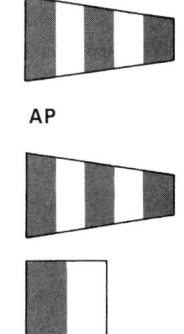

AP

POSTPONE

A postponed race is delayed before its scheduled start but may be started or *abandoned* later.

A race can be *postponed* only if it has not been started. Once a race has been started, it can only be stopped by *abandoning* it. To signal a *postponement*, the race committee will make two consecutive sound signals and display flag

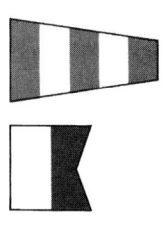

AP over A

94 UNDERSTANDING THE RACING RULES OF SAILING THROUGH 2024

M is surfing waves in order to increase her speed in an attempt to arrive at the next mark and ultimately the finishing line as soon as possible. Therefore, her luffs are justifiable changes in her proper course; and when she bears away she is keeping clear of L. M has not broken any rule.

AP, flag AP over H (meaning return to the harbor and await further instructions) or flag AP over A (meaning no more races that day). See Race Signals.

PROPER COURSE

A course a boat would choose in order to *sail the course* and *finish* as soon as possible in the absence of the other boats referred to in the rule using the term. A boat has no *proper course* before her starting signal.

This is the most subjective definition in the book. It is also very important, particularly in applying rule 17 (On the Same Tack; Proper Course). The concept is very straightforward: your *proper course* is the course you think will get you from the starting line to the finishing line as quickly as possible, taking into account all the factors that will affect your speed. Typically, different sailors will have different ideas on what their fastest course is; thus different boats will have justifiably different *proper courses*.

THE DEFINITIONS   95

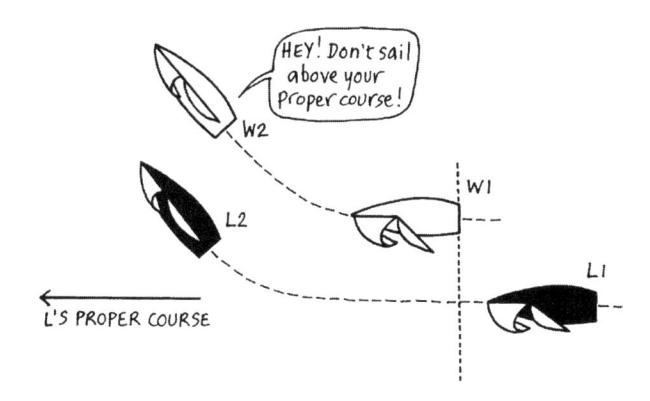

L became overlapped from clear astern and then luffed above her proper course solely to make it more difficult for W to stay ahead of her. In W's absence L would not have luffed at all. Therefore, L has broken rule 17 by sailing above her proper course.

One way to visualize this concept is to imagine a Time Trial. You and nine other sailors show up to race around a fixed-length triangle course, one at a time; the one with the fastest time wins. Around the windward-reach-reach course there are wind shifts, grandstands and a small man-made island on the second reach for the press and photographers. You start. You've already calculated the fastest path up the first beat, accounting for wind shifts, waves, current, time lost while tacking and so on. Down the first reach, as you approach the grandstand area you notice it's creating a huge wind shadow so you bear away to avoid the light air and break through to leeward as quickly as possible. On the second reach, you've calculated that passing to leeward of the press island is the shortest, fastest route to the leeward mark. You finish.

The next boat starts. But this boat goes a different way up the beat. And it doesn't think the grandstand's wind shadow is that bad, so it doesn't bear off as much. And finally it passes the press island to windward and finishes. Both boats were trying to *finish* as quickly as possible and so they were both sailing *proper courses*. In fact, all the boats may have had different opinions as to the fastest course that day. The course each boat sailed was a *proper course*.

Clearly it is possible that there may be several *proper courses* at any given moment, depending upon the particular circumstances involved. However, because it is often difficult to prove when someone is actually on a *proper course* as opposed to sailing extra high or low for tactical purposes, Case 14 suggests, "Which of two different courses is the faster one to the next mark

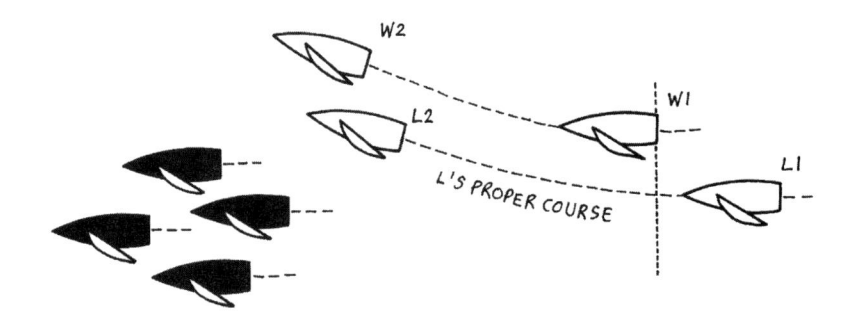

L is "limited" to sailing no higher than her proper course because she became overlapped from clear astern. However, L decides that she will arrive at the gybe mark sooner by luffing and sailing to windward of the pack in front of her. Because she would do this even in the absence of W, it is a legitimate proper course for L and W must keep clear under rule 11.

cannot be determined in advance and is not necessarily proven by one boat or the other reaching the next mark ahead." For protest committees, two reasonable criteria for judging a *proper course* are whether the boat sailing it has a logical reason for its being a *proper course* and whether she applies it with some consistency. (See also Case 134.)

"Isn't my proper course my fastest course to finish in the absence of all the other boats in the race?"

No. The phrase "*in the absence of the other boats referred to in the rule using the term*" clarifies which boats to "remove" when determining whether a course is a *proper course* or not. It does not mean "in the absence of all the boats in the race." Let's say you and another boat are sailing down a reach. You catch up and become *overlapped* to *leeward* of the other boat (W). Rule 17 (On the Same Tack; Proper Course) tells you that you cannot sail above your *proper course* while *overlapped* with W. Because W is the "other boat" referred to in rule 17, your *proper course* is your fastest course in the absence of W.

As you and W continue down the reach, you begin catching up to a group of boats in front of you going slowly. Now you have to decide whether to head up and try to pass the group to windward, or bear away and try to pass them to leeward. You decide that you will arrive at the gybe *mark* faster by heading up and passing the group to windward, but by heading up, you will collide with the *windward* boat. In this case, heading up can be considered your *proper course* because you would do so even in the absence of W.

The point is: your *proper course* should be based on what will get **you** to the next *mark* and ultimately to the finishing line as quickly as possible, not on a tactical consideration such as heading up to cut off a nearby *windward* boat.

"If I am subject to rule 17 and my spinnaker collapses or I come off my foils because my wind is being blocked by the windward boat, can I head up to fill my spinnaker or begin foiling again?"

If you are sailing on your *proper course* and then your wind is affected by the windward boat, you may not head up without breaking rule 17. The reason is that your *proper course* is based on the windward boat not being there, in which case your wind would not have been affected.

Notice also that there is no *proper course* **before** the starting signal. That is because a *proper course* is the course sailed to *finish* as soon as possible. Obviously, you can't start racing toward the finishing line until you are allowed to *start*; therefore, there is no *proper course* until after the starting signal is made.

PROTEST

An allegation made under rule 61.2 by a boat, a race committee, a technical committee or a protest committee that a boat has broken a *rule*.

For the most part, allegations and decisions on whether boats have broken any *rules* are handled after the race in a hearing called by a protest committee. The procedure to ask for such a hearing is called a *protest*. Rules 60 (Right to Protest; Right to Request Redress or Rule 69 Action) and 61 (Protest Requirements) clearly outline the rights and requirements for boats, race committees, protest committees and technical committees that wish to protest.

Note that a "request for redress" under rule 62 is not a *protest*. For you to "request redress," you must make your request in writing and state why you are claiming it. If the request is based on an incident in the racing area, it has to be delivered no later than the protest time limit or two hours after the incident, whichever is later. Other requests have to be delivered as soon as reasonably possible after learning of the reasons for making the request. However, on the last scheduled day of racing a request for redress based on a protest committee decision shall be delivered no later than 30 minutes after the decision was posted. In any event you don't need to fly a protest flag (rule 62.2, Redress).

Note also that a report to the protest committee alleging a breach of rule 69.1(a) (Misconduct) is not a *protest* either (see rule 69.1(c)). Upon receiving such a report, the protest committee will decide whether to call a hearing (rule 69.2(b)).

RACING

A boat is *racing* from her preparatory signal until she *finishes* and clears the finishing line and *marks* or retires, or until the race committee signals a general recall, *postponement* or *abandonment*.

It is important to know when you are *racing* because you can only be penalized for breaking a rule of Part 2 (When Boats Meet) when you are *racing*, with the exception of rule 14 (Avoiding Contact) when the incident results in serious damage or injury, and rule 23.1 (Interfering with Another Boat) (see the preamble to Part 2). You begin *racing* at your preparatory signal. In a "5–4–1–GO" sequence, the four-minute signal is the preparatory signal (Rule 26, Starting Races). In a "3–2–1–GO" sequence, it's usually the two-minute signal (see the US prescription Appendix U, Audible-Signal Racing System). Check the sailing instructions for the race to find out when your actual preparatory signal is. You are no longer *racing* when you have *finished* and cleared the finishing line and *marks*. Appeal 16 reads, "…when no part of a boat's hull, equipment or crew is still on the finishing line, she has cleared it."

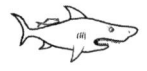

"When am I considered to be clear of the finishing marks?"

You have "cleared the finishing *marks*" when you are no longer at risk of hitting them during or just after an incident that occurred while you were *finishing*. Case 127 says, "A boat clears the finishing line and marks when the following two conditions are met: no part of her hull, crew or equipment is on the line, and no finishing mark is influencing her choice of course." See Appeal 26.

"Once my bow crosses the finishing line and I've "finished," do I need to cross the finishing line completely?"

Absolutely not. Rule 28.1 (Sailing the Race) states, "*After **finishing** she need not cross the finishing line completely.*" So if you are beating to an upwind finishing line in light air and adverse current, all you need to do is get your bow across the line, then you can bear away and sail away from the line and *marks*.

ROOM

The space a boat needs in the existing conditions, including space to comply with her obligations under the rules of Part 2 and rule 31, while manoeuvring promptly in a seamanlike way.

This definition is central to applying rule 15 (Acquiring Right of Way); rule 16 (Changing Course); rule 18 (Mark-Room); rule 19 (Room to Pass an Obstruction); and rule 20 (Room to Tack at an Obstruction).

"Room" is "space." It is the space on the water a boat "needs" at the time. For instance, when the term is used in rules 15 and 16, it is the space the keep-clear boat needs to *keep clear* of the right-of-way boat. When the term is used in the definition *Mark-Room*, it is the space the inside boat needs to sail to and around the *mark*. When used in rule 19, it is the space the inside boat needs to pass between the outside boat and the *obstruction*.

Note the word "promptly" which means "performed readily, quickly, almost immediately." This builds in a time element to the definition. Therefore when a *leeward* boat (L) luffs near a *windward* boat (W), rule 16.1 requires L to give W *room* to *keep clear*, but W must respond "promptly" or risk losing the protection of *room*. The same is true when a *port-tack* boat (P) tacks close in front of, or to *leeward* of, a *starboard-tack* boat (S) and rule 15 applies.

To expand on "seamanlike," I would say "seamanlike" means "responsible, prudent, safety conscious." In other words, it is "seamanlike" never to put your or another boat's crew, boat or equipment at risk of damage or injury. Furthermore, "seamanlike" describes the way competent, but not expert, sailors handle their boat. Case 21 says, "["seamanlike way"] implies that an outside boat must provide enough space so that the inside boat need not manoeuvre in an extraordinary or abnormal manner."

Note that "room" includes the space a boat needs to comply with the rules in Part 2, which include the right-of-way and *mark-room* rules, and rule 31 (Touching a Mark). For instance, if three boats are approaching a *mark*, and the inside boats are entitled to *mark-room*, the outside boat has to give the middle boat "room" to comply with her obligation to give the inside boat "room" to sail between her and the *mark*. (See Case 114.)

"Does the definition Room take into account the experience or the number of the crew on board the boat?"

No. Case 103 addresses this head on by saying, "Neither the experience of IW's crew nor their number is relevant in determining 'room'…the interpretation of 'seamanlike way' must be based on the boat-handling that can reasonably be expected from a competent, but not expert, crew of the appropriate number for the boat."

Furthermore, Appeal 20 talks about tactical *mark* roundings and says in essence that *room* does not include all the space an inside boat might like to take to make a tactically desirable rounding.

RULE

(a) The rules in this book, including the Definitions, Race Signals, Introduction, preambles and the rules of relevant appendices, but not titles;

(b) World Sailing Regulations that have been designated by World Sailing as having the status of a *rule* and are published on the World Sailing website;

(c) the prescriptions of the national authority, unless they are changed by the notice of race or sailing instructions in compliance with the national authority's prescription, if any, to rule 88.2;

(d) the class rules (for a boat racing under a handicap or rating system, the rules of that system are 'class rules');

(e) the notice of race;

(f) the sailing instructions; and

(g) any other documents that govern the event.

This is the complete list of the *rules* that govern a race. Note that the notice of race and the sailing instructions are *rules* so it is important to read them carefully before entering a race. The notice of race and sailing instructions can change certain racing rules, **but they must refer specifically to the rule being changed** and state the change (see rules 85.1, Changes to Rules; 86.1(b), Changes to the Racing Rules; and Appendix J1.3(1) and J2.1(1), Notice of Race and Sailing Instructions). Note that one of the rules the notice of race and sailing instructions cannot change is rule 42 (Propulsion). Note also that the term "racing rule" means a *rule* in *The Racing Rules of Sailing* (RRS) (see the Introduction in the RRS: Terminology).

THE DEFINITIONS **101**

Also note that class rules are only permitted to change certain rules of *The Racing Rules of Sailing*, specifically: rule 42 (Propulsion); rule 49 (Crew Position); rule 51, (Movable Ballast); rule 52 (Manual Power); rule 53 (Skin Friction); rule 54 (Forestays and Headsail Tacks) and rule 55 (Setting and Sheeting Sails). They too **must refer specifically to the rule being changed** and state the change (see rules 85.1, Changes to Rules and 86.1(c), Changes to the Racing Rules). Class rules that conflict with other racing rules do not apply.

SAIL THE COURSE

A boat *sails the course* provided that a string representing her track from the time she begins to approach the starting line from its prestart side to *start* until she *finishes*, when drawn taut,

(a) passes each *mark* of the course for the race on the required side and in the correct order,

(b) touches each *mark* designated in the sailing instructions to be a rounding *mark*, and

(c) passes between the *marks* of a gate from the direction of the course from the previous *mark*.

This new definition is essentially the "string rule" language from the previous rule 28. It clarifies what it means to "sail the course," a phrase used in rule 28.1 (Sailing the Race) and throughout the rule book. Note that the race committee is required to score a boat NSC (Did not *sail the course*) without a protest hearing if it knows a boat did not *sail the course* in compliance with rule 28.1 (see rule A5.1, Scores Determined by the Race Committee).

START

A boat *starts* when, her hull having been entirely on the pre-start side of the starting line at or after her starting signal, and having complied with rule 30.1 if it applies, any part of her hull crosses the starting line from the pre-start side to the course side.

You cannot *start* until after the starting signal for your class. If any part of your hull is on the course side of the starting line at the starting signal, you must get your hull completely behind the line to *start* correctly (rule 28.1, Sailing the Race, and rule 29.1, Individual Recall). If you don't, the race committee is required to score you OCS (on the course side) or DNS (Did not *start*) without needing to protest you (rule A5.1, Scores Determined by the Race Committee). If you feel the race committee has incorrectly scored you OCS or DNS, you can request redress under rule 62.1(a) (Redress).

Notice that you *start* when, your hull having been entirely on the pre-start side of the starting line at or after the starting signal is made, **any** part of your hull first crosses the starting line. There is no mention of crew or equipment. If your bow person is calling the line from the pulpit and inadvertently sticks his or her hand over the line just before the gun, or if your crew, by going out on the trapeze, mistakenly puts his or her head over the line one second before the gun, it does not matter. It is only the hull that matters. The same is true if anchored and your anchor and anchor line are over the starting line. See the discussion of the definition *Finish* for more explanation of what the "hull" is.

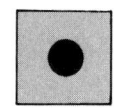

The definition refers to rule 30.1 (Starting Penalties; I Flag Rule), commonly referred to as the "one minute rule" or "round-an-end rule." Notice that the race committee can signal the I Flag Rule on any start it wants simply by displaying flag I as the preparatory signal. When it is lowered one minute before the starting signal, accompanied by one long sound signal, the one-minute period of rule 30.1 has begun. The purpose of the rule is to keep people from charging over the line early and making it difficult for the race committee to have a fair start. The way it works is, if you are on the course side of the starting line or its extensions during the minute before your starting signal, you must sail back to the pre-start side of the line outside one of the starting marks across the extension of the starting

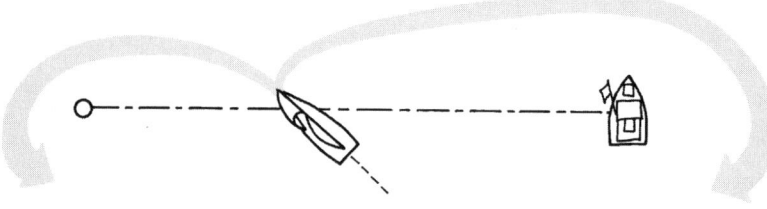

When rule 30.1 (the "I Flag Rule") is in effect, a boat that is on the course side of the starting line at any time during the final minute before the starting signal must sail outside one of the starting marks and across the extension of the starting line before starting. Typically the fastest way to do this is to sail around the closest end of the starting line. She may do this immediately if she chooses; i.e., she does not need to wait for the starting signal before going around an end.

line before starting. Typically the quickest way to do this is to sail around one end of the starting line or the other at some point before *starting* correctly. Notice you can sail around an end immediately; you don't have to wait for the starting signal to be made.

Notice that anytime you are sailing back towards the pre-start side of the starting line or its extensions **after** your starting signal, you have to *keep clear* of any boats not doing so until you are completely on the pre-start side (rule 21.1, Starting Errors; Taking Penalties; Backing a Sail).

Notice also the more stringent starting penalties available to race committees in rules 30.2 (Z Flag Rule), 30.3 (U Flag Rule) and 30.4 (Black Flag Rule).

SUPPORT PERSON

Any person who

(a) provides, or may provide, physical or advisory support to a competitor, including any coach, trainer, manager, team staff, medic, paramedic or any other person working with, treating or assisting a competitor in or preparing for the competition, or

(b) is the parent or guardian of a competitor

This definition, along with several other rules, brings a *support person* under the jurisdiction of the *rules*. This permits protest committees to call a hearing to consider whether a *support person* has broken a *rule* (see rule 60.3(d)), and to penalize a *support person* as well as the boat being supported (see rule 64.5, Decisions Concerning Support Persons).

Furthermore, rule 4.1(b) (Acceptance of the Rules) states, "(b) *A support person by providing support, or a parent or guardian by permitting their child to enter an event, agrees to accept the rules.*" And rule 4.3(d) states, "*Acceptance of the rules includes agreement by each competitor and boat owner to ensure that their support persons are aware of the rules.*"

Note that rule 1.1 (Helping Those in Danger) now states, "*A boat, competitor or support person shall give all possible help to any person or vessel in danger.*" Furthermore, *support persons* must comply with applicable World Sailing Regulations (see rule 6, World Sailing Regulations).

The primary misconduct rule is Rule 69.1(a) (Misconduct: Obligation not to Commit Misconduct; Resolution). It states, "*(a) A competitor, boat owner* or **support person** *shall not commit an act of misconduct. (b) Misconduct is: (1) conduct that is a breach of good manners, a breach of good sportsmanship, or unethical behaviour; or (2) conduct that may bring, or has brought, the sport into disrepute."*

> *"Does that mean that if I am racing, I am responsible for making sure my parents and coaches know the rules; and I can be disqualified if someone supporting me breaks a rule?"*

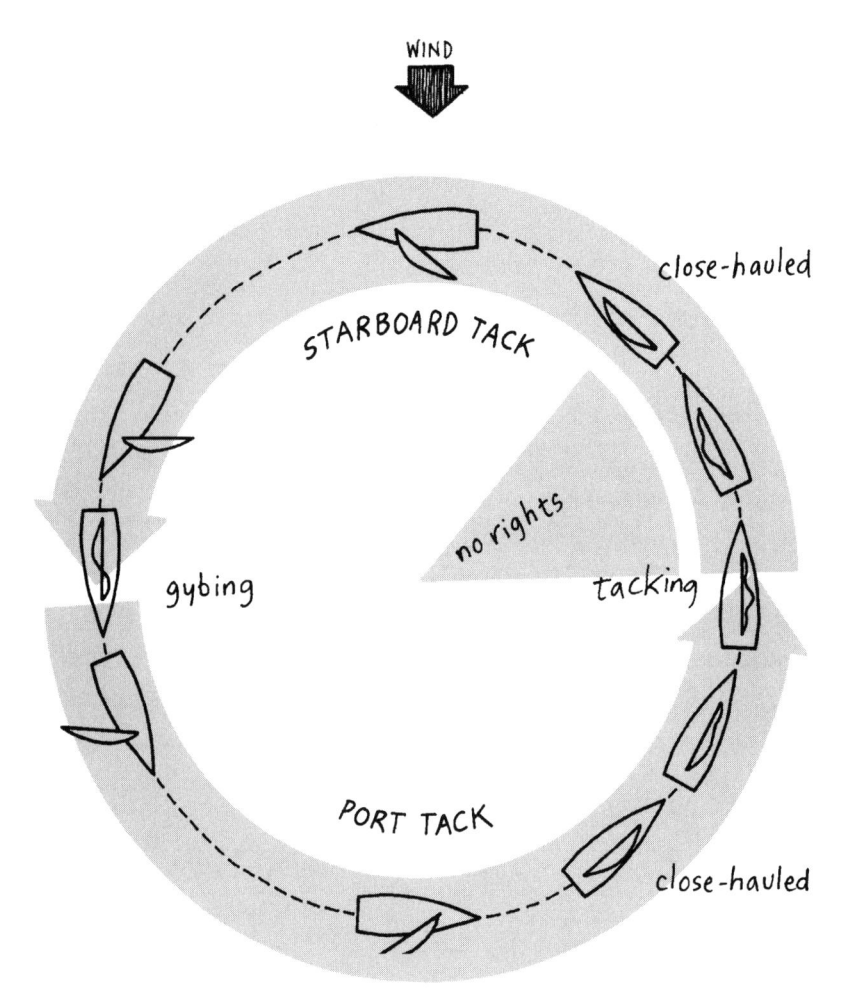

Yes and Yes! You are in effect an "agent" for your support people, as well as your crew and boat owner (see rule 4.4, Acceptance of the Rules), and as such you are required to not only make sure they know the *rules*, but that they follow the *rules*. Rule 64.5(b) states, "*The protest committee may also penalize a boat that is a party to a hearing under rule 60.3(d) or 69 for the breach of a rule by a support person by changing the boat's score in a single race, up to and including disqualification, when the protest committee decides that (1) the boat may have gained a competitive advantage as the result of the breach by the support person, or (2) the support person committed a further breach after the protest committee warned the boat in writing, following a previous hearing, that a penalty may be imposed.*"

TACK, STARBOARD OR PORT

A boat is on the *tack, starboard* or *port,* corresponding to her *windward* side.

When *racing*, you are **always** on either *starboard* or *port tack*, even when you are in the act of tacking or gybing. Your *tack* (*starboard* or *port*) is determined by your *windward* side; i.e., if your port side is your *windward* side, you are on *port tack*. For discussion on how to determine your *windward* side, see the definition *Leeward* and *Windward*.

Let's look at a boat (P) tacking from *port tack* to *starboard tack*. At some point during her tack, P will pass head to wind. At the moment she passes head to wind her starboard side becomes her *windward* side; therefore she is instantly on *starboard tack*. However, rule 13 (While Tacking) requires her to *keep clear* of other boats until she is on a close-hauled course; and rule 15 (Acquiring Right of Way) requires her to initially give other boats *room* to *keep clear* once she gets the right of way.

WINDWARD

See *Leeward* and *Windward*.

ZONE

The area around a *mark* within a distance of three hull lengths of the boat nearer to it. A boat is in the *zone* when any part of her hull is in the *zone*.

As boats near a *mark*, rule 18 (Mark-Room) provides specific instructions regarding which boats are entitled to *mark-room*, which must give *mark-room* to others, etc. These instructions begin to apply when the boats first enter the *zone*.

The Zone is an imaginary area with the mark at its center, and extending out a distance equal to three hull lengths of the boat that is nearest the mark (unless team or match racing in which case the zone is two lengths, radio sailing racing in which case it is four lengths or kiteboard racing in which case it is 30 meters).

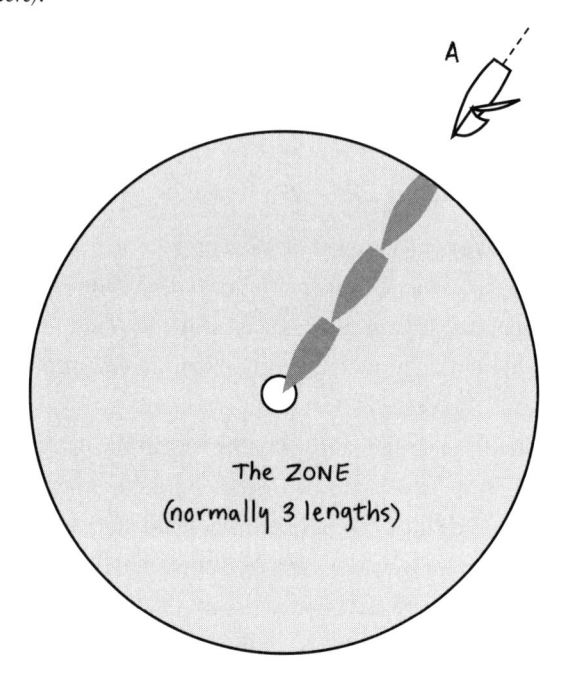

The ZONE
(normally 3 lengths)

The *zone* is essentially a circle with the *mark* at its center whose radius is three hull lengths of the boat that is nearest to it. Therefore, if a 24-foot boat and a 30-foot boat are approaching a *mark* and the 24-foot boat is nearer the *mark*, the *zone* is 72 feet (3 feet x 24 feet) from the *mark*. Obviously, if the *mark* were a boat, then the shape of the *zone* would be more oblong.

Note, a boat is in the *zone* based on her hull and not her spinnaker or bowsprit. The "hull" is the boat's main body or shell. Things attached to the hull like racks, or things protruding from the hull like bowsprits or prods for the spinnaker, are not part of the "hull" (see the discussion of the definition *Finishing*). Furthermore, the use of the term "hull length" is intended to clarify that the *zone* is based solely on the length of the hull, and not the additional length of bowsprits, etc.

Finally, note that the *zone* in team and match racing is "two lengths" (rules C2.4, Match Racing Rules, and D1.1(a), Team Racing Rules), in radio sailing racing it is "four lengths" (rule E1.1, Radio Sailing Racing Rules), in kiteboard racing it is a distance of 30 meters (Appendix F, Changes to the Definitions) and in windsurfing fleet racing there is no *zone* (Appendix B, Changes to the Definitions).

6

Part 2, Preamble and Section A
When Boats Meet—Right of Way

When boats that are **both** *racing* meet, the rules that apply are in Part 2 of the rule book.

PREAMBLE TO PART 2

The rules of Part 2 apply between boats that are sailing in or near the racing area and intend to *race,* are *racing,* or have been *racing.* However, a boat not *racing* shall not be penalized for breaking one of these rules, except rule 14 when the incident resulted in injury or serious damage, or rule 23.1.

When a boat sailing under these rules meets a vessel that is not, she shall comply with the International Regulations for Preventing Collisions at Sea (IRPCAS) or government right-of-way rules. If the notice of race so states, the rules of Part 2 are replaced by the right-of-way rules of the IRPCAS or by government right-of-way rules.

The preamble clarifies **which** *rules* apply **when** and to **whom**. Note that the "preambles" rank as *rules* (see the definition *Rule*). If the rules of Part 2 apply to you and you are approaching a vessel that is clearly not in any way a part of a race, e.g., a cruising boat or commercial tug, then you are required (note the word "shall") to comply with the Inland Navigational Rules (INR) (in U.S. waters) or the International Regulations for Preventing Collisions at Sea

(IRPCAS) (outside of a country's waters) or other applicable government right-of-way rules. If you don't, you can be protested under rule 60 (Right to Protest; Right to Request Redress or Rule 69 Action) and penalized under rule 64.2 (Penalties). (See Cases 67 and 109.)

When the Inland Navigational Rules (in U.S. waters) or the International Regulations for Preventing Collisions at Sea (outside of a country's waters) are to replace the *The Racing Rules of Sailing*, e.g., when the race will continue after sunset, the notice of race must specifically contain the numbers of the applicable INR or IRPCAS and state the time(s) or places(s) they will apply, as well as any night signals to be used by the race committee (Appendix J1.2(12), Notice of Race and Sailing Instructions: Notice of Race Contents).

Sailors wishing a complete copy of the INR or IRPCAS should contact the US Sailing office for information on how to get one.

"Is it true that the rules of Part 2 apply between boats that are racing in different races?"

Yes. The rules of Part 2 apply between boats in different races as long as they both fit the description in the preamble of Part 2. Rule 63.8 (Hearings Involving Parties in Different Events) reads, *"A hearing involving **parties** in different events conducted by different organizing authorities shall be heard by a protest committee acceptable to those authorities."*

Also, notice that when you intend to *race*, the rules of Part 2 only apply from when you begin to sail in or near the racing area until you have left the racing area; and they only apply between boats intending to *race*. This distinction may be important in resolving a financial claim after a serious collision when the boats were not actually *racing*.

"I realize I am technically 'racing' after my preparatory signal, but what happens if I foul a boat before or after I am racing?"

The preamble to Part 2 says, *"a boat not **racing** shall not be penalized for breaking one of these rules, except rule 14 when the incident resulted in injury or serious damage, or rule 23.1."* Rule 14 (Avoiding Contact) is the rule that requires all boats to avoid contact if reasonably possible. If you don't avoid contact when you could have, and there is injury or "serious damage," then you can be penalized (see discussion of "injury and serious damage" under rule 44, Penalties at the Time of the Incident). Rule 23.1 (Interfering with Another

Boat) says that even if you aren't *racing*, you can't interfere with a boat that is; see the discussion of rule 23.1.

Note, rule 44.1 (Taking a Penalty) says, *"A boat may take a Two-Turns Penalty when she may have broken one or more rules of Part 2 in an incident while racing* (emphasis added)." Therefore, if you break a *rule* before your preparatory signal (i.e., before you are *racing*), other than rule 14 when injury or serious damage results or rule 23.1, apologize and continue on. But if you break rule 14 or rule 23.1, you can't take a Two-Turns Penalty, and you can be protested and penalized under rule 64.2 (Penalties). Note, rule 64.2 says *"If a boat has broken a rule when not **racing**, her penalty shall apply to the race sailed nearest in time to that of the incident."* So if you cause "serious damage" between races and want to take a penalty, you should retire from the race sailed nearest in time to the incident.

Of course, if there is any damage at all, you and/or the other boat may choose to protest so that the protest committee can find the facts and make a decision as to who was at fault. If there was no injury or serious damage, neither one of you can be "penalized" under rule 64.2 (Penalties); but the facts and decision of the protest committee may be useful in determining who pays for the damage (rule 67, Damages).

Remember, under the definition of *racing*, you are *racing* from your preparatory signal until you have *finished* and cleared the finishing line and finishing *marks* or retired. So if your preparatory signal is four minutes before your starting signal and you foul someone with three and a half minutes to go, you can be disqualified if you don't take a penalty (which you can do right away; you don't need to wait until after the starting signal). Remember also that you are no longer *racing* the moment your entire boat clears the finishing line and finishing *marks* (US Sailing Appeals 16 and 26, Case 127 and rule 28.1, Sailing the Race).

Note, however, that if you are not *racing* and break any other *rules*, other than those in Part 2 (When Boats Meet) and Part 4 (Other Requirements When Racing) and rule 31 (Touching a Mark), you will receive a penalty under rule 64.2 (Penalties). For instance, you will be penalized before or after you are *racing* for breaking the sailing instructions, or for violating the principles in rule 2 (Fair Sailing), or for committing misconduct under rule 69 (Misconduct), or for not complying with the rules of Part 6 (Entry and Qualification) which include rules 75 (Entering an Event) and 78 (Compliance with Class Rules:

Certificates). And your penalty will be applied to the race sailed nearest in time to that of the incident (rule 64.2, Penalties).

"If five minutes before my preparatory signal I'm near the starting line on starboard tack and despite my best effort to avoid the collision my boat gets holed by a port tacker who is also intending to race, and as a result I can't sail in the race, do I have any recourse under the rules?"

You sure do. You should protest them under rule 10 (On Opposite Tacks) and rule 14 (Avoiding Contact), and request redress under rule 62.1(b) (Redress). Both of you were intending to *race* and were sailing in the racing area; therefore you were both governed by *The Racing Rules of Sailing* (preamble to Part 2, When Boats Meet). The *port-tack* boat (P) was required to *keep clear* of you while you were on *starboard tack* under rule 10, and both of you were required to avoid contact if reasonably possible. The protest committee is required to hold a hearing, find facts and determine which boat, if either, broke any rules (rules 63.1, Hearings; 64.2, Penalties; and 65.1, Informing the Parties and Others).

P cannot be penalized for breaking rule 10 as she was not *racing* at the time. But if P is found to have broken rule 14 and caused "serious damage," P can be disqualified (see the preamble to Part 2). However, if P is found to have broken rule 10 or rule 14, the protest committee must turn to your request for redress (rule 63.1). If you were found not to have broken rule 14, you should be granted redress as your race score or place was made significantly worse (you were unable to race!) through no fault of your own due to the physical damage caused by P, a boat that was penalized for breaking a rule of Part 2. Furthermore, the question of financial responsibility for damages may be helped by a finding of facts and fault by the protest committee (see rule 67, Damages).

"If I'm racing and a boat definitely fouls me, and later in the race I am converging with them and I don't have the right of way, do I have to keep clear of them even though they were wrong in the first incident?"

You bet! When competitors know they have broken a *rule*, they are expected to promptly take a penalty (see Basic Principles: Sportsmanship and the Rules in the "Introduction of the RRS").

But while a boat continues to race, she maintains all her rights just as any other boat. Case 1 reads, "Boats A, B, and C are racing with others. After an incident between A and B, boat A hails 'Protest!' and displays her protest flag, but boat B does not take a penalty. Later, B protests a third boat, C, after a second incident. The protest committee hears A's protest against B and disqualifies B. Does this disqualification invalidate B's protest against C?

ANSWER: No. When a boat continues to race after an alleged breach of a rule, her rights and obligations under the rules do not change. Consequently, even though A's protest against B is upheld, the protest committee must hear B's protest against C and, if B's protest is valid and the protest committee is satisfied from the evidence that C broke a rule, she must be disqualified."

PREAMBLE TO SECTION A

A boat has right of way over another boat when the other boat is required to *keep clear* of her. However, some rules in Sections B, C and D limit the actions of a right-of-way boat.

The rules of Part 2 are written to clearly say which boat must *keep clear* of the other. (See the definition *Keep Clear* for a full discussion of the meaning of this phrase.) For example, rule 10 (On Opposite Tacks) says, *"When boats are on opposite **tacks**, a **port-tack** boat shall **keep clear** of a **starboard-tack** boat."* Therefore, in learning the rules, it is helpful to learn which boats do **not** have the right of way in meeting situations, as these are the boats with the requirement to stay out of the other's way. Note, "shall" when used in the *rules* means "must;" i.e., it is a mandatory requirement.

There are just four basic right-of-way rules (rules 10–13), and they are found in Section A. They cover the three basic relationships boats can be in (on the opposite tack, on the same tack or changing tacks), and they are:

- on *opposite tacks*..................... *port tack keeps clear* of *starboard tack*
  – rule 10

- on same the *tack*, overlapped........ *windward keeps clear* of *leeward*
  – rule 11

- on the same *tack*, not overlapped... *clear astern keeps clear* of *clear ahead*
  – rule 12

- changing *tacks* by tacking............ boat tacking *keeps clear* of other boats
  – rule 13

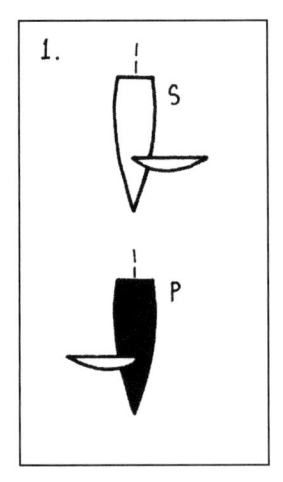

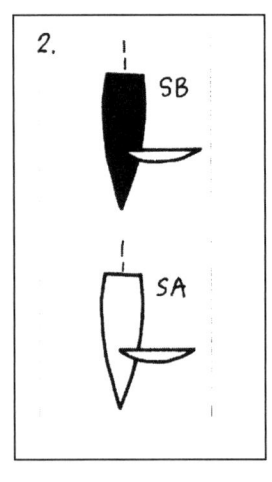

In position 1, the boats are on opposite tacks; therefore S has right of way over P under rule 10.

In position 2, both boats are on the same tack; therefore SB must keep clear of SA under rule 12.

RULE 10 — ON OPPOSITE TACKS

When boats are on opposite *tacks*, a *port-tack* boat shall *keep clear* of a *starboard-tack* boat.

This basic rule applies to boats that are on **opposite** *tacks*. When boats are on the **same** *tack*, rules 11 *(windward/leeward)* and 12 *(clear astern/clear ahead)* apply. Thus, if on a downwind leg a *starboard-tack* boat comes up from behind and runs into a *port-tack* boat (assuming no damage or injury), who will be penalized under the rules? The *port-tack* boat under rule 10, because the two boats are on *opposite tacks*.

"If I'm on a beat converging with a port-tack boat and she hails "Hold your course," is that hail binding on me?

No. Appeal 27 reads, "In response to the questions regarding a boat that has been hailed to hold course, it is permissible to hail, but the rules do not recognize such a hail as binding on the other boat. S can tack or bear away at any time she is satisfied that a change of course will be necessary to avoid a collision."

My opinion is that in order for the *port-tack* boat to be liable for failure to *keep clear*, it is important that as they approach each other, the *starboard-tack* boat hold her course as long as she can do so with safety. I recommend that when *port-tack* boats are about to cross close in front of *starboard-tack* boats, P should hail "Hold your course" or otherwise alert S that P is there, she realizes it'll be close, and she wants S to hold her course for as long as possible.

PART 2, SECTION A: WHEN BOATS MEET — RIGHT OF WAY 115

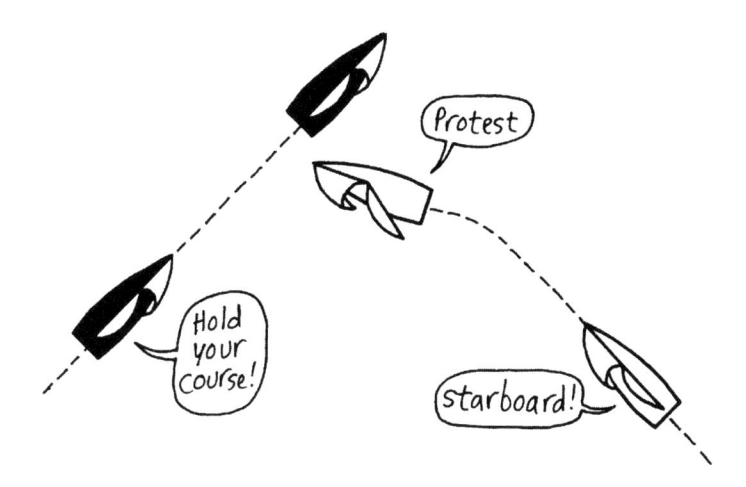

Though it is common for P to hail "Hold your course" to assure S that P is aware that she's there and to encourage S to give her every opportunity to try and cross, S is in no way bound by that hail to actually do so. S may bear away or tack at any time she has a reasonable concern that her change of course is necessary to avoid a collision.

"Okay, but do I have to hit the port-tacker to prove there was a foul; and if there is no contact, whom is the 'onus of proof' on?"

S does NOT have to hit P to prove that P failed to *keep clear*. S should avoid the collision and protest. Though the rule itself contains no specific "onus" (i.e., an assignment of responsibility to one boat or the other to prove the other boat's guilt), Case 50 discusses the whole issue, including the question of "onus of proof:" "Rule 10 protests involving no contact are very common, and protest committees tend to handle them in very different ways. Some place an onus on the port-tack boat to prove conclusively that she would have cleared the starboard-tack boat, even when the latter's evidence is barely worthy of credence. No such onus appears in rule 10. Other protest committees are reluctant to allow any rule 10 protest in the absence of contact, unless the starboard-tack boat proves conclusively that contact would have occurred had she not changed course. Both approaches are incorrect.

"A starboard-tack boat in such circumstances need not hold her course so as to prove, by hitting the port-tack boat, that a collision was inevitable. Moreover, if she does so she will break rule 14 (Avoiding Contact). At a protest hearing, S must establish either that contact would have occurred if she had held her course, or that there was enough doubt that P could safely cross ahead to create a reasonable apprehension of contact on S's part and that it was

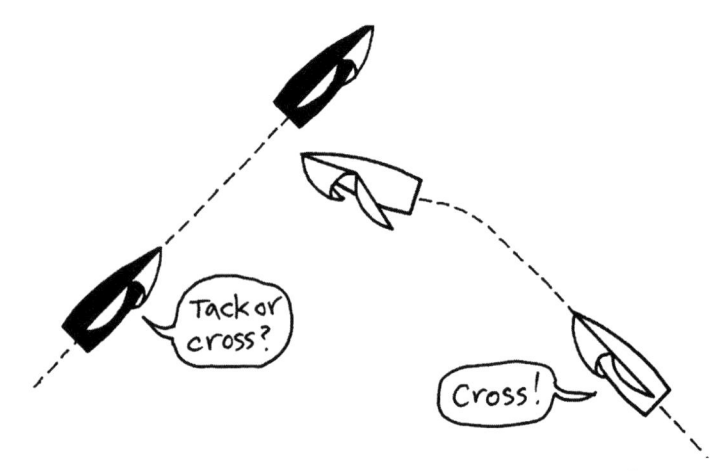

A long standing universally accepted tactic is for S to "wave" P across for tactical reasons (S is on the layline, or unable to tack, or simply wants to continue sailing on starboard tack). P often initiates the communication by calling "Tack or Cross?". S indicates to P that P can safely cross with a hand gesture and/or hail. S typically bears away soon enough to allow her to smoothly head up and pass close astern of P, which is before S may actually "need" to bear away to avoid hitting P. However, regardless of where she bears off, S would never protest P in this situation because S is "waving" P across, and it would be considered unsportsmanlike to protest in this situation.

unlikely that S would have 'no need to take avoiding action' (see the definition Keep Clear).

"In her own defence, P must present adequate evidence to establish either that S did not change course or that P would have safely crossed ahead of S and that S had no need to take avoiding action. When, after considering all the evidence, a protest committee finds that S did not change course or that there was not a genuine and reasonable apprehension of collision on her part, it should dismiss her protest. When, however, it is satisfied that S did change course, that there was reasonable doubt that P could have crossed ahead, and that S was justified in taking avoiding action by bearing away, then P should be disqualified."

In Case 88, P and S were converging on an upwind leg. When three and then two lengths away, S hailed "Starboard" but P held her collision course. When just under two lengths away, and fearing a collision, S luffed to try to minimize the contact at the same moment P bore away sharply. S then bore away sharply to pull her transom out of P's way. P passed astern of S within two feet; there was no contact. The protest committee dismissed S's rule 10 protest against P and S appealed.

In its decision, the appeals committee says, "Rule 10 required P to 'keep clear' of S. 'Keep clear' means something more than 'avoid contact;' otherwise the rule would contain those or similar words. Therefore, the fact that the boats did not collide does not necessarily establish that P kept clear. The definition Keep Clear in combination with the facts determines whether or not P complied with the rule. In this case, the key question raised by the definition is whether S was able to sail her course 'with no need to take avoiding action.'" After listing all the considerations it took into account, the appeals committee concluded that S did have a need to take avoiding action, and disqualified P for breaking rule 10.

"I've seen starboard-tack boats intentionally wave port-tack boats across them. Can you discuss that?"

Sure. There are many times in a race when a *starboard-tack* boat (S) is approaching a *port-tack* boat (P) where P cannot cross S. For tactical reasons, S does not want P to tack in front or close to leeward of her. Maybe S is on the starboard-tack layline to the windward *mark*, or S cannot tack away because of boats to windward of her, or maybe S just wants to continue sailing on *starboard tack* for strategic reasons. S will tell P it is safe to cross her, and will bear away and avoid hitting P if need be.

The safest way for S to communicate this to P is to make eye contact with the skipper of P and make a clear hand gesture "waving" P across. A hail such as "Cross" can also be made. Often P will initiate this communication by hailing "Tack or Cross?" Beware of hailing "Go!" because "Go" sounds like "No." But until P is 100% certain that S is "waving" her across, P should plan on *keeping clear* by tacking or ducking S.

If S has to bear away to avoid P, typically she does so at a time where she can do a smooth early bear away and be luffing up to a close-hauled course as she passes P's stern. This bear away will be done before she "needs" to bear away to avoid contact with P. Therefore, P has *kept clear* and not broken rule 10 (On Opposite Tacks) (see the definition *Keep Clear*). However, regardless of where she bears off, S would never protest P in this situation because S is "waving" P across. This is a long standing and universally accepted tactic, and it would be considered unsportsmanlike to protest in this situation (see rule 2, Fair Sailing).

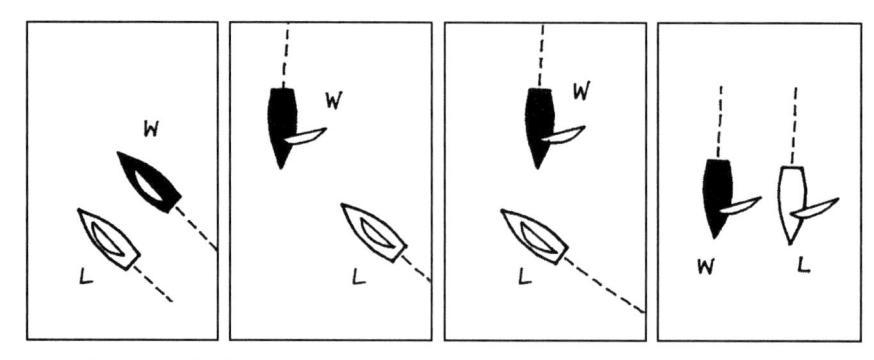

118 UNDERSTANDING THE RACING RULES OF SAILING THROUGH 2024

In each situation, both boats are on the same tack. The white boat is the leeward boat and the black boat must keep clear under rule 11.

RULES 11 AND 12 — ON THE SAME TACK

Rules 11 and 12 are the basic rules for boats on the **same** *tack*. When boats are on the same *tack* they can either be *overlapped* or not *overlapped*. If they are *overlapped*, they are either a *windward* boat or a *leeward* boat. If they are not *overlapped*, they are either clear ahead or clear astern.

RULE 11 — ON THE SAME TACK, OVERLAPPED

When boats are on the same *tack* and *overlapped*, a *windward* boat shall *keep clear* of a *leeward* boat.

When boats on the same *tack* are *overlapped*, rule 11 applies. When boats are on much different angles of sail, it is often difficult to know which is the *leeward* boat. The boat that will hit the other's *leeward* side or be hit on her own *windward* side is the *leeward* boat. As a good rule of thumb, the boat that is on the point of sail closer to the wind is typically the *leeward* boat; i.e., between a boat sailing downwind and a boat sailing close-hauled, the close-hauled boat is usually the *leeward* boat.

"I realize that when I'm the windward boat I have to keep clear of the leeward boat, but how far away do I need to stay?"

Far enough away so that while the *leeward* boat (L) is sailing on a straight line, you do not hit L or force L to take any avoiding action to miss you; e.g., have to change her course, ease her spinnaker pole forward or require any of her crew to duck or move to avoid being hit.

Furthermore, you need to be far enough away so that the *leeward* boat can change course in **both** directions without **immediately** making contact with you. If you allow yourself to get so close to L that she is physically unable to change her course without immediately hitting you, you are not *keeping clear* under the definition *Keep Clear* and are breaking rule 11.

Note that the word "if" in the second part of the definition suggests that L does not need to actually hit you to prove she couldn't change course without hitting you. If the protest committee decides that L couldn't change course without immediate contact, then you have broken rule 11 simply by your extreme close proximity to L.

More importantly, **anytime** L cannot sail her course without a need to take action to avoid you, you have not *kept clear* and have broken rule 11. Therefore, you will be smart not to allow yourself to get so close that you will possibly interfere with L in the least. Notice also that when L is head to wind, it is quite possible that you will be required to go **beyond** head to wind (i.e., change *tacks*) in order to *keep clear*. If this is the case, you must do so. Also, if you are converging with L and both of you are sailing on what you each believe to be your *proper course*, rule 11 requires you to *keep clear* of L.

RULE 12 — ON THE SAME TACK, NOT OVERLAPPED

When boats are on the same *tack* and not *overlapped*, a boat *clear astern* shall *keep clear* of a boat *clear ahead*.

In 1949 the rule read, "A yacht Overtaking another shall keep clear while she is Clear Astern." Now the rules only talk about boats that are *clear ahead* or *clear astern*; however, the concept is still the same. A boat, as in cars on the road, coming up from behind another boat on the same *tack*, must not hit her.

Rule 12 clearly identifies a boat or boats *clear ahead* as right-of-way boats, therefore making them *obstructions* to boats coming up from behind (definition *Obstruction*). Case 41 reads, "While BW and BL are overtaking A, rule 12 requires both BL and BW to keep clear of A. Therefore, A is an obstruction to both BL and BW."

Note, rule 12 applies only to boats when they are on the **same** tack. If a *starboard-tack* boat (S) is astern but on a collision course with a *port-tack* boat (P), P must get out of S's way even though S is the "overtaking" boat.

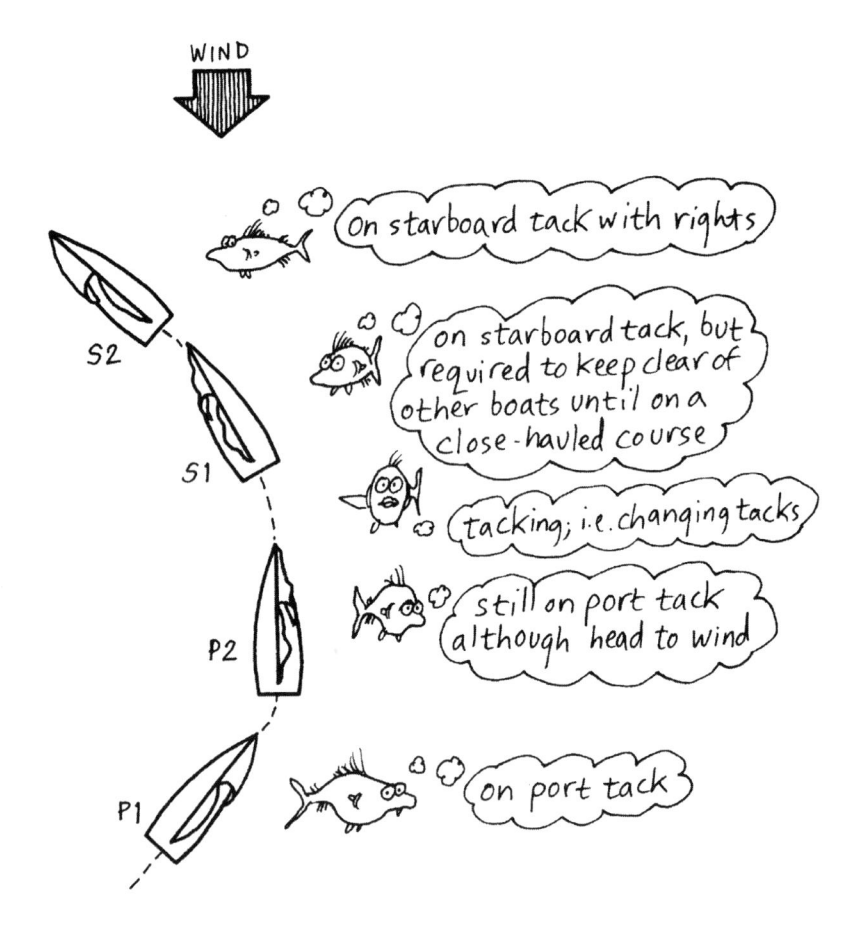

120 UNDERSTANDING THE RACING RULES OF SAILING THROUGH 2024

[Diagram showing boats S2, S1 labeled "On starboard tack with rights" and "on starboard tack, but required to keep clear of other boats until on a close-hauled course"; boat between S1 and P2 labeled "tacking; i.e. changing tacks"; P2 labeled "still on port tack although head to wind"; P1 labeled "on port tack". Wind arrow points down from top.]

Because the boats are on **opposite tacks,** S is the right-of-way boat under rule 10 (On Opposite Tacks).

RULE 13 — WHILE TACKING

After a boat passes head to wind, she shall *keep clear* of other boats until she is on a close-hauled course. During that time rules 10, 11 and 12 do not apply. If two boats are subject to this rule at the same time, the one on the other's port side or the one astern shall *keep clear.*

Remember that under the definition *Tack, Starboard* or *Port,* you are always on one *tack* or the other. So if you are on *starboard tack* and turn your boat towards the wind, the moment your boat passes head to wind you are instantly on *port tack.*

PART 2, SECTION A: WHEN BOATS MEET — RIGHT OF WAY

HEY, you're still tacking because your sails aren't full

Actually, L has right of way because she is on a close-hauled course

Rule 13 provides a transitional rule that applies when a boat is changing *tacks* by tacking. "Tacking" is the maneuver by which a boat changes *tacks* with the bow passing head to wind. Generally that involves an approximately 90-degree turn from a close-hauled course on one *tack* to a close-hauled course on the other *tack*.

Rule 13 simply says that while you are tacking, you must *keep clear* of other boats from the moment you pass head to wind until you are on a close-hauled course (on **either** *tack*). A "close-hauled course" is the course a boat will sail when racing upwind and sailing as close to the wind as she can. Notice that to be on a close-hauled "course," the sails don't need to be full nor does the boat need any headway (see Case 17). Note that once you pass head to wind, rule 13 turns off rules 10, 11 and 12. Therefore, after you pass head to wind and before you're on a close-hauled course, if another boat (that is not also subject to rule 13) hits you or has to change her course to avoid you, you have not *kept clear* and have broken rule 13.

In the rare instance where two boats are tacking near each other and both are past head to wind but neither is close-hauled yet, the one on the other's port side must *keep clear*; or put another way, the boat on the right has the right of way. The same applies if the boats are not *overlapped*; the boat behind must *keep clear*.

"Gybing" is the maneuver by which a boat changes *tacks* with the bow turning away from the wind. For instance, when sailing downwind on *port tack*, the moment the foot of your mainsail crosses the centerline and can stay on the new side with no human force applied, you are on *starboard tack* (see the definition *Leeward* and *Windward* for a complete discussion on determining a boat's *tack* when sailing directly downwind or by the lee). Because the act of "gybing" is generally so momentary, there is no special transitional rule for "gybing" except for in match racing (see Appendix C, rule C2.6).

"When I tack or gybe into a right-of-way position, do I have to give other boats room to keep clear of me?"

Absolutely yes. For a full explanation of the obligations of boats that acquire right of way, see the discussion of rule 15 (Acquiring Right of Way) in chapter 7.

"Will you be discussing how the rules work in Slam Dunks?"

You bet. That explanation occurs at the end of the discussion of rule 17 (On the Same Tack; Proper Course) in chapter 7.

Part 2, Section B
When Boats Meet — General Limitations

The International Rules for the Prevention of Collisions at Sea (IRPCAS) and other government rules are designed to keep boats apart. *The Racing Rules of Sailing* are designed to allow boats to get very near each other, with certain limits to keep the racing safe and fair. The rules that **limit** the actions of the boats, including the right-of-way boats, are rules 14–17, found in Section B of Part 2.

In other words, a right-of-way boat cannot just go anywhere she wants. One example is that a right-of-way boat can be penalized when she's involved in contact that causes any damage or injury (rule 14). Another is that whenever a right-of-way boat changes her course, she is required to give the other boat *room* to *keep clear* (rule 16.1). Therefore, it is equally important to know what limitations the rules place on boats, including right-of-way boats, in various situations.

RULE 14 — AVOIDING CONTACT

A boat shall avoid contact with another boat if reasonably possible. However, a right-of-way boat, or one sailing within the *room* or *mark-room* to which she is entitled, need not act to avoid contact until it is clear that the other boat is not *keeping clear* or giving *room* or *mark-room*.

This is a very strong rule regarding contact. It talks to all boats in a race, including right-of-way boats, and tells them to avoid any contact whatsoever if reasonably possible. The intent of the rule is to minimize the amount of collisions that occur during a race, and particularly the intentional ones. Collisions can be dangerous, expensive, frustrating to all sailors and particularly intimidating to newcomers and novice sailors. They are not part of the sport.

When two or more boats converge, the possibility of contact exists. The rules clearly assign the right of way and the requirement to *keep clear* or to give *room* or *mark-room* in each situation where boats could hit. Furthermore, when one boat is required to *keep clear*, the other shouldn't do anything to make the situation more dangerous. Rule 14 makes it clear that the right-of-way boat or one entitled to *room* or *mark-room* can hold her course until it becomes "clear" that the other boat is not going to *keep clear* or give *room* or *mark-room*. At that moment, however, the right-of-way boat or one entitled to *room* must take action herself to avoid contact if reasonably possible. For instance, when a *port-tack* boat is crossing a *starboard-tack* boat, if S holds her course and hits P, with no attempt to avoid the contact, P has broken rules 10 (On Opposite Tacks) and 14, and S has broken rule 14 (see Case 123).

However, rule 43.1(c), Exoneration, states that a right-of-way boat or one sailing within the *room* or *mark-room* to which she is entitled is exonerated (freed from penalty) if the contact does not cause "damage or injury." "Damage" is what a boat suffers; "injury" is what a person suffers (see Case 110). Therefore, if the contact causes no physical damage or injury to any boat or person, the right-of-way boat or the one sailing within the *room* or *mark-room* to which she is entitled can be found to have broken rule 14 but she is exonerated by rule 43.1(c) and cannot be penalized for breaking the rule (see rule 43.2, Exoneration).

On the other hand, if there is any damage or injury at all to **any** boat or person involved in the incident, no matter how slight, and regardless of whether the damage or injury has any effect on the speed or handling of the boat or whether the damage or injury was to the right-of-way boat, the right-of-way boat or the boat sailing within the *room* or *mark-room* to which she is entitled will be penalized if it was found that it was reasonably possible for them to have avoided the contact.

Note that if the keep-clear boat fails to avoid contact, she technically can be disqualified under this rule; however, this is a moot point because she will be disqualified under the Section A rule she broke, and a boat can only be

PART 2, SECTION B: WHEN BOATS MEET — GENERAL LIMITATIONS **125**

disqualified once in a race. Likewise, if she took a penalty for breaking one or more rules in the incident, she cannot be further penalized under rule 64.2. See rule 64.2(a) (Penalties).

"If I'm involved in contact that causes damage or injury, can I take a Two-Turns Penalty or Scoring Penalty (put up a yellow flag) to avoid disqualification?"

If there is just "damage," then Yes! But if anyone got "injured" or if the damage was "serious," then No! Rule 44.1 (Penalties at the Time of an Incident) permits a boat that may have broken any rule in Part 2 while *racing* to take a penalty at the time of the incident. The penalty is the Two-Turns Penalty unless the sailing instructions specify the use of some other penalty (rule 44.1). So if you are a right-of-way boat or an inside boat entitled to *mark-room* and you cause damage in an incident, you can quickly do two turns in the same direction including two tacks and gybes and continue in the race. If you are the keep-clear boat, you can also do two turns which absolves you of all Part 2 and rule 31 (Touching a Mark) rule breaches you may have committed in the incident (even if you broke more than one rule in the incident; see rules 44.1 and 64.2(a)).

There are two exceptions however. Rule 44.1(b) says, *"if the boat caused injury or serious damage or, despite taking a penalty, gained a significant advantage in the race or series by her breach her penalty shall be to retire."* In other words, you can't absolve yourself with a Two-Turns Penalty if anyone got injured in the incident or there was "serious" damage, or if you gained a significant advantage, despite taking a penalty, by breaking a *rule*.

See the explanation of rule 44 for a discussion on how to properly do a Two-Turns Penalty and what constitutes "serious damage" in chapter 12.

"I understand that if I'm the right-of-way boat, I can be penalized for causing any damage or injury at all; what constitutes 'damage or injury'?"

Case 110 says that "'Injury' in the racing rules refers only to bodily injury to a person, and 'damage' is limited to physical damage to a boat or her equipment." Case 19 offers an interpretation of the term "damage:" "It is not possible to define 'damage' comprehensively, but one current English dictionary says 'harm…impairing the value or usefulness of something.' This definition suggests questions to consider.

Examples are:

1. Was the current market value of any part of the boat, or of the boat as a whole, diminished?
2. Was any item of the boat or its equipment made less functional?"

In my opinion, a related question to number 1 above is, "Did the contact result in something needing to be repaired or replaced?"

Regarding "injury," I think an "injury" is something that physically hurts a person more than just briefly, and that ordinarily affects the person's ability to function normally and/or requires the person to be attended to at some point. A related question would be "Does the person need attending to; and/or is the effect on the person brief or longer lasting?"

Clearly, boats will have contact that will cause no damage or injury to either boat or crew. Examples will include two boats having light side-to-side contact on the starting line or while rounding a *mark*, or incidents where the crews fend off and the hulls never touch. On the other hand, there will be contact that clearly causes "damage or injury:" a hole or dent in the boat, a torn sail, a bent stanchion, a nick out of the rudder, a broken finger, etc. The hard calls will be the situations where the gel coat gets lightly scratched, the sailors hear the fiberglass "crunch" though there is no visible sign of "damage" or a crew member gets a temporary soreness from fending off, etc. Protest committees will need to exercise their best judgment in these situations. Notice that the judgment that "damage or injury" occurred is not a "fact found;" it is a conclusion based on the "facts found" and therefore subject to appeal.

"As I understand the rule, even if I'm involved in contact that causes damage or injury, but it was not reasonably possible for me to avoid the contact, I won't be penalized under this rule; correct?"

Correct. The rule acknowledges that there may be times when it is simply not reasonably possible for a boat to avoid contact. However, this should not be viewed as a rationale for not making every effort to avoid collisions. Ultimately, whether or not it was reasonably possible to have avoided the contact will be decided by the protest committee.

The dictionary defines "reasonable" as "agreeable to reason; possessing sound judgment; not extreme or excessive." In judging whether it was "reasonably possible" for a boat to have avoided contact, it is implicit, to me, that as two boats near each other, the right-of-way boat settles on a straight-line or compass course or risk breaking rule 16.1 (Changing Course); and the keep-clear boat begins to take avoiding action. However, when, in her judgment, the right-of-way boat has a reasonable apprehension that contact will occur if she continues to hold her course, she may change her course to avoid the collision (Case 50). Rule 14 reinforces this by telling right-of-way boats and boats sailing within the *room* or *mark-room* to which they are entitled that they need not act to avoid contact until it is "clear" that the other boat is not *keeping clear*.

Therefore, as boats approach each other, they must continually assess the situation in terms of "what are the probable chances that I may hit this other boat or vice versa?" This judgment should factor in:

- what the response(s) have been from the other boat,
- whether the other boat is keeping a good lookout,
- what the sailing conditions are like and how well a boat of the class involved maneuvers in such conditions,
- who the sailors in the other boat are, and
- is there anything at all peculiar about the way the other boat is being handled?

In judging whether it was "reasonably possible" for a boat to have avoided contact, I'd consider whether the contact could have been avoided given the sailors' best attempts at avoiding or minimizing the impact of the collision, factoring in the amount of warning they had that a keep-clear boat might not *keep clear* or give *room* or *mark-room*, the time they had to consider what their best attempt might be, and the amount and difficulty of the boat and sail handling involved. Also factored in to a much lesser degree would be the competency of the sailors and the condition of their equipment and boat; i.e., their steering gear, cleats and so on. However, the rules do not make allowances for poor seamanship, and I would be hesitant to excuse a boat due to poor sailing skills or less than adequately functioning equipment. In other words, in my opinion, "reasonable" is defined in terms of what a competent, but not expert, sailor could be expected to do in a similar situation.

Case 87 addresses a situation where a *port-tack* boat (P) and a *starboard-tack* boat (S) are sailing upwind on a collision course. S expected that P would bear off and pass astern of her, but instead P "made no attempt to avoid S and struck her amidships at right angles, causing considerable damage. The protest committee disqualified both boats, P under rule 10 and S under rule 14. S appealed."

In its decision, the appeals committee says, "In P's case...P broke both rule 10 and rule 14. In S's case...[she] was required by rule 14 to avoid contact if it was 'reasonably possible' to do so. However, rule 14 allowed S to sail her course in the expectation that P would keep clear as required, until such time as it became clear that P would not do so...For that reason, the time between the moment it became clear that P would not keep clear and the time of the collision was a very brief interval, so brief that it was impossible for S to avoid contact. Therefore, S did not break rule 14."

Case 26 concerns a collision where P, a 5-0-5, and S, a Soling, were rounding the same leeward *mark* in opposite directions. Needless to say, the 5-0-5 received most of the damage as the Soling's bow sliced through P's hull and side buoyancy-tank just aft of the mast, the force of the impact knocking P's crew overboard unhurt. The decision reads, "P, as the keep-clear boat, failed to keep a lookout and to observe her primary duties to keep clear and avoid contact. She broke both rule 10 and rule 14. An important purpose of the rules of Part 2 is to avoid contact between boats. All boats, whether or not holding right of way, should keep a lookout, particularly when approaching a mark.

"When it became clear that P was not keeping clear, S was required by rule 14 to act to avoid contact with P (see rule 14)...S could have luffed and avoided contact with P. Such a change of course by S would have given P more room to keep clear and would not have broken rule 16.1. The contact caused damage. Therefore, S broke rule 14 and...must be penalized for having done so." (See Appeal 52.)

Case 27 is an illustration of when it was not reasonably possible for a boat to avoid contact. It involves two boats sailing upwind on *port tack* approaching the starboard-tack layline. "AS, a hull length to leeward and a hull length ahead of BP, tacked as soon as she reached the starboard-tack lay line. Almost immediately she was hit and damaged by BP travelling at about ten knots." The Decision states, "When AS passed through head to wind, BP became the right-of-way boat under rule 13 and held right of way until AS assumed a close-hauled course on starboard tack. At that moment AS, having just acquired right of way under rule 10, was required by rule 15 to give BP room to keep clear.

BP took no action to avoid a collision, but what could she have done? Given her speed and the distance involved, she had perhaps one to two seconds to decide what to do and then do it. It is a principle of the right-of-way rules, as stated in rule 15, that a boat that becomes obligated to keep clear by an action of another boat is entitled to sufficient time for response. Also, while it was obvious that AS would have to tack to round the mark, no rule required BP to anticipate that AS would break a rule."

Another scenario in which it may not be reasonably possible for boats to avoid contact is in light air when boats have very little steerageway and large powerboat waves enter the racing area and toss the boats about.

In conclusion, to penalize a right-of-way boat or one sailing within the *room* or *mark-room* to which she is entitled under rule 14, two things must be decided. One, was the boat involved in contact that caused "damage or injury;" and two, was it "reasonably possible" for the boat to have avoided the contact? If either there was no "damage or injury," or if it is decided that the boat couldn't have reasonably avoided the contact, then the boat should not be penalized under rule 14. As a juror, I would have to be satisfied from the weight of the evidence submitted (in other words there is no onus) that a boat was negligent or had shown very poor judgment or seamanship before I penalized them. On the other hand, I expect jurors would not be very tolerant of situations where the right-of-way boat intentionally hits the keep-clear boat to prove the foul, causing any damage or injury as a result.

"If I'm on port tack, and a starboard-tacker hits me and causes damage or injury, and the damage or injury causes me to get a significantly worse score as a result, I realize that I have to take a Two-Turns Penalty because I was on port tack; but can I request redress because of the damage or injury?"

You can, but whether or not you receive it will depend on the facts found by the protest committee. Rule 62.1(b) (Redress) says that a boat is entitled to request redress when her *"score or place in a race or series has been or may be, through no fault of her own, made significantly worse by… injury or physical damage because of the action of a boat that was breaking a rule of Part 2 and took an appropriate penalty or was penalized…"*. In the hearing, the protest committee must first decide if S broke rule 14; and if so, whether the injury or physical damage itself made your score or place significantly worse (see

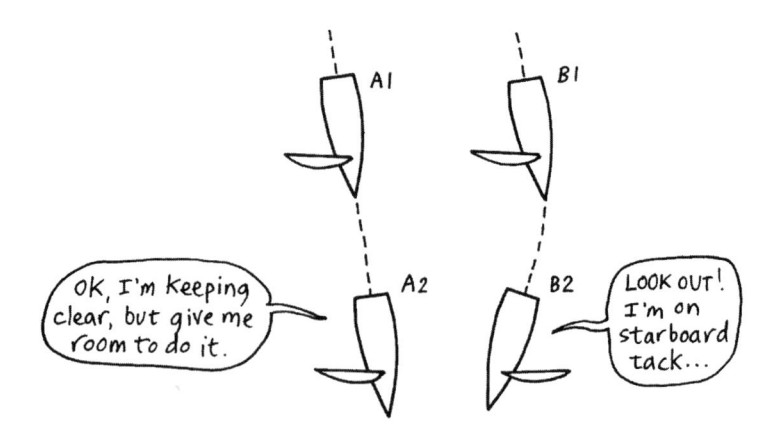

[A1 boat, B1 boat shown above; A2 boat says "OK, I'm keeping clear, but give me room to do it." B2 boat says "LOOK OUT! I'm on starboard tack..."]

Case 110). Next it must decide if you contributed to the receiving of damage or injury. It may decide that you broke rule 14 as well because you misjudged the crossing and therefore failed to avoid the contact (see Case 123).

RULE 15 — ACQUIRING RIGHT OF WAY

When a boat acquires right of way, she shall initially give the other boat *room* to *keep clear*, unless she acquires right of way because of the other boat's actions.

This rule states one of the oldest and most fundamental principles in the rules, and it makes perfect sense. When a boat takes action that gives her the right of way over you, she must give you the chance to respond and *keep clear* of her. For example, you are sailing on a run on *port tack* with another *port-tack* boat just to windward. As the *leeward* boat, you have the right-of-way (rule 11, On the Same Tack, Overlapped) and everything is under control. You have the "sword," so to speak, and the *windward* boat must stay out of your way. Suddenly, the *windward* boat gybes. Now she is on *starboard tack* and you are on *port tack*. She now has the right-of-way; i.e., she now has the "sword" (rule 10, On Opposite Tacks), but she can't just gybe and hit you; her actions are limited by rule 15.

Case 24 describes a scenario where a boat (B) comes up from astern and becomes *overlapped* to *leeward* of the boat *clear ahead*. When B becomes *overlapped* she gains the right of way under rule 11, but also the limitation under rule 15 which "embodies the principle in the rules that when the right of way shifts from one boat to another, the boat with the newly acquired right

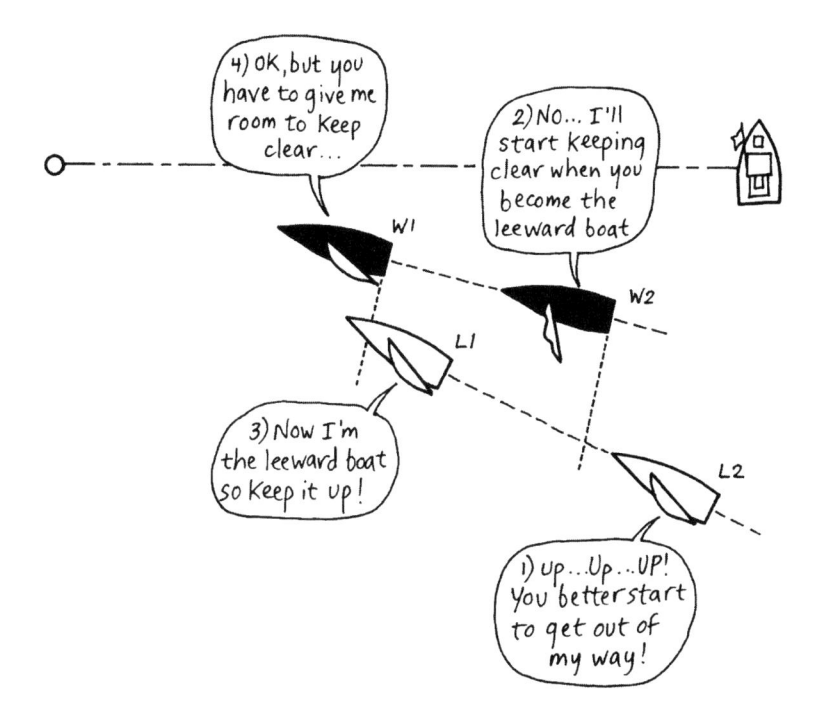

PART 2, SECTION B: WHEN BOATS MEET — GENERAL LIMITATIONS 131

> 4) OK, but you have to give me room to keep clear...

> 2) No... I'll start keeping clear when you become the leeward boat

> 3) Now I'm the leeward boat so keep it up!

> 1) Up...Up...UP! You better start to get out of my way!

of way must give the other boat space and time for response, and thus a fair opportunity to manoeuvre to keep clear." (See also Case 53.)

Note that a right-of-way boat does not have to anticipate that she will lose her right of way. Case 53 is clear on this point: "Allowing adequate time for response, when rights and obligations change between two boats, is implied in rule 15 by its requirement to allow the newly obligated boat 'room to keep clear'." Therefore, in the example above, the *leeward* boat need not anticipate her requirement to *keep clear* as a *port-tack* boat before the *windward* boat gybes to *starboard*.

However, the use of the word "initially" clearly states that the protection of "*room* to *keep clear*" is not continuing. In the old video game *Deluxe Asteroids*, a tiny rocket ship tries to blast apart large rocks that will blow up the ship if they hit her. When there are just too many rocks about to hit, the player can press a button, putting a protective force shield around the ship. At first, the rocks bounce off the shield, but after a few seconds the shield begins to fade and disappear.

The room to respond to a newly acquired obligation to *keep clear* is a temporary "shield" for the new keep-clear boat. It is very strong initially, but fades in strength as the seconds go by. Also, for you to be entitled to the protection of the 'shield' you must, at the moment you become the keep-clear boat, make a prompt and careful attempt to begin to get clear of the right-of-way boat. If you delay at all, you lose the protection of "*room* to *keep clear*" and you run the risk of fouling the right-of-way boat.

LET'S LOOK AT SOME COMMON SITUATIONS on the race course where this principle of transition comes into play:

Becoming *overlapped* to leeward of a boat from *clear astern* (common during pre-start maneuvering and when sailing downwind):

Two boats on the same *tack* are sailing near each other, one clear astern (BL) of the other (AW) and catching up. While BL is approaching AW, she must *keep clear*. When she becomes *overlapped* to leeward of AW, rule 12 *(clear astern/clear ahead)* ceases to apply and she **instantly** becomes the right-of-way boat under rule 11 *(windward/leeward)*. This is when rule 15 requires her to initially give AW *room* to *keep clear* of her. Remember that AW does not need to anticipate that BL will gain the right of way; therefore she does not need to take any evasive action **before** the *overlap* is created. And if AW luffs within the first few seconds of the *overlap* and her stern hits BL's bow, typically it will be decided by a protest committee that BL failed to give AW the space she needed to turn out of BL's way; i.e., that BL broke rule 15.

Rule 15 does not change the fact that W is required to *keep clear* of L. Case 53 makes the point that the keep-clear boat must respond promptly: "After L became overlapped to leeward of W, W immediately trimmed her sails, headed up, and thereafter kept clear. By taking these actions, W fulfilled her obligations under rule 11." Case 7 states, "…L was bound by rule 15 to allow W room to keep clear, but that obligation is not a continuing one, and in this case the overlap had been in existence for a considerable period during which W certainly had room to keep clear." (See Case 24 and Appeal 43.)

"If I'm on the starting line and a boat from astern puts her bow so close to leeward of me that she couldn't head up without immediately hitting me, but then she immediately bears away and gives me room to head up and keep clear of her, does she comply with rule 15, and am I exonerated for my momentary breach of rule 11?"

PART 2, SECTION B: WHEN BOATS MEET — GENERAL LIMITATIONS   **133**

In position 1, SL is past head to wind; therefore she is on starboard tack. However, rule 13 requires that she keep clear of SW until she is on a close-hauled course. If SW has to change course to avoid hitting SL before SL is on a close-hauled course, SL breaks rule 13.

In position 2, SL is on a close-hauled course; therefore, as the leeward boat, she is now the right-of-way boat. SW must now promptly try to avoid hitting SL, but SL must initially give her room to do so under rule 15.

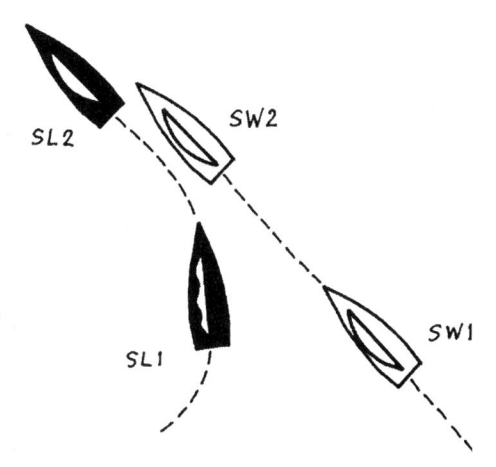

Yes and Yes. Rule 15 states that the rule goes into effect "when" the right-of-way boat acquires the right of way. When a boat *clear astern* (B) establishes an *overlap* within inches of a boat *clear* ahead (A), A is by definition not *keeping clear* at that moment because if B headed up she would immediately make contact with A (see the definition *Keep Clear*). When B establishes the *overlap*, rule 15 requires B to initially give A *room* to *keep clear*. As long as B immediately bears away and gives A the space A needs to head up and *keep clear* of her, then B has complied with rule 15. And as long as A promptly takes action to *keep clear* of B in a seamanlike way (by turning her boat away from B and trimming her mainsail), she is sailing within the *room* to which she is entitled, and is exonerated by rule 43.1(b) (Exoneration) for her momentary breach of rule 11 (On the Same Tack, Overlapped) (see Case 146 and Appeal 119).

Tacking into a right-of-way position to leeward of a right-of-way boat (commonly known as "lee-bowing"):

While a boat is tacking near another boat, rule 13 (While Tacking) requires her to *keep clear* of the other boat from the time she passes head to wind until she is on a close-hauled course. But, once she is on a close-hauled course, and if she has become the right-of-way boat, rule 15 applies. For a good analogy (though this may not be the actual highway law), picture yourself coming up the entrance ramp to a three-lane highway. Cars driving down the right-hand lane must stay clear of other cars in the right-hand lane in front of them. While you're on the ramp you cannot interfere with cars driving in the right-hand lane. If, while you are moving across the white line into the right-hand lane, a car hits you or swerves to miss you, you are in the wrong. But once you get **all four wheels** across the line, you are now technically in the right-hand lane yourself and cars coming up from behind have to keep clear of you. However, these cars are not required to begin to avoid you or even to **anticipate** avoiding you until you are completely in the lane. Once you are in the lane they have to try reasonably hard to miss you. If they can't, then you've moved on too close in front of them.

The same is true in sailboats. Let's say I'm on *starboard tack*, you're approaching me on *port tack*, and you want to tack on my lee-bow or in front of me. If I could hit you before you passed head to wind (i.e., before you began to cross the white line), you'd be wrong under rule 10 *(port/starboard)*. If I could hit you after you'd passed head to wind but before you were aiming on your close-hauled course (i.e., while you were crossing the line), you'd be wrong under rule 13 (a boat past head to wind must *keep clear*). However, the moment you get to your close-hauled course (i.e., completely in my lane) and you are either *clear ahead* or to *leeward* of me, you have the right of way under either rule 12 *(clear astern/clear ahead)* or rule 11 *(windward/leeward)* and I have to promptly take action to *keep clear* of you. This is when rule 15 requires you to initially give me the *room* (space and time) I need to *keep clear* of you. Of course, in most situations it will take me only a second or two to react enough to luff or bear away slightly to avoid a collision.

"In protests involving the situation where P tacks very close to leeward of S, it seems that P and S may often disagree on whether P was actually on a close-hauled course before S changed course to avoid her; or whether P, after acquiring right of way, actually gave S room to keep clear. Are there any onuses to help resolve these disagreements?"

No. In resolving these disagreements, most protest committees apply the principle in Case 50 (see rule 10 discussion), which is that they first put responsibility on S to satisfy the committee that the boats were close together. Then they put the responsibility on P to satisfy them that P was on a close-hauled course before S changed her course; and that once she was on a close-hauled course, she gave S *room* to *keep clear*. This responsibility on P is often difficult to win against. Hails to the effect of "complete–2–3–4, now you're changing course" and a witness are very helpful.

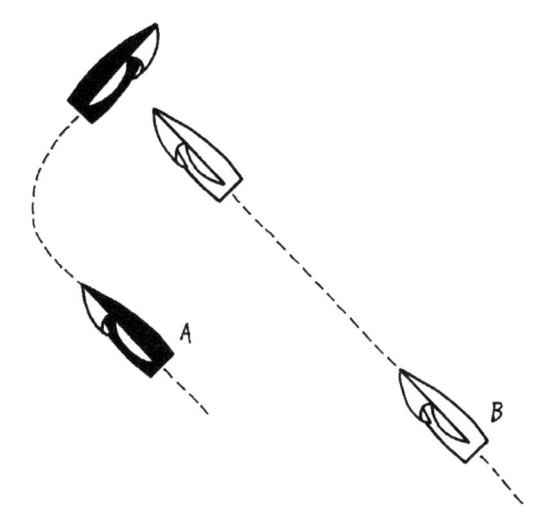

PART 2, SECTION B: WHEN BOATS MEET — GENERAL LIMITATIONS **135**

Because B acquires right of way as a result of A's tack, rule 15 does not require B to give A any room to keep clear.

Appeal 78 describes a situation where three *port-tack* boats (L, M and W) were sailing upwind and L (the leeward-most boat) tacked to *starboard* thereby acquiring the right of way. The middle boat (M) tacked to *starboard* and kept clear of L, but she tacked so close to the windward boat (W) that she and W could not avoid colliding, therefore breaking rule 15. The Appeals Committee said that L, by depriving M of the space necessary to maneuver without breaking a Part 2 rule, failed to give M *room* to *keep clear* (see the definition *Room*). L broke rule 15 against M and is disqualified. M is exonerated by rule 43.1(b) (Exoneration) for breaking rule 15 against W.

Gybing into a right-of-way position:

The same is true when gybing. If two boats are running side by side on *port tack* and the *windward* boat gybes, essentially the moment the foot of the mainsail crosses her centerline she is on *starboard tack* and the other boat (P) must promptly maneuver to get clear. However, S must plan to initially give P the *room* she needs to *keep clear*.

Completing penalty turns or starting after being over early:

Again, the principle applies when a boat is completing penalty turns for fouling another boat or touching a *mark* (rule 44, Penalties at the Time of an Incident). While making her penalty turn(s), she is required to *keep clear* of boats not doing so (rule 21, Starting Errors; Taking Penalties; Backing a Sail). The moment she completes her last turn, she is no longer bound by rule 21. If she suddenly acquires the right of way over a nearby boat, she must give this boat *room* to respond. The same applies when she returns to the correct side of the starting line to *start* after being on the course side of the starting line at the gun (rule 21).

"What is the reason for the last phrase of the rule, 'unless she acquires right of way because of the other boat's actions'?"

Good question! This is to protect boats that suddenly become right-of-way boats solely because of an action by the other boat. For example, you are sailing upwind on *starboard tack* just to windward and slightly behind a boat to leeward. Suddenly, the *leeward* boat tacks and is now directly in front of you on *port tack*! Without the last phrase in rule 15, you would be required to give the boat that tacked *room* to *keep clear* of you, because you have just acquired the right of way! Clearly this would be unacceptable, hence the phrase. Therefore, in the example above, assuming you had to take action to avoid contact, the boat that tacked broke rule 10 *(port/starboard)*, and rule 15 did not apply to you.

Another situation where this applies is when two boats on the starting line are on the same *tack* and the boat *clear ahead* (A) bears away and creates an *overlap* with the boat *clear astern* (B). The moment the boats are *overlapped*, B becomes the right-of-way boat under rule 11 *(windward/leeward)*. In this case, B was holding her course and it was A's action that gave B the right of way. Therefore rule 15 does not apply to B, and if A were to suddenly luff and strike B's bow with her port stern quarter, A would be penalized for breaking rule 11 (On the Same Tack, Overlapped).

RULE 16 — CHANGING COURSE

RULE 16.1

When a right-of-way boat changes course, she shall give the other boat *room* **to** *keep clear.*

Rule 16.1 contains one of the most fundamental principles in the rules. Simply put, when a right-of-way boat changes her course near a keep-clear boat, she

PART 2, SECTION B: WHEN BOATS MEET — GENERAL LIMITATIONS

must be aware of the space and time the keep-clear boat will need to stay clear of her, assuming the keep-clear boat reacts and maneuvers promptly in a seamanlike way; and she must be sure to give her that **space** and **time**.

Let's get into this extremely important rule. Rule 16.1 is clearly talking to right-of-way boats (see Case 52). When two boats are about to collide, the keep-clear boat has the obligation to *keep clear*. The only way she can decide how to do this is if she can accurately figure out where the right-of-way boat is going. It would be chaos if just as a *port-tack* boat was reaching by a *starboard-tack* boat, S could suddenly and unexpectedly turn and hit P. The purpose of rule 16.1 is to protect keep-clear boats from unpredictable or last-second changes of course by right-of-way boats which, in essence, prevent the keep-clear boat from being able to *keep clear*.

"So if I'm on starboard tack near a port-tack boat, rule 10 doesn't allow me to steer any course I want to?"

Absolutely not. That is exactly what rule 16.1 is designed to prevent. Case 60 says, "Tactical desires do not relieve a boat of her obligations under the rules. A (the right-of-way boat in the case) was free to adopt any course she chose to reach the leeward mark, but she did not have the right to luff into the path of B (the keep-clear boat) so close to B that B could not keep clear."

However, rule 16.1 does not shift the right-of-way between two boats; it is simply a common-sense "limit" on the right-of-way boat requiring her to limit her course changes when a keep-clear boat is close by and trying to *keep clear*.

Notice that rule 16.1 only applies to a "change of course." It in no way applies to a change in your boat's speed, sail trim or angle of heel. When P reaches by just to windward of S such that S momentarily loses her wind, thereby straightening up and hitting P's mast, P is wrong under rule 10 (On Opposite

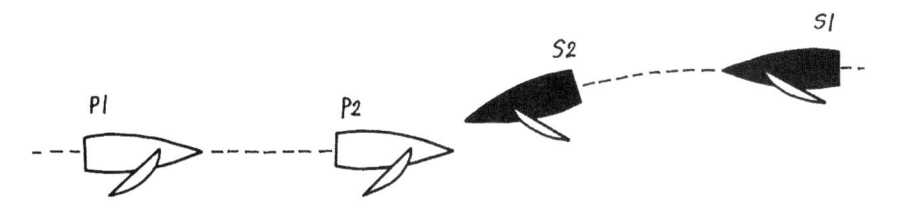

S has the right of way over P. But rule 16.1 requires that S not change her course so close to P that P does not have room to keep clear. So despite having the right-of-way, S needs to be careful when changing course near P.

Tacks). Of course, rule 2 (Fair Sailing) is available to P if she suspects that S deliberately tried to hit her in an unfair manner (see the discussion of rule 2).

"If I'm making a smooth turn toward a keep-clear boat, am I considered to be 'changing course' if I continue the arc of my turn?"

Yes. Appeal 33 says, "…a boat changes course when she sails the arc of a circle or any other course where she changes direction, whether or not she moves her helm… To change course means to change the direction in which the boat is heading…".

That tells us that "course" in rule 16.1 refers to the boat's straight-ahead or "compass" course. Therefore, whenever a boat is turning, it is changing "course." It also refers to its fore and aft or "directional" course; i.e., when a boat that was moving forward begins to move astern, it has also changed "course" (see Appeal 33; see also rule 21, Starting Errors; Taking Penalties; Backing a Sail).

"Okay, so if I'm a right-of-way boat and want to change course near another boat, what exactly does rule 16.1 require that I give her?"

You need to give her "*room* to *keep clear*" of you. She is *keeping clear* of you when you can sail your straight-ahead course with no need to take action to avoid hitting her; and if you are *overlapped*, if you can also change course in both directions without immediately hitting her. The *room* you have to give her is the "space" and "time" she needs to get far enough away from you so that you can sail your course, assuming she acts promptly in a seamanlike way (see the definition *Room*).

Note that "promptly" means "performed readily, quickly, almost immediately" which builds in the time element. Therefore when a right-of-way boat changes course, rule 16.1 requires nearby boats to respond "promptly" or risk losing the protection of *room*.

However, "seamanlike" means "responsible, prudent, safety conscious." Therefore, you have to be sure that your course change doesn't force the keep-clear boat to put their or your boat's crew, boat or equipment at risk of damage or injury by the need to make a sudden, hurried or extreme maneuver. For instance, forcing a *windward* boat to sail head to wind with a spinnaker up in heavy air may be considered "unseamanlike" as it may put their spinnaker at great risk of tearing.

PART 2, SECTION B: WHEN BOATS MEET — GENERAL LIMITATIONS 139

"Does 'room' take into account the experience or the number of the crew on board the boat?"

No. Case 103 addresses this head on by saying, "Neither the experience of IW's crew nor their number is relevant in determining 'room'…the interpretation of 'seamanlike way' must be based on the boat-handling that can reasonably be expected from a competent, but not expert, crew of the appropriate number for the boat."

Also note that the definition *Room* makes it clear that your course change can't force a keep-clear boat to foul another boat or touch a *mark*. You need to be aware of the space the keep-clear boat has around her to get away from you.

"If a port-tack boat is bearing away to go astern of me, can I hunt down (bear away) and force them to bear away more to avoid me?"

Absolutely not. Rule 16.2 is known as "the anti-hunting" rule.

RULE 16.2

In addition, on a beat to windward when a *port-tack* boat is *keeping clear* by sailing to pass to leeward of a *starboard-tack* boat, the *starboard-tack* boat shall not bear away if as a result the *port-tack* boat must change course immediately to continue *keeping clear.*

The idea here is that if P has conceded that S is ahead in the race, and is steering a course that will take her behind S (she's "ducking" S), S can't bear away (turn away from the wind) so close to P that P would "immediately" need to change her course to continue to avoid S. This permits P to safely pass close to leeward of S without the risk of hull or spar contact if S were permitted to bear away and "hunt" P as she was ducking.

So, there are basically two questions the right-of-way boat will need to consider before changing course near another boat (these will be the same two questions the protest committee will have to answer in a protest involving rule 16):

1) When I change my course, will the other boat have enough "space" and "time" to get away from me "promptly" without having to make an "unseamanlike maneuver" to do so (rule 16.1)?

2) If it is after the starting signal and we're on a beat to windward, and if I am on *starboard tack* converging with a *port-tack* boat that is about

to safely pass behind me, will I be able to bear away without making the port-tacker have to make an "immediate" course change to continue safely passing behind me (rule 16.2)?

If the answer to either of these questions is "No," then the right-of-way boat will break rule 16.1 and/or rule 16.2 if she changes course near the other boat.

Clearly, the questions must be answered depending on the circumstances at the time, and for that reason it is impossible to project a hypothetical distance apart. The major considerations will be:

1) the distance between the boats;
2) the speeds and sizes of the boats;
3) the angles at which they are converging;
4) the visibility between the boats;
5) the amount of course change by the right-of-way boat;
6) the amount and difficulty of the boat handling required by the keep-clear boat to *keep clear*; and
7) the reasonableness of the keep-clear boat's attempt to *keep clear*.

Having said all this, I will say that as a conservative and safe rule of thumb in most boats, any course change by the right-of-way boat when closer than two lengths from the keep-clear boat is risky.

"The rule does not say "after the starting signal," so why did you use that phrase above; and when is a boat "on a beat to windward?"

A boat is "on a beat to windward" when the course she would sail in the absence of other boats to get to the windward mark as soon as possible is close-hauled or above, or she is sailing below close-hauled because she has overstood the close-hauled layline to the mark (see Case 132). Before the starting signal, boats are not "on a beat to windward."

LET'S LOOK AT SOME COMMON SITUATIONS when rules 16.1 and 16.2 will come into play.

When a *port-tack* boat (P) and a *starboard-tack* boat (S) are converging on a beat:

Situation 1: P will cross S by half a boat-length or so. When about two lengths apart, S hails "Starboard" and makes a medium fast luff toward P. P, who has

PART 2, SECTION B: WHEN BOATS MEET — GENERAL LIMITATIONS **141**

been watching S, continues for a couple of seconds, realizes she cannot cross S safely, and makes a routine tack to *starboard tack* on S's lee-bow. S could continue straight-ahead, but decides to tack away to avoid P's bad air.

Resolution: When the boats are converging, P is required to *keep clear* under rule 10 (On Opposite Tacks). When S changes her course near P, she is required to give P *room* to *keep clear* (rule 16.1). P is able to tack in a seamanlike way to continue *keeping clear* of S. S is able to sail her course without concern of hitting P. Therefore S gives P the *room* she needs to *keep clear*, and P does *keep clear*. Neither boat breaks a *rule*.

Situation 2: Same scenario as above but the boats are a bit closer together when S luffs towards P. P tacks immediately in response to S's luff. P's tack is a routine tack to *starboard tack* on S's lee-bow. S tacks away to clear her air.

Resolution: Note that rule 16.2 does not apply (because P is not sailing to pass to leeward of S), so the fact that P had to "immediately" change course to avoid S is not, in and of itself, proof of a breach of rule 16.1 by S. If in fact P's tack was "seamanlike," then P properly *kept clear* under rule 10, and S properly gave P *room* to *keep clear* under rule 16.1. But part of sailing in a "seamanlike way" is looking before changing course. Keeping in mind that P does not need to anticipate the fact that S "might" change course near her, if S gets so close to P before luffing that P will need to tack immediately, typically P will not have time to look over her shoulder to see if she is clear to tack, let alone prepare her crew for the tack, and S will break rule 16.1 if P fails to *keep clear*. This is particularly true in a fleet race, as opposed to a match race where there are no other boats besides P and S.

Situation 3: P will cross S by half a boat-length or so. When about one length apart, S hails "Starboard" and makes a medium fast luff toward P, putting the two boats on a collision course. P holds her course to get across S as quickly as she can (tacking would make matters worse because she would be turning directly in front of S). To avoid contact, S immediately bears away and protests.

Resolution: The first job of the protest committee will be to determine if P actually *keeps clear*. Clearly she doesn't because S needs to take action to avoid hitting her (see the definition *Keep Clear*). Therefore, P breaks rule 10 (On Opposite Tacks). However, when S changes course she is required to give P *room* to *keep clear*. Because P was sailing within that *room* (space), P is exonerated by

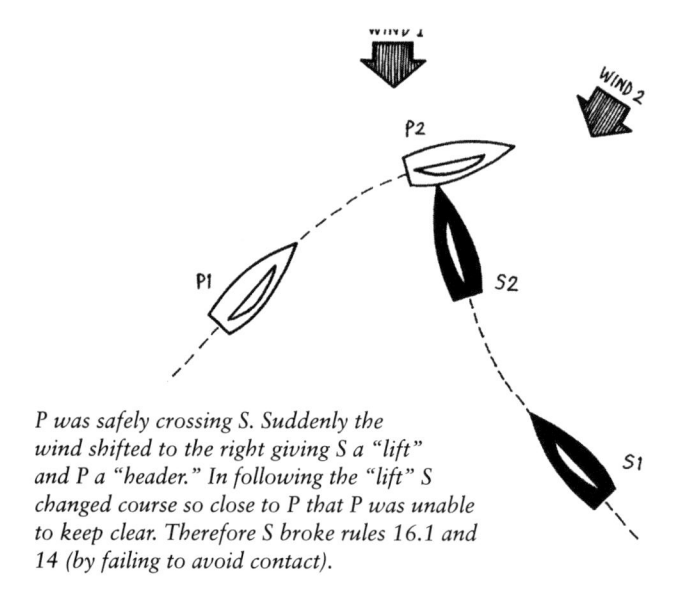

142 UNDERSTANDING THE RACING RULES OF SAILING THROUGH 2024

P was safely crossing S. Suddenly the wind shifted to the right giving S a "lift" and P a "header." In following the "lift" S changed course so close to P that P was unable to keep clear. Therefore S broke rules 16.1 and 14 (by failing to avoid contact).

rule 43.1(b) (Exoneration). Its next task is to decide if, after S changes course, she gives P *room* to *keep clear*. By bearing away immediately S gives P *room* to *keep clear* and therefore complies with rule 16.1 (see Case 146). Neither boat is penalized. Note: Had S hit P, or forced P to make an "unseamanlike maneuver" to *keep clear*, then S would **not** have given P *room* to *keep clear* and would have broken rule 16.1, as well as rule 14 (Avoiding Contact). P would still be exonerated by rule 43.1(b) if she had broken rule 10.

Situation 4: P bears away to "duck" (pass to leeward of) S. When a length and a half away, S bears away towards P and P has to immediately bear away further to avoid S. S luffs back up to close-hauled and P safely passes close astern of her. P protests.

Resolution: By bearing away, P is *keeping clear* of S by sailing a course to pass to leeward of S. When S changes her course, P needs to immediately bear away further to *keep clear* of S. By causing P to have to immediately change her course to continue *keeping clear*, S breaks rule 16.2. This is so even though S gives P space to *keep clear* in a seamanlike way; i.e., S does not break rule 16.1. (See Case 92.)

BOTTOM LINE: Rule 16 is very strict, and S must be very careful with her course changes when near P. Again, course changes when closer than two lengths from the keep-clear boat are risky.

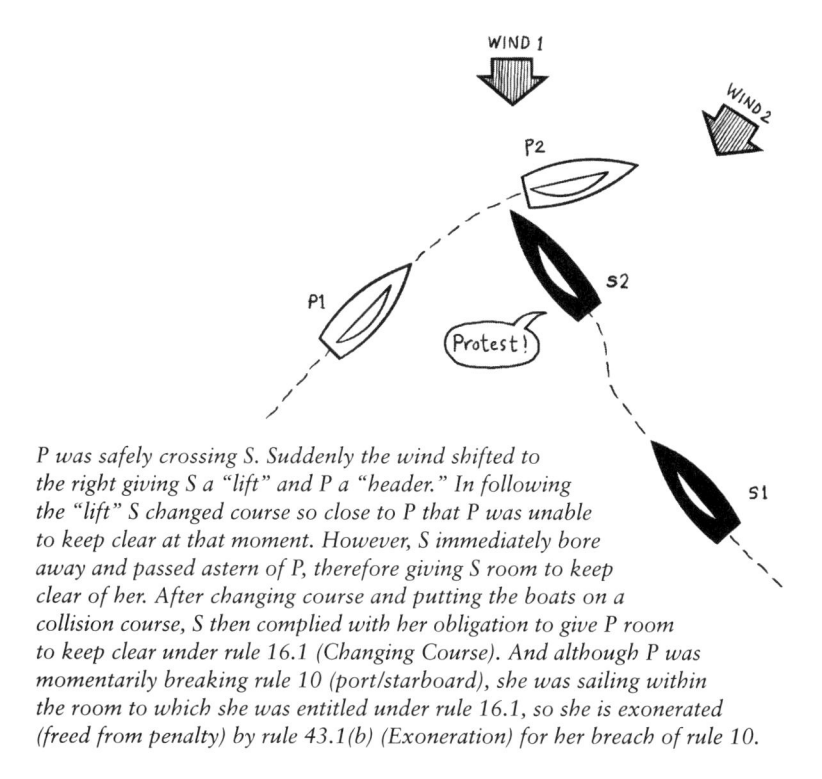

PART 2, SECTION B: WHEN BOATS MEET — GENERAL LIMITATIONS **143**

P was safely crossing S. Suddenly the wind shifted to the right giving S a "lift" and P a "header." In following the "lift" S changed course so close to P that P was unable to keep clear at that moment. However, S immediately bore away and passed astern of P, therefore giving S room to keep clear of her. After changing course and putting the boats on a collision course, S then complied with her obligation to give P room to keep clear under rule 16.1 (Changing Course). And although P was momentarily breaking rule 10 (port/starboard), she was sailing within the room to which she was entitled under rule 16.1, so she is exonerated (freed from penalty) by rule 43.1(b) (Exoneration) for her breach of rule 10.

"I assume from all this that if I get a wind shift on a beat, I can't follow the shift and hit a port-tack boat that is just crossing my bow?"

That's absolutely right. Rule 16.1 applies to any course change, regardless of the reason (with one exception when rounding a mark; see the discussion of rule 43.1(b), Exoneration, in chapter 8). If you find yourself in the situation where P is crossing you and you get a favorable wind shift and want to head up and pass close astern of P, but you know that P doesn't have *room* to tack away after you head up, simply let P know, with a hail or a wave, that she can continue on across you as you head up to pass close astern of her.

"Do I have to hail before changing my course? And if I do warn the other boat with a hail that I am about to change course toward them, does that count as 'giving room'?"

No and No. First, the rule does not require a hail. Second, the rule begins "When a boat changes course," which means that the test of whether you gave *room* will begin **after** you actually change your course. However, a clear hail alerting the keep-clear boat that you are about to change course is strong evidence that you intend to give her *room* to *keep clear* when you do change course, and is therefore strongly recommended.

When a port-tack boat (P) and a starboard-tack boat (S) are on a downwind leg:

Situation 1: P will cross S by half a boat-length or so. When one length away, S bears away such that the boats are now on a collision course. P immediately makes a routine gybe to *keep clear* of S, and protests.

Resolution: Again note that rule 16.2 does not apply because the boats are not on a beat to windward. When S changes her course, the question is whether P is able to get out of her way in a seamanlike way (rule 16.1). P makes a routine gybe and therefore is able to properly *keep clear* of S in a seamanlike way. Neither boat breaks a *rule*.

Situation 2: P and S are converging and P is sailing a course that will take her astern of S. When one and a half lengths apart, S luffs slightly which causes P to have to immediately luff slightly to continue safely passing astern of S, which she does. P protests.

Resolution: Because the boats are not on a beat to windward, rule 16.2 does not apply. When S changes course she is required to give P *room* to *keep clear* under rule 16.1, which she does. Neither boat breaks a *rule*.

When a *leeward* boat (L) and a *windward* boat (W) are sailing on the same *tack*:

Situation 1: L is sailing along on a reach. W catches up and *overlaps* her to windward, but far enough away so that L can change her course toward her (luff) without immediately hitting her. L begins to luff medium fast and W promptly responds and *keeps clear*. At some point during the luff, L gets closer to W (either because W slows down her response rate, or L increases her luffing rate, or because the boats are simply getting closer as they rotate up). L realizes that if she continues her luff she will get so close to W that she could then immediately hit W if she luffed even more. She stops her luff and protests.

Resolution: When L luffs (changes course toward W), W must respond "promptly" (i.e., very quickly) and make her best effort to get out of L's way. Furthermore, L can luff as quickly as she chooses **provided** she allows W the

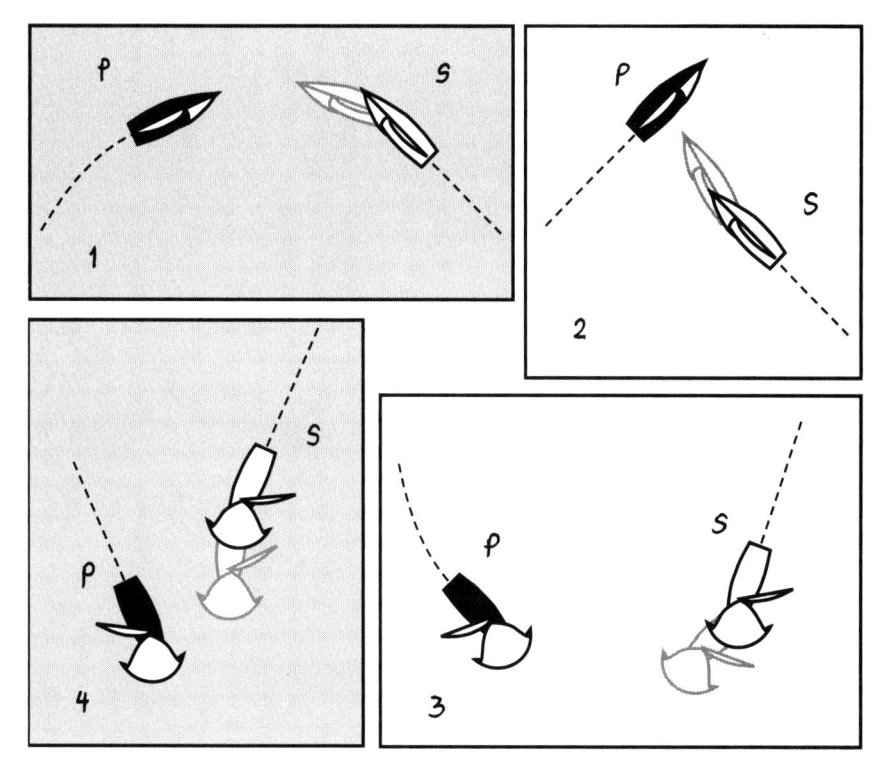

PART 2, SECTION B: WHEN BOATS MEET — GENERAL LIMITATIONS **145**

In diagram 1, the starboard-tack (right-of-way) boat (S) is bearing away while a port-tack boat (P) is keeping clear by sailing to pass to leeward of S. If P needs to "immediately" change course to continue keeping clear in reaction to S's course change, S breaks rule 16.2.

In diagram 2, the starboard-tack (right-of-way) boat (S) is changing course while a port-tack boat (P) is keeping clear by sailing to pass to windward of S. In this case rule 16.2 does not apply. If P can react to S's course change in a seamanlike way and keep clear of S, even if it requires an "immediate" course change, P must do so and S does not break rule 16.1.

In diagrams 3 and 4, the boats are not on a beat to windward. Therefore rule 16.2 does not apply; and if P can react to S's course change in a seamanlike way and keep clear of S, even if it requires an "immediate" course change, P must do so and S does not break rule 16.1.

room (space and time) needed to get out of her way, assuming W is responding promptly. However, L can never luff so suddenly or fast that, despite W's best efforts, W physically cannot *keep clear* of her and there is contact.

The first job of the protest committee will be to determine if W actually *keeps clear* of L. Clearly she does because L can always sail her course; i.e., her straight-ahead course, with no apprehension of collision. Furthermore, throughout the incident L can always change course in either direction without

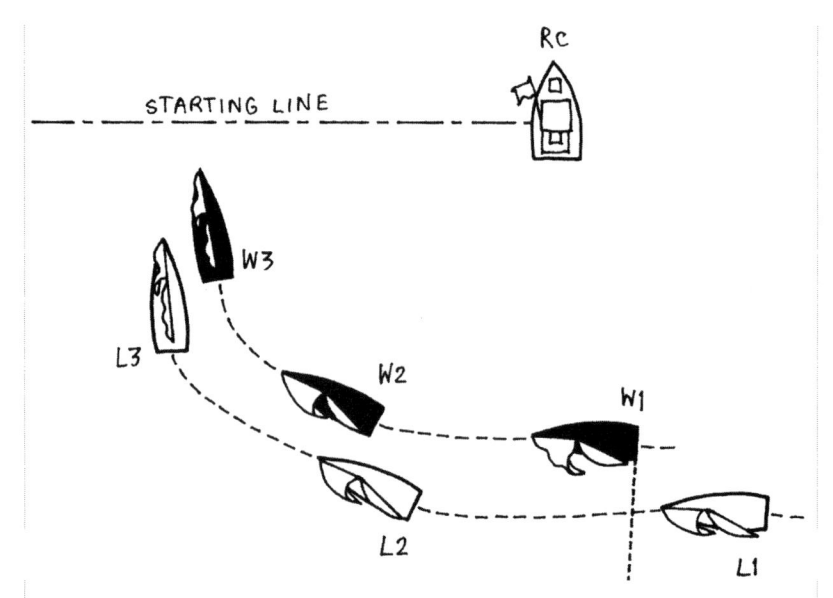

When L becomes overlapped to leeward of W and then luffs, L must initially give W room to keep clear when she first becomes overlapped (rule 15); and then L must give W any additional room W needs to keep clear when she luffs (rule 16.1).

making immediate contact with W. Once it is decided that W has *kept clear* throughout the incident, it then means that L has complied with rule 16.1. Neither boat breaks a *rule*.

Note: If L had allowed herself to get so close to W that L could not change course any more without immediately making contact with W, it would have been a much different situation. This is often called the "lock-up" position. First, by definition W was not *keeping clear* (see part (b) in the definition *Keep Clear*), and she breaks rule 11 (On the Same Tack, Overlapped). However, when L changes course she is required to give W *room* to *keep clear*. Because W was sailing within that *room* (space), W is exonerated by rule 43.1(b) (Exoneration). As long as L bears away immediately, L gives W *room* to *keep clear* and therefore complies with rule 16.1. Neither boat is penalized (see Case 146). However, if there is contact, then this *protest* will be resolved by the protest committee's determination of whether W was maneuvering promptly in a seamanlike way or not (an admittedly difficult protest at best). If yes, then L failed to give her enough *room* to continue *keeping clear* and is disqualified under rule 16.1 (and W is exonerated by rule 43.1(b)); if no, then W failed to *keep clear* by her own actions and is disqualified under rule 11.

"If L luffs, then stops luffing to give W more room to respond, is L still bound by rule 16.1 to give W room to keep clear when L begins luffing again?"

Yes. Rule 16.1 applies to L whenever she changes her course. The use of the word "initially" in rule 15 (Acquiring Right of Way) makes the requirement in rule 15 a temporary one at the outset of the overlap. However, rule 16.1 does not contain the word "initially." Therefore, throughout her luff L must give W *room* to *keep clear*; and each time L stops and then changes her course again, she must give W *room* to *keep clear* once again. W, on the other hand, will put herself at great risk by remaining too close to L over an extended period of time, and should make every effort to get well clear when L first luffs.

"What if, despite the fact that L has given W plenty of room, W allows herself to get so close to L that L can't change course at all without hitting W?"

Part (b) in the definition *Keep Clear* tells W that she is not *keeping clear* if she allows herself to get so close to L that L can't change course in **both directions** at that moment without **immediately** making contact with her. Note the use of the word "if" in the definition suggests that L does not need to actually hit W to prove she couldn't change course without contact in both directions. If the protest committee decides that L couldn't have changed course in both directions without immediately hitting W, then W has broken rule 11 (On the Same Tack, Overlapped) simply by her extreme close proximity to L.

Furthermore, any time L has a reasonable apprehension that contact with W may occur if she holds her course, W fails to *keep clear* and breaks rule 11; and when W allows herself to get that close to L, L will generally be justified in being concerned about the masts touching, the boats being tossed together by waves, etc., etc.

However, when L is luffing and her bow is getting closer to W's stern quarter, there will come a point that, due to the way boats rotate, it will become impossible for W to *keep clear* if L continues to luff (the "lock-up" position). At that point, L must cease her luff and allow W the *room* she needs to move away from L before she continues her luff again (see Appeal 108).

"Is it true that the rules regarding the rate of L's luff are the same before and after starting?"

Yes. Rule 16.1 is the rule that deals primarily with the rate of L's luff, and there is absolutely no difference in the application of rule 16.1 before or after *starting*.

"What if a boat to windward of W, or some other object, restricts her ability to respond to a luff by L?"

This is commonly the situation as boats begin to tightly line-up in the final minute before a start or as they approach a crowded downwind *mark*. The room that rule 16.1 requires L to give W often must include time for W to wait for boats to windward of her to respond, or for W to sail past an object (e.g., something in the water) that prevents her from *keeping clear* of L. A hail by W to the effect, "I am trying to *keep clear* but I have these other boats, or the race committee boat, to windward of me!" will be useful and is strongly encouraged.

Situation 2: W is slowly sailing along the starting line about a minute before starting. L catches up from *clear astern* and becomes *overlapped* to leeward of W. After about five seconds, L begins to slowly luff toward W.

Resolution: Prior to the overlap, W, as the boat *clear ahead*, is the right-of-way boat under rule 12 (On the Same Tack, Not Overlapped); therefore she doesn't need to take any action in anticipation of L's leeward *overlap*. When L becomes *overlapped*, L is required by rule 15 (Acquiring Right of Way) to initially give W *room* to *keep clear*. This includes the "space" and "time" necessary for W to trim her sails and otherwise get steerageway to get away from L. After W has had *room* to *keep clear*, L may luff, provided she gives W any **additional** *room* W needs to *keep clear* under rule 16.1. The bottom line is that when *leeward* boats "come in the back door" (i.e., establish leeward *overlaps* from *clear astern* on *windward* boats) and then want to luff, they must plan to be very patient. (See Cases 7, 24 and 53.)

"Can L bear away with no limitation and hit W with her transom?"

No, with one exception discussed below. When L bears away near W, L must comply with rule 16.1 as well; i.e., she must bear away in a way that gives W *room* to *keep clear*. Normally, if L bears away slowly and with some caution not to swing her stern into W's *leeward* side, L will not break rule 16.1. And if W has left herself so close to windward of L that L can't luff or bear away

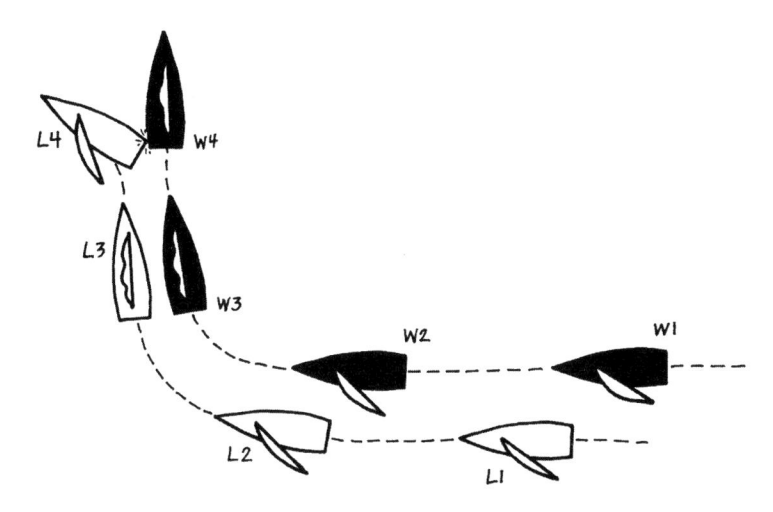

PART 2, SECTION B: WHEN BOATS MEET — GENERAL LIMITATIONS **149**

When L bears away, she cannot do so as suddenly and fast as she pleases. She is required by rule 16.1 to give W room to keep clear (unless she is changing course to round a mark; see rule 43.1(b)). She is also required by rule 14 to avoid contact. If, however, W has allowed herself to get so close that L can't luff or bear away at that moment without immediately hitting W, W has failed to keep clear and has broken rule 11 by her extreme close proximity to L.

without immediately hitting her, W has failed to *keep clear* and has broken rule 11 (On the Same Tack, Overlapped).

"If I am on starboard tack, can I bear away around the windward mark with no limitation regarding boats that are approaching the mark on port tack?"

No! Rule 16.1 applies to your course change and you are required to give those *port-tack* boats *room* to *keep clear* of you (usually by passing to windward of them). Note, rule 18 (Mark-Room) doesn't apply because the *port-tack* boats are approaching the *mark* and you are leaving it (see rule 18.1(c), When Rule 18 Applies).

"Are there any exceptions to rule 16?"

Well, in fact, there is one exception to rule 16, and that is found in rule 43.1(b) (Exoneration). This will be discussed in detail in the discussion of rule 18 (Mark-Room) in Chapter 8. But in a nutshell, rule 43.1(b) says that a boat is exonerated (freed from penalty) if she breaks rule 16.1 in an incident with a boat that is required to give her *mark-room*, when she is changing course to round a *mark*. So as a *leeward* boat (L) which is entitled to *mark-room* is bearing away around a windward *mark*, she does not need to give an *over-*

lapped windward boat (W) *room* to *keep clear* of her transom as she bears away. She does however have to avoid contact with W under rule 14 (Avoiding Contact).

"Sounds like there could be some difficult protests involving rule 16.1; are there any onuses to help resolve these disputes?"

No. In a dispute over whether W *kept clear* or whether L provided enough *room* to *keep clear*, neither the *rules* nor the appeals place any "onus" on either boat. The protest committee will have to determine the facts and use its best judgment. Remember that a *windward* boat's right to "*room* to *keep clear*" under rule 16.1 is a 'shield' and not a 'sword' for W. Also, to be entitled to the protection of *room*, W must respond as soon as she can to L's change of course and make a reasonable attempt to get clear. From there it will be up to the protest committee to decide from the weight of the evidence on (a) the wind and sea conditions, (b) the nature of the incident and (c) the exact actions of both boats as to whether or not W had '*room* to *keep clear*.' Hails by both boats at the time will be very helpful in resolving such conflicts and are strongly encouraged. And to be safe, I always assume that the benefit of any doubt will go to the right-of-way boat (L), so *windward* boats should stay extra clear. Having said that, I always encourage *leeward* boats never to hit *windward* boats because then at least they will not be penalized if the protest committee finds in favor of the *windward* boat.

RULE 17 — ON THE SAME TACK; PROPER COURSE

If a boat *clear astern* becomes *overlapped* within two of her hull lengths to *leeward* of a boat on the same *tack*, she shall not sail above her *proper course* while they remain on the same *tack* and *overlapped* within that distance, unless in doing so she promptly sails astern of the other boat. This rule does not apply if the *overlap* begins while the *windward* boat is required by rule 13 to *keep clear*.

Rule 16.1 (Changing Course) is about limiting **how fast** a right-of-way boat can turn near a keep-clear boat; rule 17 is about limiting **where** a *leeward* boat (L) can sail when near a *windward* boat (W). Note that rule 17 simply puts a "limit" on where L can sail when near W in certain situations. It does not shift any right-of-way to W. When near each other, W must remember that rule 11 (On the Same Tack, Overlapped) requires her to *keep clear* of L wherever L is sailing. The concept in rule 17 is simple: either L is "limited" to sailing no higher than her *proper course* or she is "free" to sail up to head to wind if she pleases; it is always one or the other for L whenever L and W are *overlapped* on the same *tack* and within two of L's lengths of each other.

Whether L is "limited" or "free" depends on the following five factors:

1) whether the boats are *overlapped* on the same *tack* (note, two boats sailing downwind on opposite *tacks* can be *overlapped* (see the definition Clear Astern and Clear Ahead; Overlap)); but rule 17 does not apply to them;
2) whether the boats are within two of L's hull lengths of each other;
3) whether L became *overlapped* from *clear astern* within two of her hull lengths of W and was on the same *tack* as W at the time;
4) whether W was subject to rule 13 (While Tacking); i.e., past head to wind but not yet close-hauled, when L became *overlapped*; and
5) whether the starting signal has been made.

A few clarifying points on the five factors listed above:

- When L is not "limited" under rule 17, she is "free" to sail up to head to wind if she pleases (commonly described as having "luffing rights"), provided if she changes course she gives W *room* to *keep clear* in a seamanlike way (rule 16.1, Changing Course). To clarify, even if L is only

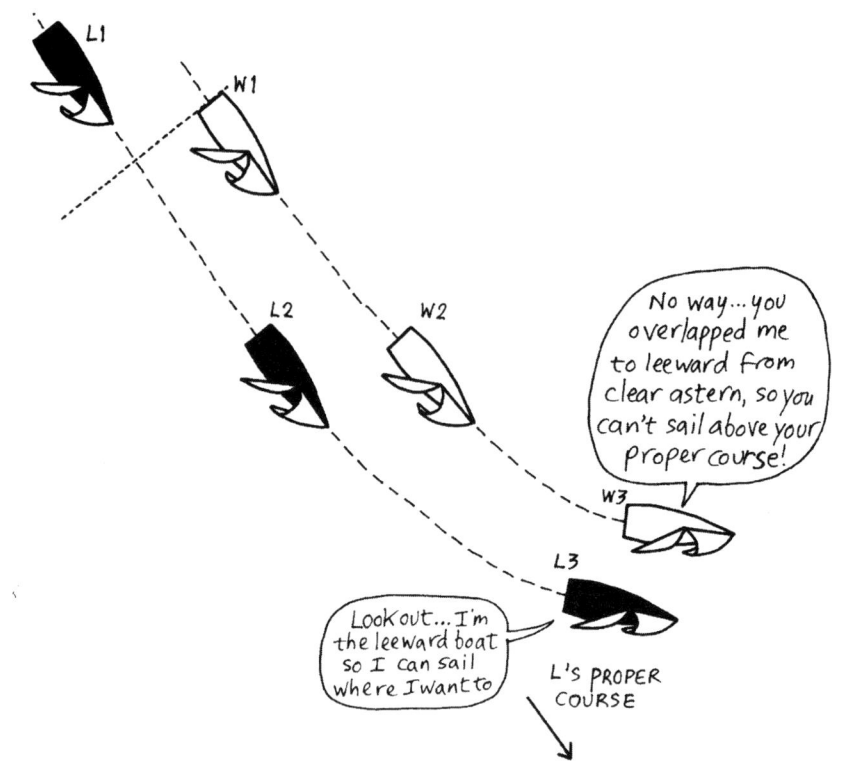

Whenever L becomes overlapped to leeward of W from clear astern within two of her lengths of W, she cannot sail above her proper course while less than that distance apart, unless she promptly sails astern of W..

overlapped with W by two feet, L can sail up to head to wind. Appeal 17 says, "A boat is head to wind when her bow is facing the wind, and the centerline of her hull is parallel to it, irrespective of the position of her sails." This clarification is helpful because often when a boat is head to wind her sails will blow momentarily to the other side giving the **illusion** that she is past head to wind and therefore subject to rule 13 (While Tacking).

Remember that when L is head to wind, it is quite possible that W will be required to go **beyond** head to wind in order to *keep clear* under rule 11 (On the Same Tack, Overlapped). If this is the case, W must do so. If it's not possible for W to *keep clear* without fouling other boats to windward of her, W should clearly alert L that she needs more *room* to *keep clear* (as required by rule 16.1).

PART 2, SECTION B: WHEN BOATS MEET — GENERAL LIMITATIONS   153

- The only time L is "limited" is when she is **on the same *tack*** as W and becomes *overlapped* **to leeward of W** from *clear astern* **within two of her lengths** of W. That's it! The "limit" does not apply when L *overlaps* W when more than two lengths apart, or when W becomes *overlapped* to windward of L, or when L becomes *overlapped* to leeward of W on the opposite *tack* and then gybes.

- Note that rule 17 uses the phrase "becomes *overlapped*." This means that any time a boat that was *clear astern* crosses a line perpendicular to the *clear ahead* boat's centerline drawn through the boat's aftermost point in normal position, it is considered that the boat has "become *overlapped*" to leeward of the boat that was *clear ahead*, regardless of how that line came to be in front of the boat *clear astern* (see the definition *Overlap*). So even in the situation where a boat *clear astern* is holding her course and a boat *clear ahead* and to windward turns down and creates an *overlap*, it is considered that the *leeward* boat has become *overlapped* with the *windward* boat.

- The "limit" in rule 17 only applies to boats that are **"*overlapped*" on the same *tack***. The terms *clear ahead, clear astern* and *overlap* apply to boats on opposite *tacks* when sailing below beam reaches or when rule 18 applies; but rule 17 does not apply to those boats. So when a *starboard-tack* boat and a *port-tack* boat are half way down a downwind leg and they are sailing side by side, neither has a *proper course* limitation. This also means that if two boats are *overlapped* on the same *tack* and rule 17 applies, and the *leeward* boat (L) gybes, now the two boats are on opposite *tacks* (i.e., they did not "remain" on the same *tack*) and rule 17 ceases to apply; and if L gybes back while remaining *overlapped* with W, rule 17 does not apply and L has "luffing rights."

- The "limit" only applies when L and W are **within two lengths of each other**. The "two lengths" distance is determined by two of L's **hull** lengths; i.e., the length of L's hull, and not the additional length of any bowsprits, overhanging mizzen booms, etc. This is particularly important when boats of different sizes are near each other. That means that if rule 17 applies and the two boats remain *overlapped* but sail more than two of L's lengths apart, rule 17 ceases to apply; and if the two boats remain *overlapped* and converge again, rule 17 does not apply and L has "luffing rights."

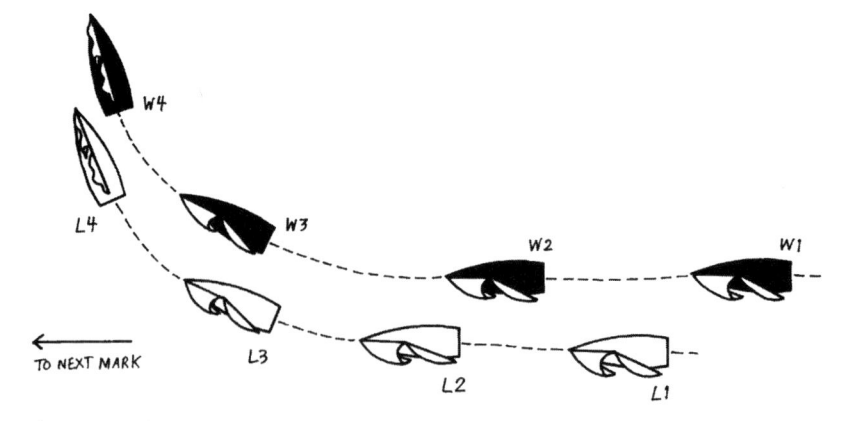

Whenever W becomes overlapped to windward of L, L can turn all the way up to head to wind for the duration of the overlap, provided she gives W room to keep clear in the process.

- The "limit" in rule 17 is that L **cannot sail above her** *proper course*. "Above" means on a course higher than the course that will get her to the next mark as soon as possible. Because a boat does not have a *proper course* until the starting signal is made, there is never any "limit" on L before her starting signal (see the discussion of definition *Proper Course*). Therefore, before the starting signal, L can sail up to head to wind at all times, regardless of how she became *overlapped*.

But at the starting signal, L will be "limited" or "free" depending on how the *overlap* began (whenever it began). Note that this applies regardless of whether the boats have actually *started*; i.e., have crossed the starting line or not. If with 20 seconds to go before the starting signal L becomes *overlapped* from *clear astern* within two lengths of W, then at the starting signal L is "limited" and must sail no higher than her *proper course*. If with 20 seconds to go W *overlaps* L to windward, then at the starting signal L continues to be "free" to sail up to head to wind if she pleases.

"So it sounds like the starting signal is the key moment in time for determining whether L is 'limited' or 'free;' and that it is pretty important for overlapped boats to remember how they first became overlapped as the starting signal approaches!"

Exactly right. Before the starting signal, L is not "limited" in any way; i.e., she can sail up to head to wind if she pleases. But after the starting signal, L is

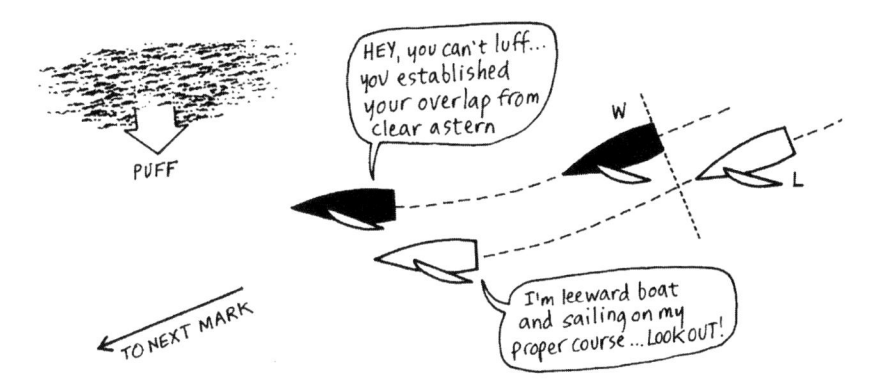

PART 2, SECTION B: WHEN BOATS MEET — GENERAL LIMITATIONS **155**

[Illustration: Two boats W (windward) and L (leeward) sailing toward next mark, with a puff of wind ahead. W says: "HEY, you can't luff... you established your overlap from clear astern". L says: "I'm leeward boat and sailing on my proper course... LOOK OUT!"]

L is slowly luffing up to a new proper course in order to get to a puff of wind sooner. Because she would do that even in the absence of W, she is not sailing above her proper course, and she is not breaking rule 17; and because she is giving W room to keep clear, she is not breaking rule 16.1. W must keep clear under rule 11.

"limited" to sailing no higher than her *proper course* if she originally became *overlapped* from *clear astern*. The advantage of having L's limitation begin at the starting signal is that it is a precise and predictable moment in time.

And the moment the starting signal is made, L instantly gets a *proper course* (see the definition *Proper Course*). At that moment it is critical for L and W to remember how they became *overlapped*! Hails when the *overlap* first begins and throughout the *overlap* are going to be critical for producing orderly starts and reducing disputes!

"Do I have to bear away to my proper course before the starting signal is made; i.e., do I have to anticipate my obligation not to sail above my proper course after the starting signal?"

No. You do not have a *proper course* before the starting signal, and therefore you are not "limited" as to where you can sail. When the starting signal is made, and if you are now "limited" because you originally became *overlapped* from *clear astern*, you are required to sail no higher than your *proper course*. The course you will sail to *finish* as soon as possible will include the course you are on at the moment the starting signal is made. If you must then bear away to a lower course to get to the next *mark* and ultimately the finishing line as soon as possible, you must do so immediately. For instance, if you are head to wind before an upwind start, your *proper course* will be to bear away to a close-hauled course or even slightly lower to build speed and sail upwind.

"What is the purpose of the last sentence in rule 17, the one about rule 13?"

This sentence specifically addresses the tactic known as the "Slam Dunk." (A detailed analysis of the Slam Dunk can be found at the end of this chapter.) Consider two close-hauled boats on opposite *tacks* (S and P) converging. P bears away to pass astern of S. When P gets near S's stern, S tacks. At some point during S's tack, P becomes *overlapped* to leeward of S. Is P "limited" or "free" under rule 17?

Well, once S passes head to wind and until she is on a close-hauled course, S is required by rule 13 (While Tacking) to *keep clear* of P. And the last sentence in rule 17 says that if P becomes *overlapped* to leeward of S while S is required by rule 13 to *keep clear* of her, then rule 17 doesn't apply. So in this case, P would be "free" for as long as the boats remained *overlapped*; i.e., she could sail up to head to wind, subject of course to rule 16.1 (Changing Course). If S was already down to a close-hauled course **before** P became *overlapped*, then P would be "limited" under rule 17 throughout the *overlap*. The net effect of this rule is that it discourages Slam Dunks, which are very aggressive and often contentious.

"What happens in the situation where L and W are both sailing their proper courses and the two boats are converging; who has to keep clear?"

W must *keep clear* of L under rule 11 (On the Same Tack, Overlapped). Rule 17 only requires that L not sail **above** her *proper course*. As long as L is **on** her *proper course*, she is complying with rule 17. Note that the phrase in rule 17 "her *proper course*" clarifies that it is L who gets to sail her *proper course*. Therefore, when L is sailing on "her" *proper course*, W must *keep clear* under rule 11, even when W's proper course may be a **lower** course than L's. (See Cases 7 and 14.)

Remember that a *proper course* is essentially any course a boat chooses to sail in order to get to the next *mark* and ultimately to *finish* as quickly as possible. Therefore it is possible that there may be several *proper courses* at any given moment depending upon the circumstances involved. It is also obvious that two *overlapping* boats sailing for the same *mark* will converge. Note also that a boat's *proper course* is not necessarily a straight-line course. It can change with changes in the breeze, current or waves, or with a change in the boat's strategy (see the discussion of definition *Proper Course*). However, whenever L wants to change her course to a new *proper course*, she must give

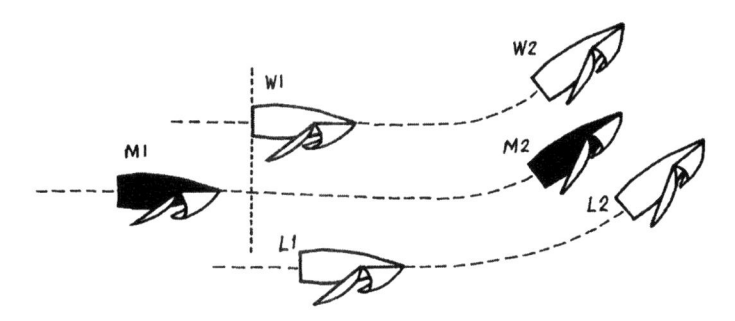

PART 2, SECTION B: WHEN BOATS MEET — GENERAL LIMITATIONS **157**

Because M becomes overlapped to leeward of W from clear astern, she is "limited" to sailing no higher than her proper course. When L luffs, M is required to keep clear of her under rule 11. Even in the absence of W, M would luff to keep clear of L. Therefore, M is not sailing above her proper course and W must keep clear of M under rule 11 and give her room under rule 19.2(b).

W *room* to *keep clear* under rule 16.1 (Changing Course). A hail that she intends to change course is strongly recommended.

If L is "limited" and W thinks that L is sailing above L's *proper course*, W must still *keep clear* (rule 11); she can then protest under rule 17. If the two boats hit, and it were decided by the protest committee that L was sailing above her *proper course*, both boats will likely be disqualified: W for failing to *keep clear* of L (rule 11), and L for illegally sailing above her *proper course* (rule 17).

"What happens when L wants to luff two or more boats and one of the middle boats is subject to rule 17 relative to a boat to windward of her?"

Good question! Let's take the situation where L and W are sailing down a reach about two lengths or so apart. Rule 17 does not apply between L and W. A boat from astern (M) catches up and becomes *overlapped* between them. When M becomes *overlapped* on W, W is clearly able to *keep clear*, so M is complying with rule 15 (Acquiring Right of Way). And W can give M *room* to pass L such that she is entitled to *room* from W to pass L (rule 19.2(b), Giving Room at an Obstruction). Now L begins to luff toward M and W. M responds by luffing. W must *keep clear* of M under rule 11 (On the Same Tack, Overlapped) and give her *room* under rule 19.2(b). And M is not breaking rule 17 because in fact M is not sailing above her *proper course*. Here's the reason. Take the two boats involved, M and W. M became *overlapped* on W to leeward from *clear astern*. Rule 17 requires M, therefore, not to sail above her *proper course*. In determining her *proper course*, the definition *Proper Course* instructs us to remove the boats referred to in the rule using the term *"proper course."* In this case, rule 17 uses the term and refers to the *windward* boat W, so we remove W. As M was sailing a course to *keep clear* of L, she would have been sailing the same course in the absence of W; therefore, M was sailing her *proper course* and not above it. (See Appeal 4.)

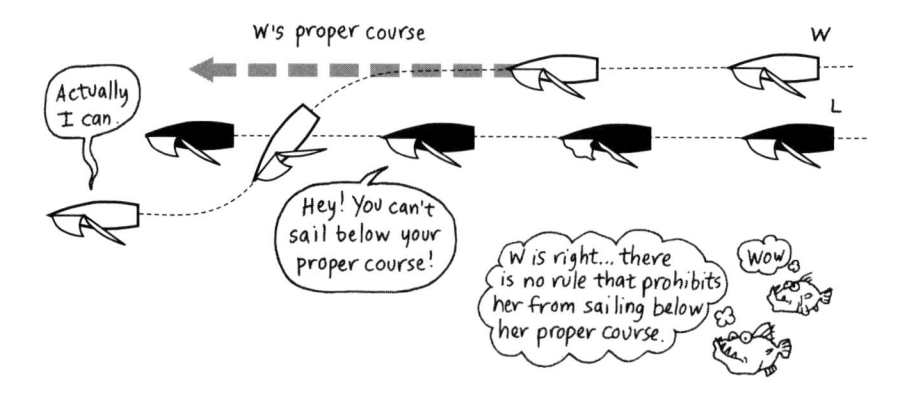

> *"What's the purpose of the phrase in rule 17, '…unless in doing so she promptly sails astern of the other boat'?"*

This is to close a very subtle, undesirable loophole in the rule. Here's a potential scenario: on a run, you sail into *leeward* of a boat that was *clear ahead* of you, but you realize that you won't be able to sail past them due to their wind shadow. You want to get out of there but you will have to luff above your *proper course* to pass astern of them. No problem. Rule 17 clarifies that you can certainly luff (i.e., sail above your *proper course*) provided you promptly sail astern of W. If you luff and then realize that your bow won't clear W's transom and have to pull your bow back down, you have broken rule 17.

> *"I thought there was a rule that said you couldn't sail below your proper course if you were to windward of another boat or clear ahead of a boat that was trying to pass you to leeward?"*

You are right; there **was**. But it was removed from the rule book entirely in the 2009–2012 rules. The reason it was removed is that it wasn't widely known, it was very difficult to prove a boat was breaking it, and with far fewer races run on triangular courses (where the rule balanced the game coming into the gybe mark), the need for the rule is far less.

PART 2, SECTION B: WHEN BOATS MEET — GENERAL LIMITATIONS **159**

If Barger tries to squeeze in between the race committee boat and L, and hits L or causes L to bear off to avoid a collision, Barger breaks rule 11.

What that means is that if two boats (W and L) are sailing downwind *overlapped*, W can sail as low as she pleases in order to more effectively slow L down by blanketing her wind, as long as she *keeps clear* of L under rule 11 (On the Same Tack, Overlapped), even if she is sailing below her *proper course*. And if one boat (A) is *clear ahead* of another (B), not only does B need to *keep clear* under rule 12 (On the Same Tack, Not Overlapped), but A can sail as low as she pleases to make it more difficult for B to become *overlapped* to *leeward* and perhaps gain an inside overlap at a *mark*, even if she is sailing below her *proper course*.

Section A and B Rules In Action

Now that we've had a thorough explanation, let's look at how the rules in Section A and B work in various common situations on the race course.

STARTING MARK SITUATIONS

For the purposes of these following explanations, it will be assumed that the starting *mark* is surrounded by navigable water, and that the boats are approaching the starting *mark* to *start*. For a full explanation of the rules at starting *marks*, see the discussion of the preamble to Section C (At Marks and Obstructions) in chapter 9.

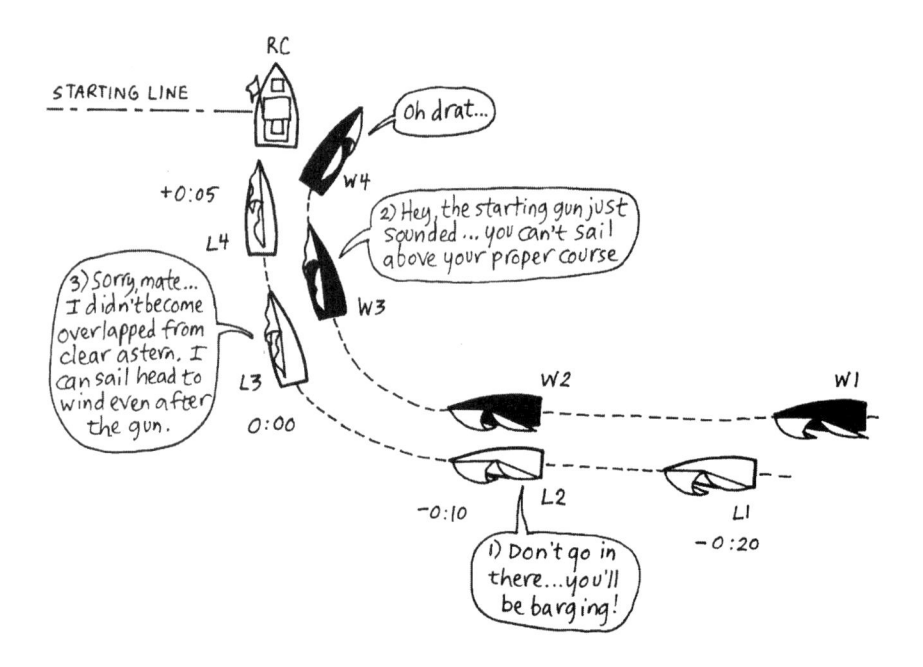

[Diagram: Starting line scenario with race committee boat (RC), showing boats W1–W4 (windward) approaching at times −0:20, −0:10, 0:00, and +0:05, and boats L1–L4 (leeward). Speech bubbles read:
- *"Oh drat…" (W4)*
- *"2) Hey, the starting gun just sounded… you can't sail above your proper course"*
- *"3) Sorry, mate… I didn't become overlapped from clear astern. I can sail head to wind even after the gun."*
- *"1) Don't go in there… you'll be barging!"]*

UPWIND STARTS including a discussion on "barging"

When boats are on their final approach to *start*, Section C rules (At Marks and Obstructions) do not apply, meaning that a *leeward*/outside boat (LO) does not have to give a *windward*/inside boat (WI) *room* to pass to leeward of the starting *mark* (say a race committee boat). If W tries to squeeze between L and the *mark* and hits L or forces L to bear away to avoid a collision, W has broken rule 11 (On the Same Tack, Overlapped). This is what is called "barging" (see Case 145).

> *"I understand that when I'm the windward boat, a leeward boat does not have to give me room to pass to leeward of the race committee boat; but does that mean she can do anything she pleases to 'shut the door' on me?"*

Absolutely not. As we've discussed above, the rules in Sections A and B apply. There are no other special rules that apply at this starting *mark*. Therefore, L must behave in exactly the same way that she must behave anywhere else on the race course. Rule 11 (On the Same Tack, Overlapped) gives L the right of way; and L can sail up to head to wind if she pleases, even when only *overlapped* with W by two feet.

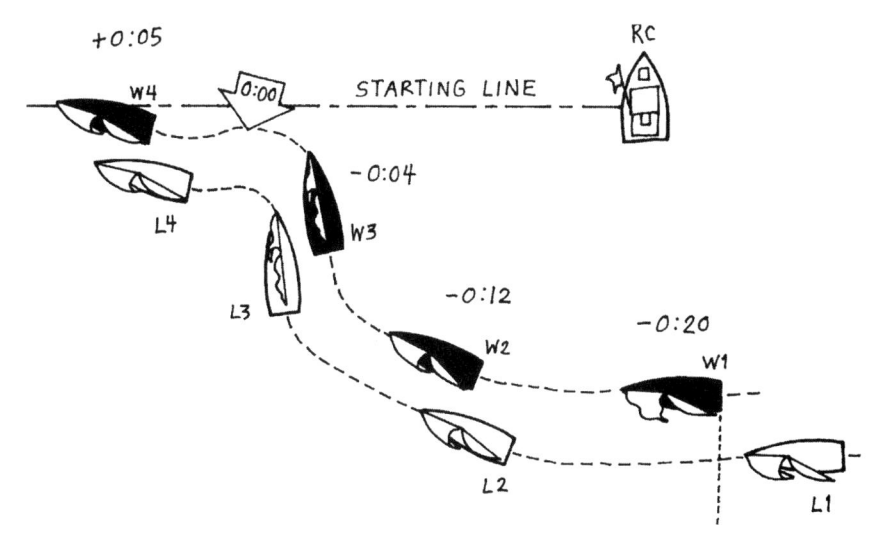

PART 2, SECTION B: WHEN BOATS MEET — GENERAL LIMITATIONS **161**

Before the starting signal, even though L becomes overlapped to leeward from clear astern, she is permitted to sail up to head to wind provided she gives W room to keep clear. However, after the starting signal, L may not sail above her proper course which, when sailing to windward, is normally a close-hauled course.

However, rule 16.1 (Changing Course) tells L when and how fast she can luff near other boats; i.e., she must give them *room* to *keep clear* whenever she changes course near them. Consider L and W approaching the race committee boat. If L holds her course W will be able to pass between L and the committee boat without touching either. Just as W sticks her bow in behind the race committee boat, L luffs slowly, but W is unable to *keep clear* due to her proximity to the race committee boat and hits both it and L. L has broken rule 16.1 by changing course (luffing) without giving W *room* to *keep clear*, and rule 14 (Avoiding Contact) by not avoiding a collision with W. If L wants to prevent W from passing between her and the committee boat, she must put herself on a course to "shut the door" **before** W gets her bow stuck in to leeward of the committee boat.

"Now, what about after the starting signal?"

If L is not "limited" under rule 17, then she can continue to sail where she pleases after the starting signal. She is under **no obligation** to turn down to her *proper course* at the starting signal. Therefore, L can sail head to wind after the gun, even if it forces W onto the wrong side of the race committee boat, before turning down to *start* herself!

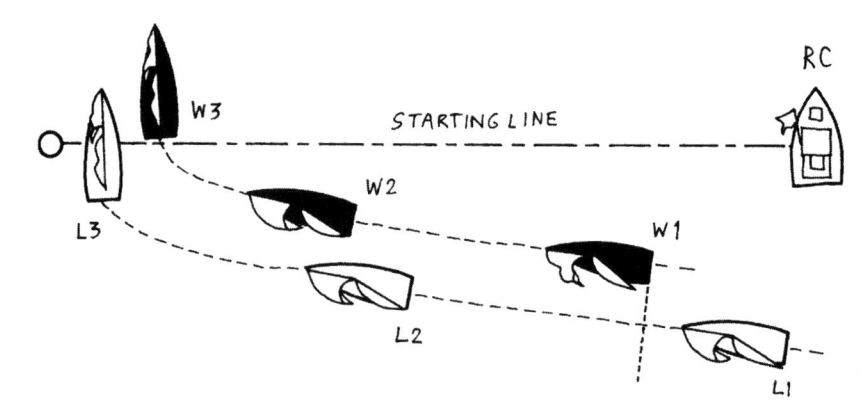

162   UNDERSTANDING THE RACING RULES OF SAILING THROUGH 2024

L becomes overlapped to leeward from clear astern on W. Before the starting signal she may sail up to head to wind whenever she pleases. After the starting signal she cannot sail above her proper course, which, when sailing to windward, is normally close-hauled. However, in order to pass the starting mark L's proper course may be to momentarily luff up to head to wind. In this case W must keep clear but L must give her room to do so.

Now, if L is "limited" under rule 17, then she must not sail above her *proper course* after the starting signal. Therefore, if she is "limited," and sailing above close-hauled before the starting signal, she must immediately turn down to her *proper course* when the starting signal is made. She does not have to anticipate this obligation; she need only react when the signal is made. However, if L is sailing her *proper course* after the starting signal, and there is no *room* for W to squeeze in between her and the committee boat, tough luck on W; W is not allowed to go in there.

"Anything special I should know when I'm starting near the leeward end of the starting line?"

Well, one thing that often happens at the leeward end of the starting line for an upwind start is that L gets into a position where she cannot make it around the starting *mark* after the starting signal goes off without sailing above close-hauled.

Remember that in this situation, sailing above close-hauled to get around the *mark* can certainly be considered L's *proper course*, and W must *keep clear* regardless of how the *overlap* began. However, L has to remember that her luff is limited by rule 16.1 (Changing Course) in that she must give W *room* to *keep clear* when she changes her course. This may be difficult when W is close by or when there is a pack of boats to windward of her.

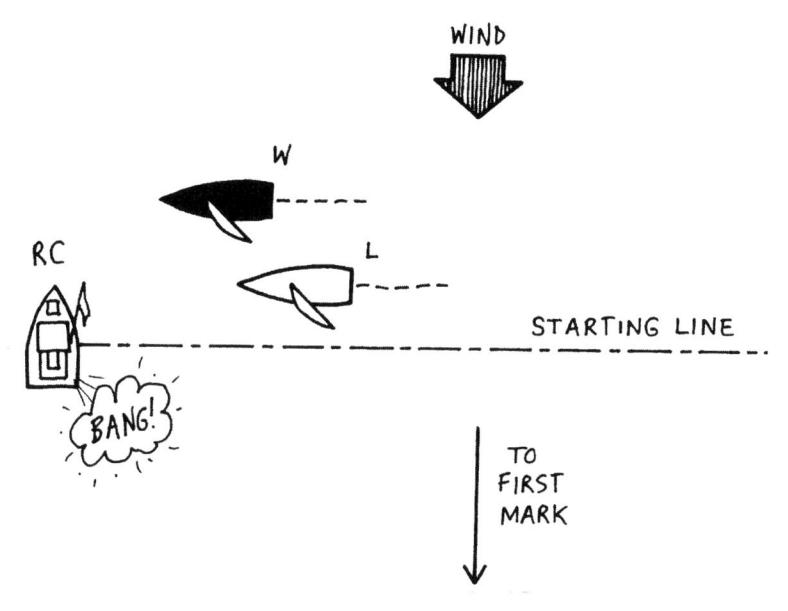

PART 2, SECTION B: WHEN BOATS MEET — GENERAL LIMITATIONS 163

Whether L is "limited" to sailing no higher than her proper course or not depends on how the overlap began. If L became overlapped to leeward from clear astern, then she cannot sail above her proper course after the starting signal. If the overlap began in any other way, L is free to sail up to head to wind, and can even cause W to pass on the wrong side of the committee boat before bearing away to start.

DOWNWIND STARTS

On downwind starts, it is especially critical that boats remember how they became *overlapped*! If L is not "limited" under rule 17, she may sail where she pleases; i.e., she is under no obligation to head for the first *mark* or sail her *proper course* at the gun. W must beware, especially before setting her spinnaker if L has not set her spinnaker yet!

As *overlapped* boats approach one of the starting *marks* (which can include the race committee boat) and the starting gun goes off, remember that L is under **no obligation** to give W *room* at the starting *mark*! If L is not "limited" under rule 17, then L can force W onto the wrong side of the *mark* before turning down to start herself. And if L is "limited," then she need only turn down to her *proper course* (not to the compass course to the first *mark*). As *proper course* is so subjective, especially around a starting line, *windward* boats will be well advised to try and avoid becoming *overlapped* to *windward* of *leeward* boats near the starting *marks*. If ever W feels L is sailing above her *proper course*, she must *keep clear* and protest.

ON UPWIND LEGS ("BEATS")

Again, coming off the starting line it will be essential that L and W remember how they became *overlapped*. If L originally became *overlapped* from *clear astern*, then she is "limited" under rule 17 and cannot sail above her *proper course* (most likely close-hauled). If she is not "limited," she can turn all the way up to head to wind and W must *keep clear*.

A common situation on beats is when a *port-tack* boat (PL) completes a tack (gets to a close-hauled course) on the "lee-bow" of a *starboard-tack* boat (SW). Because PL did not become *overlapped* from *clear astern*, she is not "limited" under rule 17 and therefore can luff up to head to wind at any time during the *overlap*, even when only *overlapped* with SW by a couple of feet. *Windward* boats will have to be a bit more cautious when rolling over *leeward* boats in this situation.

If P tacks in front of S, and S chooses to *overlap* her to leeward, then S must comply with rule 15 (Acquiring Right of Way) and furthermore must not sail above her *proper course* during the *overlap* unless she chooses to luff and pass astern of P (rule 17, On the Same Tack; Proper Course).

"Can you walk me through how the rules apply to a Slam Dunk?"

Sure. The Slam Dunk is an aggressive and often contentious tactic used upwind by S to gain control over P. It is more commonly used in match and team racing than in fleet racing. The relationship between S and P is rapidly changing in this maneuver such that the rules analysis gets quite complicated. However, the last sentence in rule 17 (On the Same Tack; Proper Course) is designed to greatly discourage S from using this tactic (see discussion of rule 17). See the illustration on the next page for a detailed analysis of the "Slam Dunk."

ON DOWNWIND LEGS (REACHES & RUNS)

L and W are sailing down a reach. L did not become *overlapped* from *clear astern* and therefore L is "free" to sail where she pleases, subject to rule 16.1 (Changing Course); i.e., she has "luffing rights." W begins to pass L and L luffs to prevent her from doing so. W is about three-quarters of the way past L and W luffs quickly and "breaks" the *overlap*. W then turns back down, thereby creating an *overla*p once again (being sure to *keep clear* under rule 11, On the Same Tack, Overlapped, and remembering that her actions have given L the

PART 2, SECTION B: WHEN BOATS MEET — GENERAL LIMITATIONS **165**

THE SLAM DUNK

Position 1: *P has borne away to sail to leeward of S. The moment P is steering a course to clear S's transom, S luffs (heads up) preparatory to tacking. As long as when she luffs (changes course), P has room to continue keeping clear, S does not break rule 16.1, even if P has to change course immediately to continue keeping clear.*

Position 2: *S is not past head to wind and is therefore still on starboard tack; P must still keep clear of her under rule 10.*

Position 3: *S has just passed head to wind. She is now on port tack, i.e., the same tack as P, and P is clear astern. S must keep clear of P under rule 13 until she is on a close-hauled course. P, now the right-of-way boat, does not need to give S room to keep clear under rule 15 if she maintains her straight-line course because she acquired the right of way by S's actions. However, if P changes course toward S, she is required by rule 16.1 to give S room to keep clear (i.e., to not prevent S from being able to keep clear or cause her to make an unseamanlike maneuver to do so).*

Position 4: *P has become overlapped with S and remains the right-of-way boat under either rule 13 or 11. If P becomes overlapped to leeward of S before S is down to a close-hauled course, P is not "limited" by rule 17, because S is required by rule 13 to keep clear of her. Therefore P can sail up to head to wind, provided she complies with rule 16.1. If S is on a close-hauled course before P becomes overlapped, then P is "limited" by rule 17 to sailing no higher than her proper course (most likely a close-hauled course) for the duration of the overlap because she became overlapped from clear astern after rule 13 no longer applied.*

Note: *Assuming P is not "limited" by rule 17, whether or not she broke rule 16.1 when she changed course will be decided by the protest committee based on its determination of whether P gave S enough space and time to cease her turn towards P and begin her turn away from P in a seamanlike way. If the collision was avoidable, P and/or S may be found to have broken rule 14; and if there was any damage or injury, P and/or S could get penalized under rule 14.*

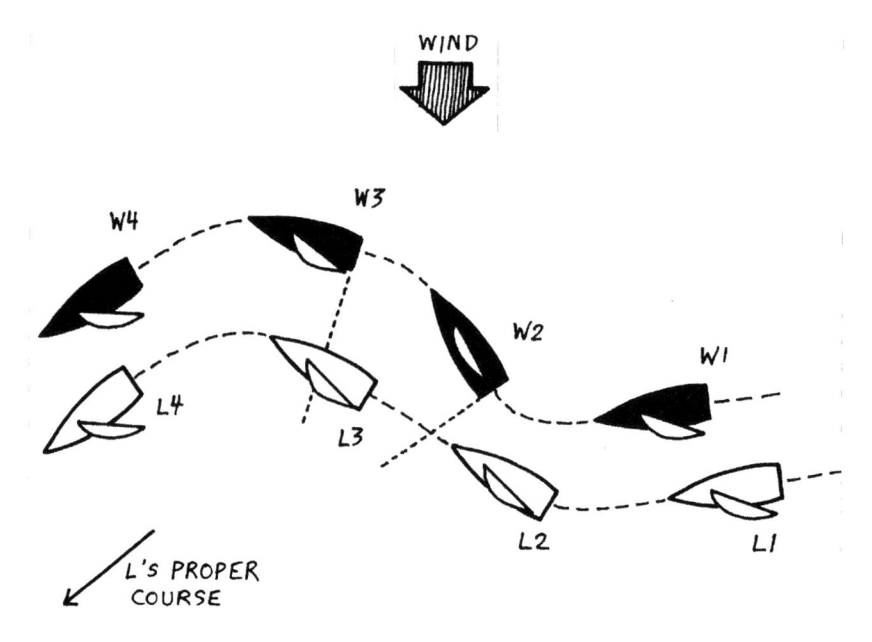

166 UNDERSTANDING THE RACING RULES OF SAILING THROUGH 2024

In this situation it is W's luffing that breaks the overlap and her bearing away that causes the overlap to begin again. When L acquires the right of way at position 3, she does not need to give W room to keep clear under rule 15 because she acquires right of way as a result of W's actions. However, rule 17 is not concerned with how the overlap was established. Therefore, because L became overlapped from clear astern, she must immediately bear away and continue to sail no higher than her proper course during the overlap.

right of way such that rule 15, Acquiring Right of Way, does not require L to "give" W *room* to *keep clear*!). Now, L has become *overlapped* to *leeward* from *clear astern* and therefore is required to immediately comply with rule 17 (On the Same Tack; Proper Course) and turn back down to her *proper course*, which includes gybing when that is necessary for L to sail her *proper course* to the next *mark*.

Anytime a boat becomes *overlapped* to *leeward* from *clear astern* within two of her lengths of a *windward* boat, she is not permitted to sail above her *proper course*. However, prior to becoming *overlapped*, L is free to sail where she pleases. Therefore, the moment the *overlap* begins, the course she will sail to *finish* as soon as possible will include the course she is on at that moment. If she must then bear away to a lower course to get to the next *mark* and ultimately the finishing line as soon as possible, she must do so immediately. Rule 15 (Acquiring Right of Way) builds in a cushion to protect W while L is bearing away.

PART 2, SECTION B: WHEN BOATS MEET — GENERAL LIMITATIONS **167**

In position 1, L is clear astern of W. When L becomes overlapped on W she is "limited" under rule 17 to sailing no higher than her proper course.

In position 2, L gybes so that the two boats are on opposite tacks and rule 17 no longer applies.

In position 3, L gybes back. Because she has remained overlapped with W, she has not been clear astern since rule 17 turned off in position 2. Therefore, L is not "limited" and can sail up to head to wind if she pleases.

In position 4, L luffs, giving W room to keep clear under rule 16.1. W fails to keep clear thereby breaking rules 11 and 14. L also breaks rule 14 (for failing to avoid contact) but is exonerated if there is no damage or injury..

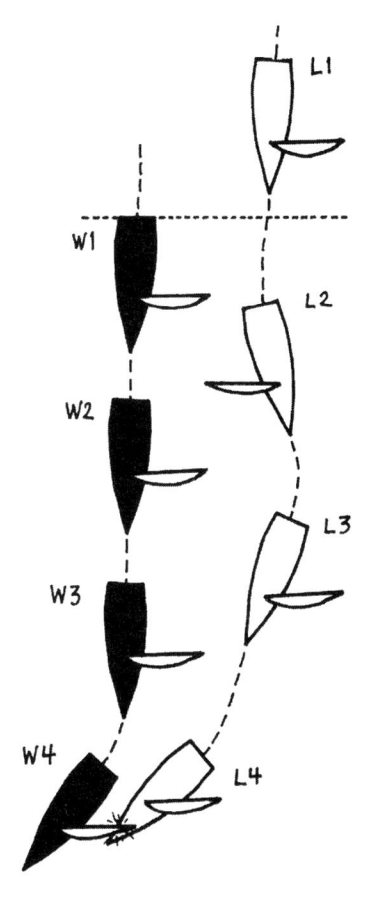

Here are three common situations where a boat can catch up from astern and sail in to leeward of a boat ahead and be "free" to sail up to head to wind if she chooses (i.e., have "luffing rights"), subject to rules 15 (Acquiring Right of Way) and 16.1 (Changing Course):

1) The boat behind (BL) *overlaps* the boat ahead (AW) more than two of her lengths to *leeward* of AW. Rule 17 (On the Same Tack; Proper Course) does not apply because the *overlap* did not begin when BL was within two of her lengths of AW. Now BL turns toward AW and maintains her *overlap* as she gets within two lengths. BL is not "limited" and can sail up to head to wind, even when she may be *overlapped* with AW by just two feet. As a defense, AW can "break" the *overlap* by heading up just after BL comes within two lengths of her; and then "create it" again by bearing off thereby causing BL to "become *overlapped* within two of her hull lengths" of AW.

2) BL overlaps AW to *leeward* within two of her lengths. At that point BL is "limited" to sailing no higher than her *proper course*. BL then gybes and gybes right back, maintaining her "overlap" throughout the maneuver (called a "double gybe"). Now, BL is not "limited" and can sail up to head to wind, even when she may be *overlapped* with AW by just two feet. The reason is that when BL gybed the first time, she did not remain on the same *tack* as AW and therefore rule 17 ceased to apply (see rule 17). When she gybed back onto the same *tack* as AW, she was still *overlapped*; i.e., she did not become *overlapped* again from *clear astern*. Therefore she was not "limited" by rule 17 (On the Same Tack; Proper Course). However, BL did acquire the right of way by her own actions, so she must initially give AW *room* to *keep clear* under rule 15 (Acquiring Right of Way); and if she changes her course toward AW, she must give AW additional *room* to *keep clear* under rule 16.1 (Changing Course).

3) Halfway down a run, a *port-tack* boat (PL) is converging with a *starboard-tack* boat (SW). PL, after passing very close astern of SW, turns down thereby creating an "overlap" on SW's *leeward* side. The boats, though on opposite tacks, are now *overlapped* because they are both sailing more than ninety degrees from the true wind (see the definition *Clear Astern* and *Clear Ahead; Overlap*). Maintaining her "overlap," PL gybes. When her boom crosses her centerline and she is on the same *tack* as SW, the two boats are already *overlapped*; i.e., PL did not become *overlapped* with SW from *clear astern* while on the same *tack* as SW. Therefore PL is not "limited" and can sail up to head to wind, even when she may be *overlapped* with SW by just two feet. However, the same "limitations" under rules 15 (Acquiring Right of Way) and 16.1 (Changing Course) apply to PL as in the example above. And SW can employ the same tactic as in example one above of breaking the *overlap* with PL just as PL is about to gybe and then re-creating it the moment PL gybes.

8

Part 2, Section C
When Boats Meet at Marks and Obstructions— Mark Room

Section C contains the rules that apply when boats converge at *marks* and *obstructions,* and are intended to provide for safe and orderly transitions from one leg to the next in these tight-quartered situations. In order for that to happen, there are times when a right-of-way boat may find herself with a **limit** on her right of way or a temporary obligation to give *room* or *mark-room* to a keep-clear boat. An example is when a *leeward* boat is on the outside of a *windward* boat while rounding a *mark* or passing an *obstruction.* The *leeward*/outside boat may have to give that *windward*/inside boat *mark-room* to round the *mark* (rule 18, Mark-Room) or *room* to pass the *obstruction* (rule 19, Room to Pass an Obstruction). Another example is when a *starboard-tack* or *leeward* boat is on the inside at a *mark*, and she has just tacked in the *zone* and she has certain obligations (rule 18.3, Passing Head to Wind in the Zone), or she must gybe to sail her *proper course* and she cannot sail any farther from the *mark* than needed to sail her *proper course* (rule 18.4, Gybing). Finally, there are times when a boat may need to tack to avoid hitting an *obstruction*, but other boats are too close for her to tack without fouling them. Rule 20 (Room to Tack at an Obstruction) gives special permission in certain circumstances that permits the boat to tack.

Section C contains three distinct rules:

Rule 18...this rule applies at *marks*, including *marks* that are also *obstructions* (other than continuing *obstructions* such as an island while boats are rounding or passing them on the same side).

Rule 19...this rule applies at *obstructions* (unless the *obstruction* is a *mark* that is not a continuing *obstruction*).

Rule 20...this rule applies when a boat sailing **close-hauled or above** wants to tack to avoid an *obstruction*.

A related rule is rule 43.1(b) (Exoneration) which is in Part 4 (Other Requirements When Racing). This rule provides exoneration (freed from penalty) to a boat that breaks a rule of Section A, or rule 15 (Acquiring Right of Way), rule 16 (Changing Course) or rule 31 (Touching a Mark) when she is taking the *room* or *mark-room* to which she is entitled.

Rule 18 is broken into the following distinct sections:

18.1...states **when** rule 18 does and does not apply

18.2...states which boats need to **give** *mark-room* to which boats

18.3...a rule about **tacking** inside the *zone*

18.4...a rule about **gybing** inside the *zone*

I'll cover rules 18.1 (When Rule 18 Applies), 18.2 (Giving Mark-Room) and 43.1(b) (Exoneration) in this chapter. I'll cover rules 18.3 (Passing Head to Wind in the Zone) and 18.4 (Gybing), as well as the exceptions to rule 18 in chapter 9. And I'll cover rules 19 (Room to Pass an Obstruction) and 20 (Room to Tack at an Obstruction) in chapter 10.

RULE 18 — MARK-ROOM

RULE 18.1 — WHEN RULE 18 APPLIES

Rule 18 applies between boats when they are required to leave a *mark* on the same side and at least one of them is in the *zone*.

This is the rule that governs boats when they are near *marks*. Though rule 18 is the longest rule in Part 2, it is very clearly written and fits very sensibly with the basic right-of-way rules in Section A. Again, the key to understanding it is not to try to memorize its every detail, but to stand back and see how the rule is trying to create orderly sailing when boats converge at *marks*.

"How do I know on which side the mark or obstruction is to be left?"

Good question. First of all, "side" in rule 18.1 refers to the boat's side, not the *mark*'s side. Therefore, when two boats are rounding or passing a *mark* going in the opposite direction (as they might when they are in different races using the same *mark* but leaving it on opposite sides, as in Case 26), rule 18 does **not** apply, and the rules of Section A and B apply. (See Appeal 123.)

As for which side to "leave" a *mark* on, the notice of race or sailing instructions tell us which side the *marks* must be passed on, but only the sailing instructions can specify the rounding *marks* (i.e., the *marks* that the boat's string must touch) (see the definition *Sail the Course (b)* and rule J2.1(4), Sailing Instruction Contents).

"Am I always required to leave all marks on a certain side?"

No. Rule 28.1 (Sailing the Race) only requires you to leave all the *marks* of the course on the required side in order to *start* and after *starting*. As for the starting *marks*, the definition *Sail the Course* says, *"A boat **sails the course** provided that a string representing a boat's track from the time she begins to approach the starting line from its pre-start side to **start** until she **finishes** shall, when drawn taut…passes each **mark** of the course for the race on the required side and in the correct order…".*

Therefore, when there are still two minutes to the starting signal, you can pass a starting *mark* on either side you wish; and because you and other boats are not "required" to leave the *mark* on the same side, rule 18 does not apply. (Note, if the starting *mark* is also an *obstruction* such as the race committee boat, rule 19, Room to Pass an Obstruction, applies when the boats are passing it on the same side but are not approaching the starting *mark* to *start*. See "Exceptions to Rule 18" in chapter 9.)

The same is true for other racing *marks* that are on your leg but that you are not required to round or pass. Rule 28.1 says, "…[a boat] *may leave on either side a **mark** that does not begin, bound or end the leg she is sailing."* So if you are on the final leg to a finishing line that is set to leeward of the leeward *mark*, the leeward *mark* does not define your leg such that you can pass it on either side. Again, rule 18 does not apply at that *mark*.

"To whom is rule 18 talking?"

Rule 18 is "talking" to all the boats involved in the rounding or passing maneuver, but fundamentally it is talking to the outside or *clear astern* boats. When rule 18 applies, outside and *clear astern* boats, whether on *port tack* or *starboard tack* and whether *leeward* or *windward* boats, must give *mark-room* to inside or *clear ahead* boats. Rule 18 also tells inside or *clear ahead* boats how much *room* they are entitled to.

Remember, rule 18 is a rule of exception. In some situations at *marks*, an outside boat otherwise holding right of way must nonetheless yield to an inside keep-clear boat and even change course to move far enough away from the *mark* to give the inside keep-clear boat the *mark-room* she needs to round or pass it. At a downwind *mark*, a *starboard-tack* boat with a *port-tack* boat inside of her and a *leeward* boat with a *windward* boat inside of her are examples of this sort of situation that put a "limit" on the right-of-way boat. So, even though you are the right-of-way boat approaching a *mark* or *obstruction*, when rule 18 begins to apply, your right of way may be temporarily "limited."

"As I approach a mark, when does rule 18 begin to apply to me?"

Rule 18 begins to apply between boats when at least one of them is in the "*zone*." The "*zone*" is the area around the *mark* within a distance of three (3) hull lengths of the boat nearer to it; and a boat is "in the *zone*" when any part of her hull (not her sails or equipment) first is in the *zone* (see the discussion of the definition *Zone* in chapter 5).

"Will the zone always be three hull lengths in every race?"

Normally the *zone* will be three lengths. But the *zone* in team and match racing is "two lengths" (rules C2.4, Match Racing Rules, and D1.1(a), Team Racing Rules), in radio sailing racing it is "four lengths" (rule E1.1, Radio Sailing Racing Rules) and in kiteboard racing it is 30 meters. There is no *zone* in windsurfing fleet racing (Appendix B, Changes to the Definitions).

"So does that mean that rule 18 does not apply between boats if none of them have reached the zone yet?"

Yes, that's right! A *leeward* boat that may be an outside boat at the *mark* that has luffing rights may luff a *windward* boat, subject to rule 16.1 (Changing Course) right up until the point either of them first reaches the *zone*. Note, this could be during or after the boats have taken their spinnakers down, etc. in preparation for the *mark* rounding.

The ZONE (normally 3 lengths)

As boats approach a mark, rule 18 turns on when one of the boats enters the zone, and not before that time.

But note that when either of the boats enters the *zone*, rule 18.2(b) (Giving Mark-Room) requires the outside boat to give the inside boat *mark-room* from that moment on, which in most situations is the space the inside boat needs to sail to the *mark* in a "seamanlike way" (see the definition *Mark-Room*). Therefore, in order to comply with rule 18.2(b), boats should anticipate this by sailing a course **prior** to entering the *zone* so that they will be in compliance with the rule at the moment the first one reaches the *zone*.

"I understand now about the significance of the 'zone;' but how do I know where the 'zone' actually is on the water?"

Well, at first it's difficult, and then after you've raced more and more it becomes easier to judge. Let's say you race a 30-foot boat. Three lengths is 90 feet. That's the distance from home plate to first base on a baseball diamond, or approximately a third of a football field. Doing 6 knots (about 10 feet per second) you'll cover three lengths in just under 10 seconds. Measure it out and mark it with two orange poles or something at your club so everyone will learn to "guesstimate" it better. And remember that when the first part of your hull is three lengths from the *mark*, the helmsman will be almost four lengths away.

"Okay, but what if two boats simply can't agree on whether an overlap was obtained or broken before reaching the zone?"

Competitors and protest committees should try their hardest to remember and determine the facts. However, realizing that there will be disputes, the rule writers built in some "guidance" to help resolve such disputes. Rule 18.2(e) reads, *"If there is reasonable doubt that a boat obtained or broke an **overlap** in time, it shall be presumed that she did not."*

In other words, if you come up from behind and claim that you got the inside *overlap* before the outside boat reached the *zone*, but the outside boat disagrees saying that you were still *clear astern* when she arrived at the *zone* and that you subsequently obtained the *overlap*, rule 18.2(e) states that if there is "reasonable doubt," it shall be presumed by the sailors that the *overlap* was **not** obtained in time. Similarly, if it goes to a protest hearing and the protest committee has "reasonable doubt," it shall presume that the *overlap* was **not** obtained in time. In other words, in a *protest* you will have to satisfy the protest committee that there is no doubt that you obtained the *overlap* in time (see Appeal 92).

By the same token, if you have an *overlap* on an outside boat at say five and then four lengths away, she will be required to give you *mark-room* under rule 18.2(b) unless she pulls *clear ahead* before reaching the *zone*. If she claims to have "broken" the *overlap* just before she reached the *zone*, but you disagree saying that you were still *overlapped* when she reached the *zone*, then it is she who must satisfy the protest committee that there is no doubt that the *overlap* was broken in time.

Satisfying the protest committee is generally very tough to do as it is usually one person's word against the other's. Hails to each other regarding the *overlap* situation as the boats near the *zone* are very helpful to the point that they are almost expected by good protest committees. Also, witnesses can be very useful, particularly independent witnesses who were positioned exactly at the *zone* and in a position to determine *overlaps*. But the bottom line is that boats that will have the "burden of proof" under rule 18.2(e) should yield on the water to be safe.

WHEN THE BOATS ARE OVERLAPPED

"When rule 18 applies between two or more overlapped boats, what rights and requirements do the inside and outside boats have?"

That's the key question, and it's covered in rules 18.2(a) and 18.2(b). Let's get into it.

When boats get to the *zone* (other than boats on opposite *tacks* at the windward *mark*), they will either be *overlapped* or not *overlapped*. Let's look at those two situations.

RULE 18.2 — GIVING MARK-ROOM

(a) When boats are *overlapped* the outside boat shall give the inside boat *mark-room*, unless rule 18.2(b) applies.

(b) If boats are *overlapped* when the first of them reaches the *zone*, the outside boat at that moment shall thereafter give the inside boat *mark-room*. If a boat is *clear ahead* when she reaches the *zone*, the boat *clear astern* at that moment shall thereafter give her *mark-room*.

Note, rule 18.2(a) and the first sentence in 18.2(b) are "talking" only to *overlapped* boats. The second sentence in rule 18.2(b) deals with boats that are not *overlapped*.

Remember, a boat is *overlapped* with another if her bow or equipment in normal position (such as the spinnaker or extended bowsprit) is on or across a line drawn abeam through the aftermost point of the other boat's hull and equipment in normal position. Also, two boats that otherwise are not *overlapped* suddenly become *overlapped* when a boat **in between them** *overlaps* both of them. So if you are approaching a *mark* to be left to port and are just *overlapped* on the port transom of the boat ahead of you, and she is just *overlapped* on the port transom of the boat ahead of her, you are technically *overlapped* with the boat ahead of her (see the definition Clear Astern and Clear Ahead; Overlap). Therefore you are entitled to *mark-room* from both boats if you are *overlapped* when the **farthest boat ahead** arrives at the *zone*.

Also remember that, by definition, two boats *overlap* when the bow or equipment in normal position of one is over the line drawn through the aftermost part of the other, even when the boats are a quarter of a mile apart.

"Can boats on opposite tacks be overlapped?"

Yes. Boats on opposite *tacks* are *overlapped* when rule 18 applies to them, or when they are both sailing more than ninety degrees from the true wind. This becomes important as boats approach the leeward *mark* on opposite *tacks* on widely differing angles. For instance, say that two boats are reaching on opposite *tacks* to a leeward *mark* to be left to starboard. When the *starboard tack* boat (S) reaches the *zone*, the *port tack* boat (P) is five lengths from the *mark*, but based on the angle of S's course, P is *overlapped* on the inside of S. Therefore, P is entitled to *mark-room* from S under rule 18.2(b) if she needs it!

However, as two boats approach a windward *mark* on opposite *tacks*, they are on a beat to windward, and rule 18.1(a) says that rule 18 does not apply to

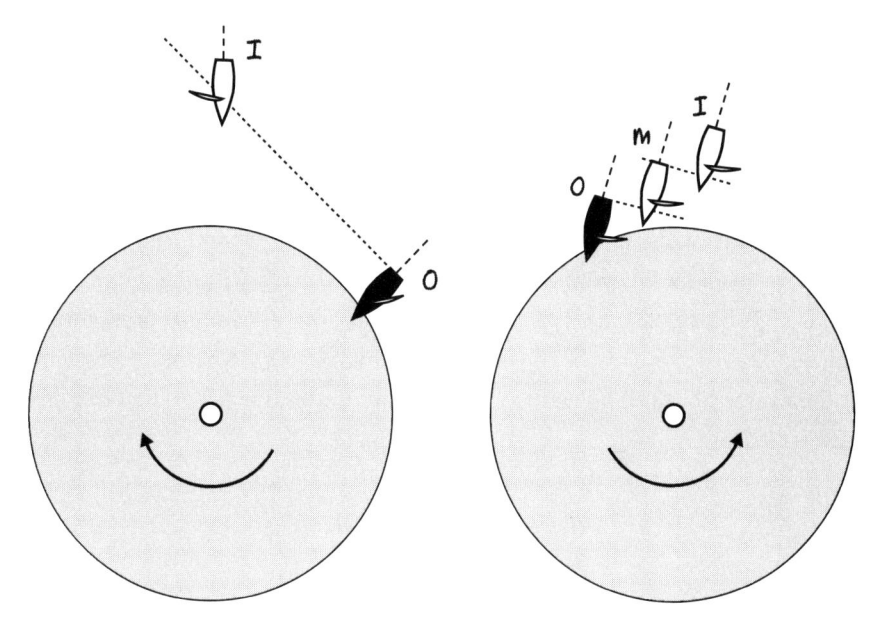

PART 2, SECTION C: WHEN BOATS MEET — RULE 18: MARK-ROOM 177

Even though I is well behind O, I has an inside overlap when O reaches the zone; therefore O must give I mark-room.

M is in between O and I and overlaps both of them; therefore, I is overlapped with O when O reaches the zone. O and M must keep clear of I and give I mark-room.

them. As they are not sailing below ninety degrees to the true wind, the terms *"clear astern," clear ahead"* and *overlap* do not apply to them, so they are not *"overlapped,"* and the *port-tack* boat must *keep* clear of the *starboard-tack* boat. See the definition *Clear Astern* and *Clear Ahead; Overlap*.

"Are there any limitations on obtaining an overlap and becoming entitled to the rights in rule 18.2(a) or 18.2(b)?"

Yes, there are two:

1) the boat astern cannot obtain an inside *overlap* and become entitled to *mark-room* once the boat ahead reaches the *zone clear ahead* of the boat astern (rules 18.2(b) and 18.2(c)); and

2) the outside boat is not required to give *mark-room* if she has been physically unable to give the inside boat *mark-room* from the time the *overlap* began (18.2(f)).

Up to 1965, a boat *clear astern* could get a legal inside *overlap* as long as it was (a) in time to enable the outside boat(s) to give *room*; (b) before the boat ahead changed her course in the act of rounding; and (c) before any part of the boat ahead came abreast of the *mark*. Things were often a tad out of control as boats came barreling up from astern yelling for "buoy room" at the last second.

In 1965 the rule writers took a creative step. Realizing that there ought to be some "cutoff point" after which a boat *clear astern* could not obtain an inside *overlap*, they devised a safety zone now simply called "the *zone*," which has proved to work very effectively. And because the "point" can be in any direction from the *mark*, the *zone* is an imaginary area with the *mark* in the center and having a radius of three of the nearer boat's hull lengths; for instance, 72 feet in a Melges 24 (see the definition *Zone*). Note the fact that it is the nearer boat's hull lengths; this becomes important when the boats are different sizes.

The second sentence in rule 18.2(b) says, *"If a boat is **clear ahead** when she reaches the **zone**, the boat **clear astern** at that moment shall thereafter give her **mark-room**."* So the game ends at the *zone*. If you are catching up from astern but don't get the inside *overlap* before the boat ahead of you gets to the *zone*, then you are not entitled to the rights in rule 18.2(b) and must give the boat ahead *mark-room* under rule 18.2(b). If you do get the inside *overlap* before she gets to the *zone*, then you are entitled to the rights in rule 18.2(b). So often the race is not to the *mark*…it is to the *zone*!

"What if I physically can't give room to the boat that just obtained the inside overlap on me?"

That's the second exception to rule 18.2(a) and 18.2(b). When a boat obtains an inside *overlap* from *clear astern*, the boat ahead has a "protective shield" if she needs it. When a boat gets an *overlap* on you just before you reach the *zone*, she becomes entitled to *mark-room* under rule 18.2(b) as an inside boat. However, you are not required to anticipate her arrival. There are times, though rare, when you may be physically unable to give her the *room* she needs to round or pass the *mark* from the time the *overlap* began, based on your situation at that moment. Rule 18.2(f) says, *"If a boat obtained an inside overlap from clear astern or by tacking to windward of the other boat and, from the time the overlap began, the outside boat has been unable to give mark-room, she is not required to give it."* In this situation, she is not entitled to *mark-room* and the applicable rules of Section A and B apply. If she becomes the right-of-way boat, she must comply with rule 15 (Acquiring Right of Way) which means she won't get inside at the *mark* because if the outside boat could have created enough *room* to do so, she would have done so in the first place. And if she is a keep-clear boat, she must *keep clear*.

One example of where this situation might occur is a tightly packed *mark* rounding in light air where a boat astern gets an inside *overlap* on a boat that is three-and-a-half boat-lengths from the *mark*, but there's just no way the outside boat can get everyone else outside of her to move away from the *mark* in time to create *room* for the new inside boat. Another example is when two boats are going so fast that by the time the outside boat can react to her new obligation and make the *room*, the inside boat is already past the *mark* on the wrong side. Twelve knots of boat-speed equals about 20 feet per second, so on a windy reach a Hobie 18 will chew up three boat-lengths in less than three seconds!

A similar situation is when you are approaching a starboard-hand windward *mark* on *starboard-tack* and you tack in the *zone*. Rule 18.3 (Passing Head to Wind in the Zone) does not apply (see the discussion of rule 18.3). If a *port-tack* boat becomes *overlapped* with you from *clear astern*, it is entitled to *mark-room* under rule 18.2(a) unless you are physically unable to give her *room*, in which case she is not entitled to *mark-room*.

Another similar situation is when you are approaching a starboard-hand windward *mark* on *starboard-tack*, and a *port-tack* boat crosses you in the *zone* and tacks to *windward* of you, or ducks you and then tacks into a *windward overlap*. Rule 18.2(a) requires you to give them *mark-room* unless you are physically unable to do so from the moment the *overlap* began.

"What if at a port-hand windward mark the boat ahead of me, or overlapped outside of me, didn't reach the zone clear ahead of me, but instead they approached on the opposite tack and then tacked inside the zone?"

If you are approaching a windward *mark* to be left to port on *starboard tack* and a boat comes in on *port tack* and tacks inside the *zone* and is *clear ahead* of you when she completes her tack, you **can** obtain an inside *overlap* and become entitled to *mark-room* under rule 18.3 (Passing Head to Wind in the Zone). Note, when rule 18.3 applies, if the boat that tacked is unable to give you *mark-room*, tough luck on her; she breaks rule 18.3. And if a boat tacks within the *zone* into an outside *overlap* on you, she must give you *mark-room* at the *mark* as well under rule 18.3. Rule 18.2 does not apply when rule 18.3 does. See the full discussion of rule 18.3 in chapter 9.

Another possible scenario is two boats (P and S) approaching a windward *mark* to be left to port on opposite *tacks*. S is about two lengths below the *starboard-tack* layline; P is close to the *port-tack* layline. When S nears the *port-tack* layline she tacks. When she passes head to wind she is within the *zone*. She completes her tack *clear ahead* of P. P, moving faster, *overlaps* S to windward about one length from the *mark*. Or in a similar approach, when S completes her tack she is *overlapped* to leeward of P. In both scenarios, S is required to give P *mark-room* under rule 18.2(a).

The reason is that after S tacks the boats are *overlapped*, but rule 18.2(a) makes no reference to **where** the boats were when they reached the *zone*. It just talks about *overlapped* boats (and remember, P and S were not "overlapped" when they were on opposite *tacks*). Because S and P are *overlapped* with S on the outside, rule 18.2(a) requires the outside boat (S) to give the inside boat (P) *mark-room*. Note that in these two scenarios, S is not *fetching* the *mark* after her tack, so rule 18.3 does not apply.

"OK, I get all that. So if I'm the outside boat, can you remind me when I have to start giving the inside boat mark-room?"

You have to start giving *mark-room* the moment rule 18 begins to apply, which is when the hull of the first of the boats involved is in the *zone*, which is normally three lengths from the *mark*. It is at this point that outside/right-of-way boats need to yield their right of way and provide the inside/keep-clear boats the space they need to sail to and around the *mark*.

"So if I'm the outside boat and required to give mark-room, how much room do I have to give the inside boat?"

Well, first you have to understand what *"room"* means; then what *"mark-room"* means. "*Room*" is "*the space a boat needs in the existing conditions, including space to comply with her obligations under the rules of Part 2 and rule 31, while manoeuvring promptly in a seamanlike way*" (see the definition Room). "*Mark-room*" is "**Room** for a boat to leave a **mark** on the required side. Also (a) **room** to sail to the **mark** when her **proper course** is to sail close to it, and (b) **room** to round or pass the **mark** as necessary to **sail the course** without touching the **mark**" (see the definition Mark-Room).

First, you have to give her *room* to round or pass the *mark* on the required side. Also, assuming the inside boat's *proper course* is to sail close to the *mark*, say within a couple of feet or so as it will be when she is rounding the *mark*, you have to give her the space she needs to sail **to** the *mark* in a "seamanlike way" (meaning safe; not putting her boat or crew at risk of damage or injury, or at risk of touching the *mark*; sailed the way competent, but not expert, sailors would sail to the *mark*) in the prevailing conditions. A boat will need more space if it is windy and wavy, and less space if it is light air and smooth; just as a boat will need more space if it has a lot of sail handling to do, and less space if it has only one sail to deal with. (See Case 21.)

Note: *room* does **not** include space for the inside boat to sail her *proper course* to the *mark*; i.e., the space the inside boat might like to set up for a tactically desirable "swing wide-cut close" type rounding, though in actual practice most outside boats are a little more forgiving. (See Appeal 20.)

Then you have to give her the space she needs to round or pass the *mark* as necessary to *sail the course*, which means just enough space to allow her to round the *mark* in a "seamanlike way" onto the course she needs to sail to begin the next leg (see the definition *Room*). Again, "seamanlike way" means the space needed to not be at risk of touching the *mark* or the outside or *clear astern* boat during her rounding, and not the space she might want to sail her *proper course*; i.e., the course she might want to sail for tactical reasons. (See Case 118.)

"What if I need to gybe; do I get room for that too?"
If you need to gybe to round the *mark* in order to *sail the course*, then yes, *mark-room* includes enough space for your boom to come across and your stern to swing when you gybe to round the *mark*. This is common at leeward *marks* when the inside boat needs to gybe to round the *mark*. (See Case 75.)

"Do I also get room to gybe around the windward mark going onto a run?"
No! If you are *clear ahead* and rounding close to the windward *mark* onto a run (where you will spend time on both *tacks*), you do not need to gybe in order to *sail the course*, even though gybing may be your *proper course*. Therefore, *mark-room* does **not** include *room* to gybe in that situation.

"How about when I'm a windward/inside boat coming into the windward mark or rounding the leeward mark; am I entitled to room to tack around the mark?"
At the windward *mark*, Yes; at the leeward *mark*, No. If you are the inside

boat and are **overlapped** to *windward* of the boat required to give you *mark-room*, and you need to tack to round the *mark* in order to *sail the course*, then *mark-room* includes *room* to tack as long as you are *fetching* the *mark* after your tack (see the definition *Mark-Room*). Note, if you are *clear ahead* in the *zone*, you are still entitled to *mark-room*, but not to *room* to tack (see the definition *Mark-Room* and Appeal 89). However, at a leeward *mark* going onto a beat to windward, you do not need to tack around the *mark* in order to *sail the course*; therefore, *mark-room* does **not** include *room* to tack.

At the windward *mark*, note that once the inside *overlapped* tacking boat passes head-to-wind, rule 18 no longer applies because the boats are now on opposite tacks on a beat to windward (rule 18.1(a)). If contact occurs during the tack, the inside boat will have a good argument that the outside boat was failing to give her *mark-room* before she passed head-to-wind; i.e., while rule 18.2(a) or 18.2(b) still applied, and that she is exonerated by rule 43.1(b) (Exoneration) for her breach of rule 13 (While Tacking). However, it is possible that a protest committee might decide that the inside boat could have tacked without causing contact (i.e., that she had *room* to tack), and therefore disqualify the inside boat for breaking rule 13 because rule 18 no longer applied once she passed head to wind. The bottom line in this situation is that the outside boat should be sure to give the inside boat enough space to make a normal tack without hitting her; and the inside boat should be careful not to hit the outside boat while she is tacking to be safe.

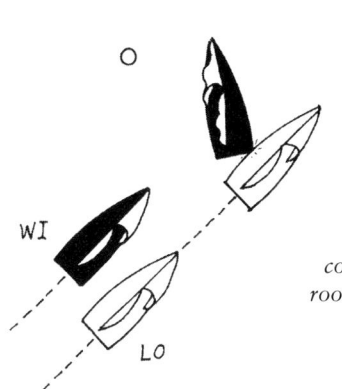

PART 2, SECTION C: WHEN BOATS MEET — RULE 18: MARK-ROOM **183**

LO must give WI mark-room under rule 18.2(b), which includes room to tack. However, the moment WI passes head to wind, she and LO are on opposite tacks and rule 18 shuts off. At that point rule 13 requires WI to keep clear of LO while tacking; and rule 14 always requires both boats to avoid contact. If WI makes a normal tack and her transom touches LO, it is likely a protest committee will decide that LO failed to give WI room to tack. To be safe, WI should try not to let her transom touch LO after she passes head to wind, and LO should give WI enough space so she can tack without contact.

"Rule 18.1 says that rule 18 no longer applies once the boat entitled to mark-room has been given mark-room. When has a boat been given mark-room?"

Rule 18.1 states, *"Rule 18 no longer applies between boats when mark-room has been given."* A boat has been given *mark-room* when it has received all the *room* (space) it is entitled to in the definition *Mark-Room* (see Cases 21 and 118). Specifically,

1) the boat has the space it needs to round or pass the *mark* on the required side;

2) if the boat's *proper course* will bring her within a couple of feet of the *mark*, the boat has the space it needs to sail "to" the *mark*;

3) the boat has the space it needs to round or pass the *mark* as necessary to *sail the course*, i.e., sail onto the course needed to begin the next leg or to *finish*; and

4) while rounding or passing the *mark*, the boat can *keep clear* of the boat giving her *mark-room* without risk of touching the *mark* or fouling another boat.

5) Additionally, *mark-room* includes *room* to tack in certain situations (see the discussion above).

Note, this might occur before she has left the *mark* astern when there are no mitigating circumstances; or it might occur after she has left the *mark* astern, for instance in strong adverse current.

"What if I am sailing short-handed or my crew is inexperienced; do I get more room as a result?"

No. A boat is not entitled to more space than usual just because her crew is short-handed or inexperienced. Case 103 addresses this head on by saying, "Neither the experience of IW's crew nor their number is relevant in determining '*room*'… the interpretation of 'seamanlike way' must be based on the boat-handling that can reasonably be expected from a competent, but not expert, crew of the appropriate number for the boat."

The moment a boat has been given *mark-room*, rule 18 ceases to apply, meaning she is no longer "sailing within the *room* or *mark-room* to which she was entitled" under rule 18.2. This means she is no longer "protected" by rule 43.1(b) (Exoneration). She is subject to the rules in Section A and B, and must comply with those rules or risk penalty.

"Can you explain what you mean by 'protected by rule 43.1(b)'?"

Sure. There are times when the inside boat is a keep-clear boat (a *windward* or *port-tack* boat) and she is sailing to and around the *mark* in a seamanlike way as she is entitled to by *mark-room*, but she nevertheless has contact with an outside right-of-way boat or the outside right-of-way boat has to change course to give her *mark-room*. In that case the inside keep-clear boat has broken rule 10 (*port/starboard*) or rule 11 (*windward/leeward*), both rules of Part 2, Section A. Or sometimes the outside boat does not give the inside boat enough *room* and the inside boat is forced to touch the *mark* breaking rule 31 (Touching a Mark). Rule 43.1(b) (Exoneration) is the rule that "exonerates" the inside boat, meaning she is freed from being penalized for her breach.

RULE 43 — EXONERATION

RULE 43.1(b)

When a boat is sailing within the *room* or *mark-room* to which she is entitled and, as a consequence of an incident with a boat required to give her that *room* or *mark-room*, she breaks a rule of Section A of Part 2, rule 15, 16, or 31, she is exonerated for her breach.

RULE 43.2

A boat exonerated for breaking a *rule* need not take a penalty and shall not be penalized for breaking that *rule*.

PART 2, SECTION C: WHEN BOATS MEET — RULE 18: MARK-ROOM

A is smart to have sailed high and then gybed on the "layline" to the offset mark where her proper course will bring her close to the mark

Yeah, she is protected by rule 43.1(a) because that's part of the "mark-room" space that B has to give her

If A had sailed past the "layline," she would have been given all the mark-room she's entitled to, and she wouldn't be protected from B at position 4

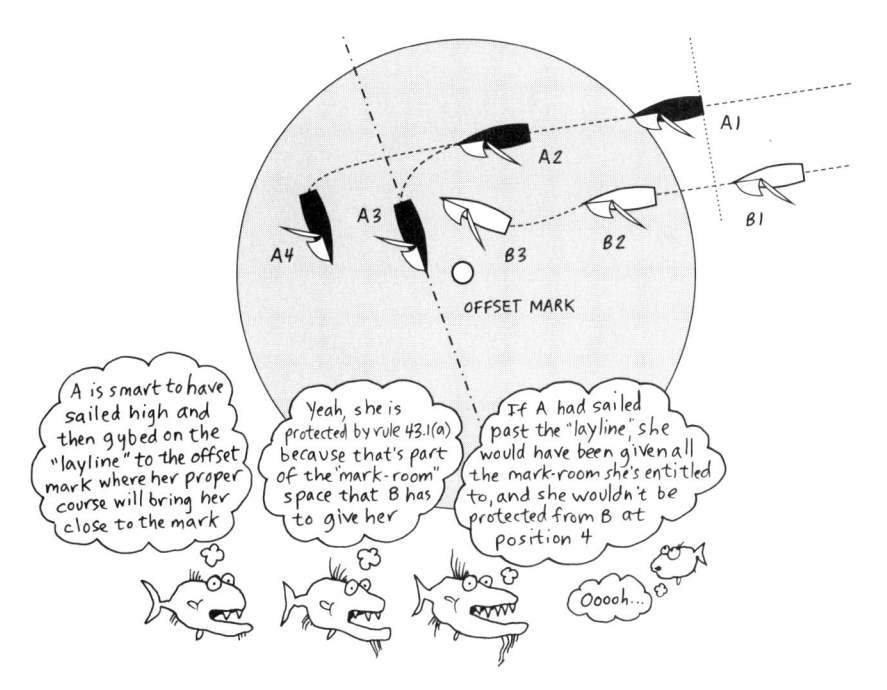

Ooooh...

"Exonerated" means freed from having to take a penalty or otherwise being penalized for breaking the rule. So if the boat ahead or the inside boat (AI) is a keep-clear boat and she is sailing within the *mark-room* to which she is entitled (meaning she is rounding the *mark* in a seamanlike way) and she fouls the other boat (BO) or touches the *mark*, BO breaks rule 18.2(b) (Giving Mark-Room) and AI is exonerated for breaking a rule of Part 2, Section A or rule 31 (Touching a Mark). And if AI is a right-of-way boat and while rounding the *mark* in a seamanlike way (i.e., within the *mark-room* she is entitled to) she has to change course and she fails to give BO *room* to *keep clear*, BO breaks rule 18.2(b) and AI is exonerated for breaking rule 16.1 (Changing Course).

This is a common sense rule. If you are entitled to *room* at the *mark*, you should be able to sail your course to and around that *mark* without concern for the boats required to give you *mark-room*. And those boats should be able to easily anticipate the course you are going to sail around the *mark* and give you the *room* you need to sail it.

"Do I need to protest the outside boat so the protest committee can exonerate me?"

No. Rule 43.1(b) tells you that you are exonerated at the time of the incident. But if someone protests the incident, the protest committee will decide if you

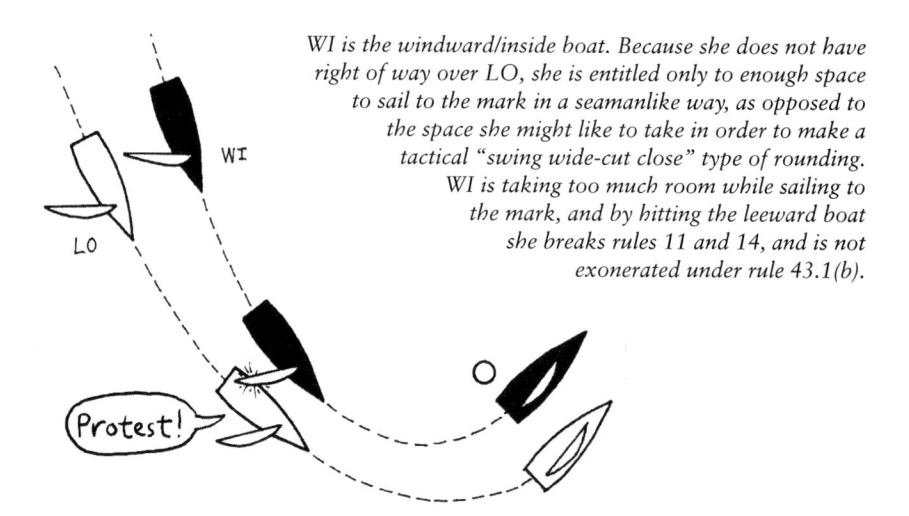

WI is the windward/inside boat. Because she does not have right of way over LO, she is entitled only to enough space to sail to the mark in a seamanlike way, as opposed to the space she might like to take in order to make a tactical "swing wide-cut close" type of rounding. WI is taking too much room while sailing to the mark, and by hitting the leeward boat she breaks rules 11 and 14, and is not exonerated under rule 43.1(b).

were entitled to exoneration; and if it decides you weren't, then it will penalize you (see rule 64.2, Penalties).

Note that exoneration for breaking rule 16 (Changing Course) only applies when rule 18 (Mark-Room) or 19 (Room at an Obstruction) applies. For instance, when boats are approaching a starting *mark* surrounded by water (like a race committee boat) to *start*, rules 18 and 19 do not apply (preamble to Section C). So both before and after the starting signal, rule 16.1 applies and right-of-way boats must give *keep clear* boats *room* to *keep clear* **anytime** they change course. The same applies at a windward *mark* when a *starboard-tack* boat (S) is bearing away around the *mark* and a *port-tack* boat (P) is approaching the *mark*. Because P is "approaching" the *mark* and S is "leaving" it, rule 18 does not apply (rule 18.1(c)), and therefore rule 16.1 does apply to S; i.e., S must be careful as she changes course near P (see discussion of rule 16).

Also note that rule 43.1(b) does **not** exonerate a boat for breaking rule 14 (Avoiding Contact), so all boats rounding *marks* must be careful to avoid any contact, and particularly any contact that causes damage or injury.

"Can you explain how this all works at an offset mark or the mark at the end of the first reaching leg on a trapezoid course?"

Sure. Commonly, fleets will sail on a short reaching leg after the windward *mark* and then round an "offset" *mark* to begin the downwind leg where boats will sail on both *tacks*, or they will round a *mark* at the end of the first reaching leg onto a downwind leg on a trapezoid course. Let's say Boats A and B are reaching on *starboard tack* to leave the *mark* to port. A enters the *zone clear ahead* of B, so B must give A *mark-room* under rule 18.2(b)). A wants to gybe and begin sailing the downwind leg on *port tack*. She knows that she is not "protected" by rule 43.1(b) (Exoneration) if she gybes around the *mark* because she does not need to gybe to begin sailing the next leg.

A sails high so that she would pass the *mark* about a length to windward of it. When A gets to the point where her *proper course* on *port tack* would bring her close to the *mark* (within a couple of feet of it), she gybes to *port tack*. Because *mark-room* includes *room* for A "to sail to the *mark*" when her *proper course* is to sail close to it, A is sailing within the *mark-room* to which she is entitled, and A is exonerated by rule 43.1(b) if she breaks rule 10 (*port/starboard*); i.e., she is "protected" by rule 43.1(b). Furthermore, when A gybes, B becomes *overlapped* inside A and becomes required to also give A *room* to sail her *proper course* under rule 18.2(c)(2) until A has been given *mark-room*.

However, if A had stayed on *starboard* tack and sailed past the point where her *proper course* on *port tack* would have brought her close to the *mark* (call it the "port layline" to the *mark*), she is no longer entitled to *room* to sail to the *mark*. While still on *starboard tack* A had been given *room* to leave the *mark* to port, and to bear away to the course needed to *sail the course* with no risk of touching the *mark*. Therefore A had been given *mark-room*, and rule 18 ceased to apply, meaning that if she gybed to *port tack* after that point, she would be required to *keep clear* of B under rule 10 (On Opposite Tacks).

Next, the question of how much *room* an outside boat must give to an inside boat depends on whether the outside boat is a "right-of-way" boat or a "keep-clear" boat.

WHEN THE OUTSIDE BOAT IS THE RIGHT-OF-WAY BOAT:

When the outside boat has the right-of-way, she only needs to give the inside boat *mark-room*, and no more space than that (see the discussion above). Note that rules 18.2(a) and 18.2(b) do not shift the right of way from the outside/right-of-way boat to the inside/keep-clear boat. But clearly the obligation to give *mark-room* conflicts with rule 10 (On Opposite Tacks) and rule 11 (On the Same Tack, Overlapped) in Section A. In other words, when a *starboard-tack* boat (S) and a *port-tack* boat (P), or a *leeward* boat (L) and a *windward* boat

(W), are rounding a *mark* with P or W on the inside, S or L has a "temporary obligation" to give P or W *mark-room*. After fulfilling that obligation, S and L will get their full rights back under rules 10 or 11.

Furthermore, if a keep-clear boat sails farther from the *mark* than allowed under *mark-room*, and she breaks a rule in Section A, she is not entitled to exoneration by rule 43.1(b) (Exoneration). For instance, when a *windward*/inside boat (WI) is slow in coming up to close-hauled around a *mark* and contact occurs between her and a *leeward*/outside boat, WI breaks rule 11 (On the Same Tack, Overlapped); and if it is found by a protest committee that she took more *room* than was needed to round the *mark*, she is not exonerated by rule 43.1(b). (See Case 25 and Appeals 3 and 20.)

Remember, the primary purpose of rule 18 is to allow boats to round or pass a *mark* without the inside boats getting wedged in between the outside boats and the *mark*, or getting forced onto the wrong side of the *mark*; and to create an orderly transition from one leg of the race to the next. As discussed above, sometimes these outside boats are going to otherwise have the right of way. Rule 18 requires them to give only enough *room* (space) for the inside boat to round or pass the *mark* in a seamanlike way. The moment the inside boat has been able to round or pass the *mark* without risk of touching the *mark* or the outside boat (i.e., has been given *mark-room*), the purpose of rule 18 has been served. At that moment the outside/right-of-way boat gets her full rights back, and the inside/keep-clear boat must *keep clear*. This is made clear in rule 18.1 which states, "*Rule 18 no longer applies between boats when* **mark-room** *has been given."*

For example, let's say that two *overlapped* boats on *port tack* are rounding the leeward *mark* onto a beat. The *leeward*/outside boat (LO) is allowing enough space for the *windward*/inside boat (WI) to round the *mark* as quickly as possible, but LO is trying to keep her bow just ahead of WI. As WI comes up to close-hauled, LO luffs at a medium rate. WI responds by luffing and tacking onto *starboard-tack*. She *keeps clear* of LO and does not hit the *mark* or tack too close to any boat about to pass the *mark*. No foul. LO gave WI *room* to round the *mark*, and when LO asserted her rights as a *leeward* boat, WI was able to *keep clear* in a seamanlike way without hitting the *mark* or fouling a boat.

Note that the circumstances will weigh heavily in determining exactly when the outside boat can assert her rights. If there are a lot of boats near the *mark*

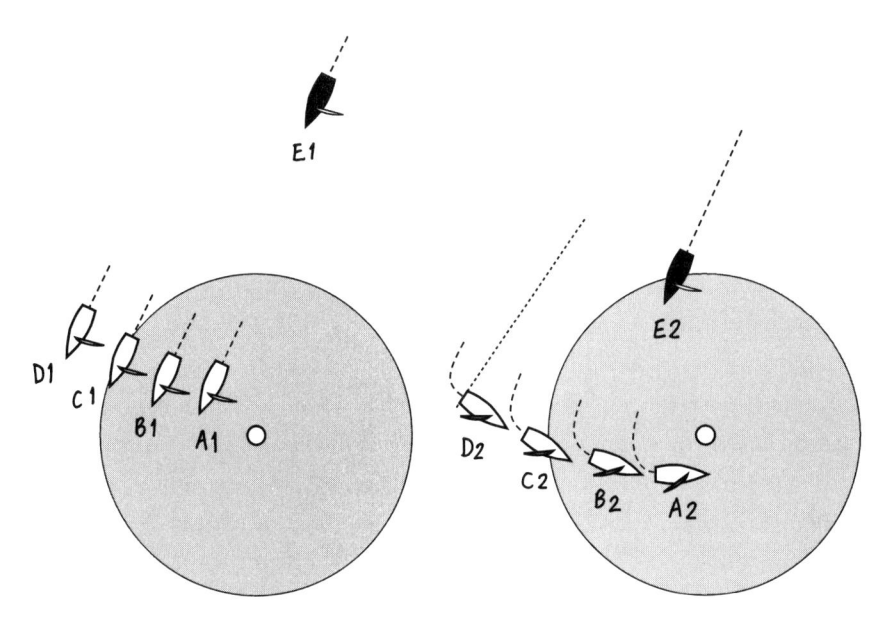

PART 2, SECTION C: WHEN BOATS MEET — RULE 18: MARK-ROOM 189

A, B, C and D are in a bunch at a mark. D is keeping clear of the three boats inside her, and as a result is outside the zone. E is well astern. In position 2, the four boats gybe and line up to pass the mark one behind the other. The position of A, B and C make it obvious that D is still outside the zone. Because E is overlapped on D's inside and is the right of way boat, D must give her mark-room and keep clear of her. E must gybe when it is her proper course to do so, unless it is a gate mark or the boats are team racing.

such that WI could not tack without fouling them under rule 15 (Acquiring Right of Way), LO will have to be careful to allow WI the *room* needed to sail between LO and the *mark* without tacking. If there is current or strong wind or waves, LO will again have to wait until WI can clear the *mark* without risk of losing speed and being pushed back into the *mark*. But if there are no mitigating circumstances, WI may be able to respond safely to LO's luff even before she has left the *mark* astern.

"Well, if I'm the inside boat and required to keep clear and the outside boat is not giving me mark-room, what should I do?"

You should sail to the *mark* in a seamanlike way expecting the outside boat to give you *mark-room* as required under rule 18.2. If there is contact between you and the outside boat or you touch the *mark*, you are "exonerated," which means freed from having to take a penalty, for breaking whichever Section A rule you broke, or rule 31 (Touching a Mark) by rule 43.1(b) (Exoneration).

Note, however, that you only get exonerated for breaking a rule in Section A

(Right of Way), or rule 15 (Acquiring Right of Way) or 16 (Changing Course), or rule 31 (Touching a Mark).

If at the moment it became clear to you that the outside boat was not going to give you *mark-room* it was possible to have avoided the contact, and if the contact resulted in damage or injury to either boat, you will also be penalized for breaking rule 14 (Avoiding Contact). In other words, both boats will be penalized in this circumstance. If no damage or injury results, then you are exonerated under rule 43.1(c) for breaking rule 14.

Note also that by avoiding the contact this may result in you not being able to round or pass the *mark* on that approach. Though the outside boat's rule breach caused you to sail on the wrong side of the *mark* on that approach, it hasn't prevented you from ultimately rounding the *mark* correctly as required by rule 28.1 (Sailing the Race); i.e., she didn't compel you to break rule 28.1. Therefore, unfortunately, you are not entitled to exoneration under rule 43.1(a) (Exoneration) or redress under rule 62 (Redress); you must circle around and try again. You should certainly win your *protest* against the outside boat, but there is nothing the protest committee can do to compensate you for the distance/places/time lost while making a second try to round or pass the *mark*.

"What happens when I have an inside overlap when the boats reach the zone, but once inside the zone the outside boat breaks the overlap?"

You are still entitled to *mark-room* under rule 18.2(b). Rule 18.2(c)(1) says, "*When a boat is required to give* **mark-room** *by rule 18.2(b), she shall continue to do so even if later an* **overlap** *is broken or a new* **overlap** *begins.*" So as long as you are *overlapped* when one of the boats reaches the *zone*, your right to *mark-room* under rule 18.2(b) is "locked in" until you have been given *mark-room*, or until you pass head to wind or sail completely out of the *zone* (rules 18.1 and 18.2(d)).

"What happens when boats on the outside that are giving room to boats on the inside never get to the zone until after they've turned and begun heading for the mark; now can a boat that was well clear astern suddenly claim room?"

Yes! Case 59 clarifies this very common situation at crowded leeward *marks*:

"QUESTION: Five boats were approaching a leeward mark dead before the wind. Four of them were overlapped in line with A nearest the mark. The fifth boat, E, was clear astern of A, B and C when those three boats reached the zone. When D came abreast of the mark and turned to round it, E became overlapped inside D. This occurred after E had already reached the zone and before D reached it. E rounded the mark behind A, B and C but inside D, which was able to give mark-room to E. Is E entitled to mark-room under rule 18.2(a) from D?

"ANSWER: Because E was clear astern of A, B and C when they reached the zone, she was required by rule 18.2(b) to give each of them mark-room. Between E and D, however, a different relationship developed. In order to leave room for the three inside boats with their booms fully extended, D had to approach the mark on a course that brought her abreast of it outside the zone. When E reached the zone, she was clear astern of D and D was still outside the zone. Therefore, rule 18.2(b) did not apply between D and E. When D changed course towards the mark, E obtained an inside overlap and rule 18.2(a) began to apply between D and E. E was entitled to mark-room under that rule, which D was able to give."

"Does the inside boat have to call for mark-room in order to get it?"

No. When you are on the inside at a *mark*, you are not required to call for *room*, although that is a prudent thing to do to avoid misunderstandings. Boats are expected to know their obligations under the *rules*, which includes outside boats at *marks*.

"Now is any of this different when the inside boat also has the right of way?"

Well, everything we've talked about regarding *mark-room* is the same; but the fundamental difference is that when the inside boat has the right of way, she can sail her "**proper course**" from the moment she enters the *zone* (and she can sail even farther from a gate *mark* than her *proper course* would take her if she is not subject to rule 17, On the Same Tack; Proper Course; see rule 18.4, Gybing). Whereas if the inside boat does **not** have the right-of-way, she can only sail a "**seamanlike**" course from the time she enters the *zone*. That permits the inside right-of-way boat to set up for a more tactical "swing wide/ cut close" type of rounding (sometimes called a "tactical" or "proper course" rounding) before she is at the *mark*, whereas the inside keep-clear boat will have to begin her rounding a little closer to the *mark*.

WHEN THE INSIDE BOAT IS THE RIGHT-OF-WAY BOAT:

When the inside boat has the right-of-way under Section A (Right of Way) of the *rules*, the outside boat must *keep clear*. This does not change just because the boats are rounding or passing a *mark*. Therefore, not only is the inside/right-of-way boat entitled to *mark-room*; she is free to sail where she pleases, with just a couple of possible limits. Therefore, the right-of-way boat has more freedom in the *zone*.

There are two situations where the inside right-of-way boat will have a "limit" as she sails to and around a *mark*:

- One such "limit" is in rule 17 (On the Same Tack; Proper Course) which limits L to sailing no higher than her *proper course* when she becomes *overlapped* from *clear astern*. Therefore, at a windward *mark*, if LI (*leeward*/inside) becomes *overlapped* from *clear astern* on the inside of a boat that has just tacked in front of her inside the *zone* (such that rule 18.3, Passing Head to Wind in the Zone, applies), LI must sail her *proper course* around the *mark*. Note that, in this situation, her *proper course* may be to sail head to wind momentarily to get up and around the *mark* (see Appeal 70).

- The other "limit" is in rule 18.4 (Gybing) which says that if an inside *overlapped* right-of-way boat must gybe to sail her *proper course* around the *mark*, she is required to sail no farther from the *mark* than needed to sail her *proper course* until she gybes; i.e., she can't continue on straight past the *mark* or luff away from the *mark* if that takes her farther from the *mark* than necessary to sail her *proper course*. (For a full discussion, including an exception at a gate *mark*, see the explanation of rule 18.4 in chapter 9.) This "limit" commonly arises at offwind *marks* whenever L or S is on the inside and her *proper course* is to gybe around the *mark*.

But the bottom line is that an inside right-of-way boat is allowed to swing a bit wider and then cut closer around the *mark*. The reason is because inside right-of-way boats always have the right to sail their *proper course* while they remain the right-of-way boat, and outside boats must both *keep clear* of them and give them *mark-room*. Setting up to round this way allows boats to make a smooth turn and will get them into the most strategically desirable position (clear air, ability to tack, etc.) as they begin the beat, which will help them to *finish* as soon

PART 2, SECTION C: WHEN BOATS MEET — RULE 18: MARK-ROOM

Before reaching the zone, S has right of way over P under rule 10. However, the moment P reaches the zone clear ahead of S, rule 18.2(b) requires S to give P mark-room.

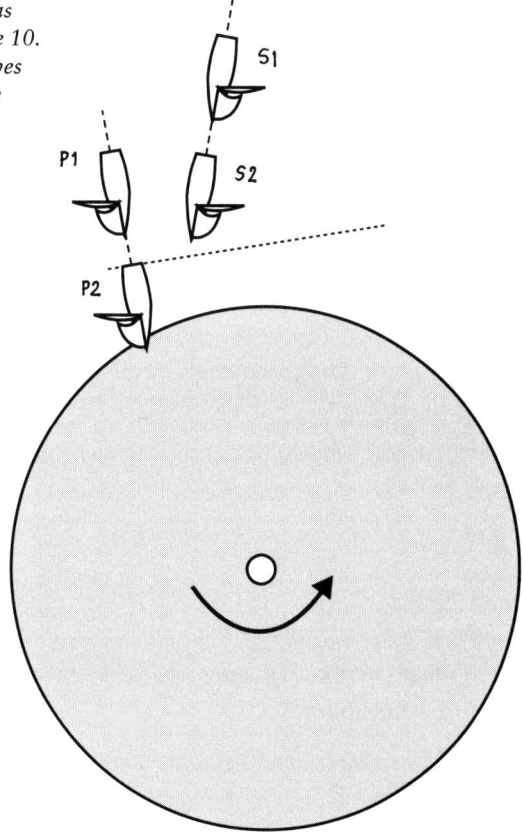

as possible (see the definition *Proper Course*).

Note, however, that the moment an inside/right-of-way boat gybes to round the *mark* and becomes an inside/keep-clear boat, she is only entitled to *mark-room*, which is the space she needs to sail "to" the *mark*. It does **not** include *room* to sail her *proper course*; and if she takes more space than she is entitled to, she will not be exonerated by rule 43.1(b) (Exoneration) if she breaks rule 11 (On the Same Tack, Overlapped).

WHEN THE BOATS ARE NOT OVERLAPPED

"Okay, I've got it so far; now how about when the boats are not overlapped when they get to the zone?"

The second sentence in rule 18.2(b) covers the situation where the boats are not *overlapped* when the boat *clear ahead* reaches the *zone*. It says, "*If a boat* is **clear ahead** when she reaches the **zone**, the boat **clear astern** at that moment shall thereafter give her **mark-room**."

So, between two boats (A and B), if they are not *overlapped* when the first of them reaches the *zone*, and assuming the *proper* course for the one ahead (A) is to sail close to the *mark* (within a couple of feet or so), the one behind (B) must give A the space she needs to sail to the *mark* in a seamanlike way; and if it is a rounding mark, the space A needs to round or pass the *mark* as needed to sail the course in a seamanlike way as well. And, if A has the right of way, then B must also *keep clear* of her, and A is not "limited" to sailing her *proper course*; i.e., she can swing as wide as she pleases as long as she stays in the *zone*.

Note that rule 18.2(b) does not shift the right of way from the boat *clear astern* to the boat *clear ahead*. If the boat *clear ahead* is the keep-clear boat, she is simply entitled to *mark-room* from the *clear astern* right-of-way boat.

"What happens when the boat ahead is on port tack approaching a downwind finishing line with a boat on starboard tack right behind her, and the port-tack boat will pass through the zone about two lengths from the finishing mark?"

Good question. First of all, the *port-tack* boat (PA) is the keep-clear boat under rule 10 (On Opposite Tacks). This does not change just because she is in the *zone* of the *mark*. Because she reached the *zone clear ahead* of the starboard-tacker (SB), she is entitled to *mark-room*. However, because her *proper course* is to sail straight across the finishing line, and because she is two lengths away from the *mark*, her *proper course* is not to sail close to the *mark*. Therefore, she is not entitled to *room* to sail to the *mark*; only to the space needed to leave the finishing *mark* on the required side (which she has plenty of). PA will need to *keep clear* of SB until she has *finished* and cleared the finishing line and *marks*, which she can easily do by either heading up or bearing away or gybing. And if she fails to *keep clear*, she breaks rule 10 and is not exonerated by rule 43.1(b) (Exoneration).

"What happens if the boat that was clear astern becomes overlapped on the inside of the other boat inside the zone?"

Note that rule 18.2(b) has a "lock-in" provision ("...*shall thereafter give her mark-room*"), and rule 18.2(c)(1) makes it clear that the lock-in provision continues to apply even if the boat *clear astern* later becomes *overlapped*, either on the inside or outside, with the boat that was *clear ahead* at the *zone*.

Rule 18.2(c)(1) says, "*When a boat is required to give* **mark-room** *by rule 18.2(b), she shall continue to do so even if later an* **overlap** *is broken or a new* **overlap** *begins…*". Therefore, if a boat is *clear ahead* when she reaches the *zone*, the boat that is *clear astern* at that moment must continue to give her *mark-room*, even if she *overlaps* her later during her rounding or passing manoeuver.

"So if I'm entitled to mark-room at a leeward mark, can I go head to wind to 'close the door' on a boat trying to sneak inside of me?"

Yes, but you have to be careful! Assuming the boat trying to sneak inside of you owes you *mark-room*, she still must give you that *room*, which is just enough space for you to round the *mark* as needed to *sail the course*. Furthermore, when she becomes *overlapped* inside of you, she must also give you *room* to sail your *proper course* while you two are *overlapped*. Rule 18.2(c)(2) says, "*When a boat is required to give* **mark-room** *by rule 18.2(b), if she becomes* **overlapped** *inside the boat entitled to* **mark-room**, *she shall also give that boat* **room** *to sail her* **proper course** *while they remain* **overlapped**."

If you break rule 16.1 (Changing Course) while taking the *room* or *mark-room* you are entitled to, you are exonerated by rule 43.1(b) (Exoneration). So as long as you don't sail **above** your *proper course*, you can "close the door" even if you break rule 16.1 in the process.

However, when rounding a leeward *mark* to start a beat, once you've sailed up to a close-hauled course (usually your *proper course*), and can sail between the *mark* and the outside boat without breaking a rule, you've been given *mark-room* and rule 18 ceases to apply (see rule 18.1). Therefore, if you choose to sail **above** close-hauled, you are no longer sailing within the *mark-room* you are entitled to, and you are **not** exonerated if you break rule 16.1. So if when you luff above close-hauled, the windward boat cannot *keep clear* of you or she is forced to touch the *mark* because she is stuck between you and the leeward *mark*, you will break rule 16.1. And you get no *room* to tack, so if you sail past head to wind, you risk breaking rule 13 (While Tacking). However, if by sailing up to head to wind you force the *windward* boat to the wrong side of the *mark* without forcing them to foul any other boats, you have not broken rule 16.1 and you have successfully "shut the door."

Let's look at some examples of this rule 16 (Changing Course) exception in action:

- A and B, two *port-tack* boats not *overlapped*, are approaching a leeward *mark* to be left to port. A reaches the *zone clear ahead* of B. As A swings wide to make a "tactical" (swing wide-cut close) rounding, B puts her bow in between A and the *mark*. As A changes course to round the *mark*, B yells that A must give her *room* to *keep clear* under rule 16.1 (Changing Course) and that B can't *keep clear* of A due to the proximity of the *mark* on her port side. B is wrong. Rule 18 applies and B is required to give A *mark-room* under rule 18.2(b) as well as *room* to sail her *proper course* under rule 18.2(c)(2). Therefore, A is free to round the *mark* and if in doing so she fails to give B *room* to *keep clear* of her, she is exonerated by rule 43.1(b) (Exoneration).

- L and W, two *overlapped starboard-tack* boats, are approaching a gybe *mark* to be left to port. They enter the *zone overlapped*. L then bears away to gybe around the *mark* and her transom hits W's *leeward* side with no damage or injury. Again, rule 18 applies and L is entitled to *mark-room*. W is wrong for breaking rules 11 and 18.2(b), and L is exonerated for her breach of rule 16.1. Note that L has broken rule 14 (Avoiding Contact), but she is also exonerated by rule 43.1(c) for her breach of rule 14 unless the contact causes damage or injury (see the discussion of rule 14 in chapter 7).

- PL and SW, two opposite *tack* close-hauled boats, are approaching a windward *mark* to be left to port. PL safely lee-bows SW (i.e., tacks to leeward of SW) outside the *zone*. As the boats enter the *zone* PL realizes she will not make the *mark* without luffing up to head to wind. When near the *mark*, PL luffs and collides with SW with no damage or injury. As PL was changing course to round the *mark*, SW breaks rules 11 and 18.2(b) as above, and PL is exonerated for her breach of rule 16.1.

In the same scenario, SW does *keep clear* of PL's luff, but as PL begins to pass the *mark* she bears away to round the *mark* and her transom swings up and hits the *leeward* side of SW, again with no damage or injury. Same answer as above. SW must *keep clear* (as well as give *mark-room*), PL is rounding the *mark*, and therefore PL is exonerated for her breach of rule 16.1.

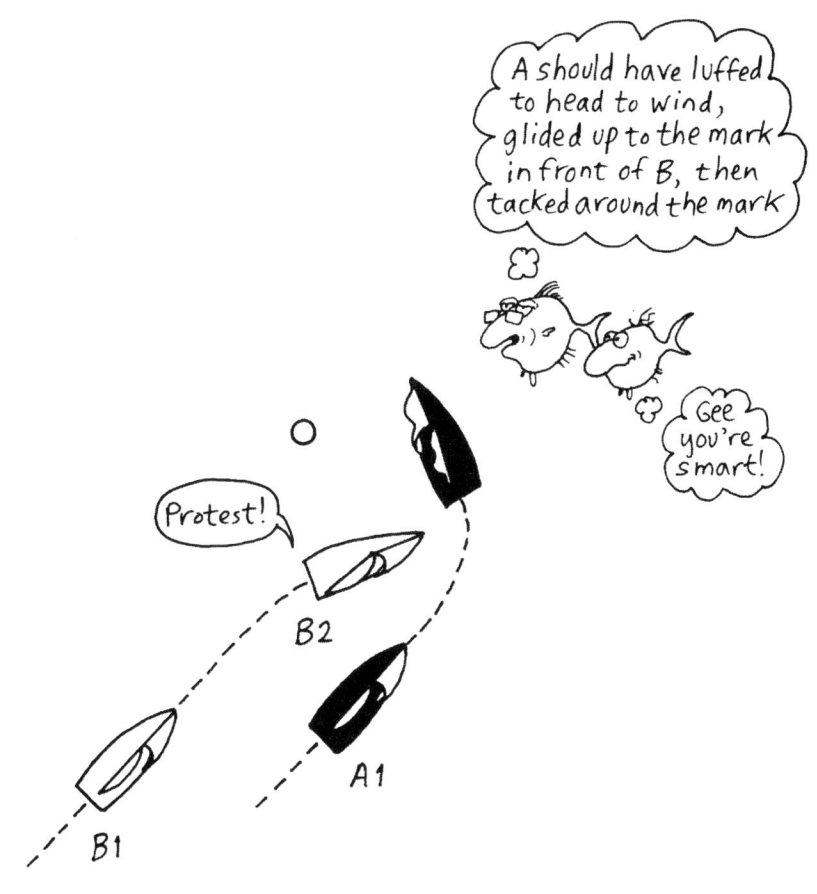

PART 2, SECTION C: WHEN BOATS MEET — RULE 18: MARK-ROOM **197**

"What if the boat ahead wants to tack around the mark?"

She must be very careful! A boat that is *clear ahead* when she reaches the *zone* that tacks around a *mark* gets no protection from rule 18.2(b) what-so-ever. In fact, rule 18.2(d) says, *"Rules 18.2(b) and (c) cease to apply if the boat entitled to **mark-room** passes head to wind...".* In other words, the moment the boat ahead passes head to wind, rule 18.2(b) instantly shuts off, and the boat is subject to the rules in Sections A and B thereafter, beginning with rule 13 (While Tacking). This can happen at a windward *mark* when the boats need to tack to round the *mark*; or at or just after a leeward *mark* when the boats are beginning the beat.

Notice also that at the windward *mark* the boat *clear astern* can sail above close-hauled to make it more difficult for the boat *clear ahead* to tack. Let's say you (A) and another boat (B) are sailing close-hauled on *port tack* into the windward *mark* to be left to port, not *overlapped*. You thought you were allowed to just tack around the *mark*. After you had passed head to wind but before you were close-hauled, B had to bear away to miss your transom. You have fouled B by breaking rule 13 (While Tacking). Notice, though, that you can luff up to head to wind just prior to tacking around the *mark*, which will make it difficult for a boat close astern to prevent you from tacking. Tactically speaking for a moment, in this situation your best move is to luff to head to wind, glide up to the *mark*, then tack around making it difficult for a boat close astern to prevent you from tacking.

Case 81 discusses the situation where two *starboard-tack* boats, A and B, are approaching a windward *mark* to be left to starboard. A enters the *zone clear ahead* and to leeward of B, then proceeds to tack to *port tack* in order to round the *mark*. B (still on *starboard tack*), collides with A (now on *port tack*), causing no damage or injury. The Appeals Committee said, "…from the time A reached the zone until she passed head to wind, rule 18.2(b)'s second sentence applied, requiring B to give A mark-room. B fulfilled [this obligation]. Shortly before position 5, when A passed head to wind, rule 18.2(b) ceased to apply (see rule 18.2(d)). At that time B acquired right of way and A became obligated to keep clear of B, first by rule 13 and later, after A was on a close-hauled course, by rule 10. Rule 15 did not apply because B acquired right of way as a result of A's tack."

"What if a boat that is entitled to mark-room in the zone sails out of the zone before rounding the mark; when she re-enters, does she retain her original rights or is it a whole new ball game?"

It's a whole new ball game. Rule 18.2(d) says, "*Rules 18.2(b) and (c) cease to apply if the boat entitled to* **mark-room**…*leaves the* **zone**." Note, it doesn't matter **why** she left the *zone*. She could have been giving *mark-room* to several boats inside her, or she could have been carried out by the current, or she may have lost control of her boat. In every case where she leaves the *zone*, she does not carry back in any rights or obligations she had before she left; it is a whole new situation.

"Now I understand when I can and cannot be entitled to 'room,' but what if an outside boat leaves enough space between her and the mark; is it a foul to sneak in there?"

Absolutely not, as long as you don't hit the *mark* or the outside boat or force the outside boat to change course to avoid hitting you. Case 63 is clear: "… when a boat voluntarily or unintentionally makes space between herself and a mark available to another that has no right to such space, the other boat may take advantage, at her own risk, of the space." (See Appeal 5.)

9

Part 2, Section C
When Boats Meet at Marks and Obstructions— Tacking and Gybing, and Other Exceptions to Rule 18

Rule 18 (Mark-Room) also has rules for when boats tack inside the zone of a windward mark (rule 18.3, Passing Head to Wind in the Zone) or have to gybe inside the zone of a leeward mark in order to sail their proper course (rule 18.4, Gybing). It also contains some exceptions, such as when boats are approaching a starting mark to start (preamble to Section C) or when a boat leaving a mark encounters a boat approaching a mark (rule 18.1(c)). I will cover all these special rules in this chapter.

WHEN ONE OF TWO OPPOSITE TACK BOATS TACKS WITHIN THE ZONE AT THE WINDWARD MARK

RULE 18.3 — PASSING HEAD TO WIND IN THE ZONE

If a boat in the *zone* of a *mark* to be left to port passes head to wind from *port* to *starboard tack* and is then *fetching* the *mark*, she shall not cause a boat that has been on *starboard tack* since entering the *zone* to sail above close-hauled to avoid contact and she shall give *mark-room* if that boat becomes *overlapped* inside her. When this rule applies between boats, rule 18.2 does not apply between them.

The concept in this rule is to improve the racing by trying to minimize the frustrating and sometimes dangerous congestion that can occur at crowded windward *mark* roundings when the *mark* is to be left to port. Problems are often caused by *port-tack* boats approaching on or near the port layline and trying to squeeze their boats in between the *starboard-tack* boats on the starboard layline and the *mark*. Too often, these *port-tackers* shoot right back up after tacking to try to make it around the *mark*, or they get hung up on the *mark* itself, or worse: they fall back onto *port tack* directly in front of the approaching *starboard-tackers*! Too many otherwise excellent close races have been ruined by these actions; and with the popular trend toward shorter courses and more races, the rule writers put this rule in the book to improve the game.

In a nutshell, rule 18.3 works like this (we'll get into the technicalities below):

If you are approaching a port-hand windward *mark* on *port tack* (which can include the port end of a windward finishing line) and tack in the *zone* near a *starboard-tack* boat (S) that has been on *starboard tack* since entering the *zone*, you must do it in a place that allows S to round or pass the *mark* without ever having to sail above close-hauled to avoid contact with you or another boat.

Furthermore, if S gets an inside *overlap* on you at **any time** during her rounding or passing maneuver, you must give her *mark-room* (*room* to round or pass the *mark*). And if you are unable to do so, tough luck on you. Rule 18.2(f) (about not having to give *mark-room* if unable to do so) does not apply because none of rule 18.2 (Giving Mark-Room) applies when rule 18.3 applies. Furthermore if S breaks rules 15 (Acquiring Right of Way) or 16 (Changing Course) while taking *mark-room*, she is exonerated under rule 43 (Exoneration). In other words, you are more or less a "sitting duck" for S!

The bottom line is: if you are going to come into a crowded windward *mark* on *port tack*, it is better to cross nearby *starboard tackers* if you can, and tack safely to *windward* of them. And if you can't cross them, then it is better to duck them than to try to tack close to leeward of them (lee-bow them). And to be safe, approach the *mark* four or more boat lengths below the *port-tack* layline so your tack to *starboard tack* is outside the *zone*.

"Okay, I'm ready to have you lead me through this rule!"

OK, let's consider just two boats to begin with. First, rule 18.3 only applies at a windward *mark* to be left to port (which can include a finishing *mark*).

PART 2, SECTION C, RULE 18: TACKING, GYBING & OTHER EXCEPTIONS **203**

Second, the two boats must have been on opposite *tacks*, and the *port-tack* boat (P) must have tacked to *starboard tack*, passing head to wind in the *zone*. Third, P must be *fetching* the *mark* after her tack. "*Fetching*" means a boat can pass to windward of a *mark* leaving it on the required side without sailing past head to wind to do so (see the definition *Fetching*). Finally, the *starboard-tack* boat (S) must have been on *starboard tack* since she entered the *zone*; if she had entered the *zone* on *port tack* and then tacked to *starboard tack*, rule 18.3 does not apply. And when rule 18.3 applies, rule 18.2 (Giving Mark-Room) does not apply (see rule 18.3).

Note that when P and S are approaching the mark, rule 18 doesn't apply at all because the boats are on opposite *tacks* on a beat to windward (rule 18.1(a), When Rule 18 Applies). Furthermore, if P passes head to wind **outside** the *zone* and then completes her tack inside the *zone*, rule 18.3 does **not** apply. However, rule 13 (While Tacking) applies, and if S needs to avoid P before she completes her tack (gets to a close-hauled course), P has broken rule 13. It can be argued that it is difficult to know exactly where the *zone* is, but that is the case when applying the *zone* in any *mark* rounding or passing situation. Sailors approaching port-hand windward *marks* on *port tack* will be well advised to be conservative when the *mark* area is congested and to complete their tacks clearly outside the *zone*.

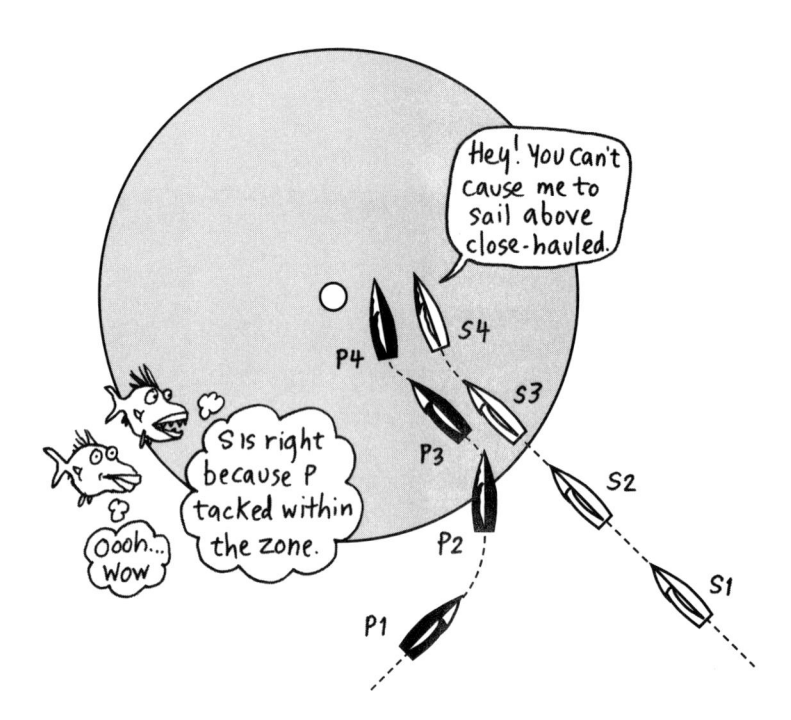

> *"I thought that if a boat tacked inside the zone, she had no rights; and if she caused me to change course at all, she broke rule 18.3."*

No! If P gets to a close-hauled course before you have to take any avoiding action, then she has complied with rule 13 (While Tacking) and **she** is the right-of-way boat. She breaks rule 18.3 only if she causes you to sail above a **close-hauled** course to avoid her during or after her tack. If you are overstood (reaching in above the starboard-tack layline) for instance, and avoid contact by luffing up to a close-hauled course, she has not broken rule 18.3.

LET'S LOOK AT SOME SCENARIOS that will involve rule 18.3.

P approaches S at a port-hand windward *mark*, and passes head to wind in the *zone* just to *leeward* of S:

Let's say that when P gets to close-hauled, the boats are now one length from the *mark*. As P (now the *leeward*/inside boat) approaches the *mark*, she realizes she won't make the *mark* unless she luffs above close-hauled. She does so, thereby clearing the *mark*, but as a result of her luff, S sails above close-hauled to avoid hitting her. P has broken rule 18.3. Note that even though she's an inside/right-of-way boat, P is not entitled to *mark-room* under rule 18.2(a) (Giving Mark-Room) because rule 18.3 specifically states that rule 18.2 does not apply. The same would be true if S sailed above close-hauled to avoid P's transom as P bore off around the *mark*.

Had S been able to round or pass the *mark* without having to sail above close-hauled to avoid P, then P would not have broken rule 18.3, and S would simply be required to *keep clear* under rule 11 (On the Same Tack, Overlapped). Note that when P bears away (changes course) to round the *mark*, she is not exonerated if she breaks rule 16.1 because rule 18.2 does not apply, meaning she is not sailing within *mark-room* at that time and she is not "protected" by rule 43.1(b) (Exoneration) (see the discussion of rule 43 in chapter 8).

P passes head to wind in the *zone* of a port-hand windward *mark* directly ahead of S; once P is close-hauled, S must change course either up or down to avoid colliding with her:

First of all, once P gets to a close-hauled course *clear ahead* of S, S is required to *keep clear* of her under rule 12 (On the Same Tack, Not Overlapped). If, despite her best efforts to avoid P beginning the moment P is close-hauled, S is unable to do so and she hits P on the transom, P has "tacked too close" and broken rule 15 (Acquiring Right of Way), and S is exonerated by rule 43.1(b) (Exoneration). It is also likely that a protest committee would decide that S was unable to avoid the contact, and therefore did not break rule 14 (Avoiding Contact). If S does have *room* to *keep clear* of P but hits P on the transom anyway, then S is not exonerated for breaking rule 12, and also breaks rule 14.

It could happen that when P gets to a close-hauled course, S can avoid hitting P but is faced with the choice of *overlapping* P to leeward and ending up in a bad position or not being able to get around the *mark* at all, or sailing above close-hauled to avoid hitting P. In my opinion, choosing to sail above close-hauled to avoid contact with P is S's only reasonable option, and therefore P has "caused" S to sail above close-hauled to avoid hitting her, breaking rule 18.3.

However, if P tacks far enough to windward of the layline such that S can clearly *overlap* P to leeward and round or pass the *mark*, then P has not "caused" S to sail above close-hauled to avoid contact with her, because it would be reasonable to expect S to bear away and round or pass the *mark*.

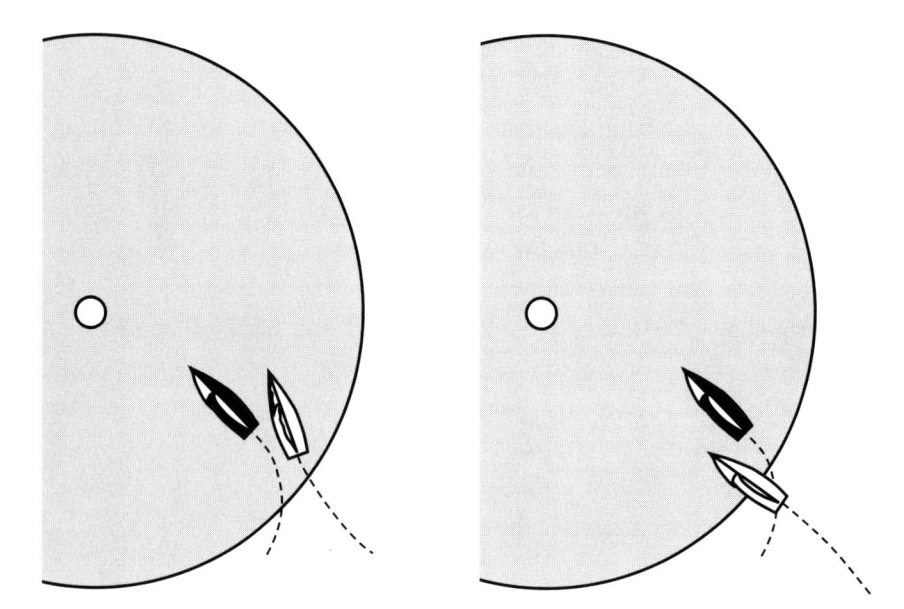

When a port-tack boat (P) passes head to wind in the zone and a starboard-tack boat (S) that has been on starboard since entering the zone approaches her, P breaks rule 18.3 if S has to sail above close-hauled to avoid hitting her, and P must give S mark-room if S becomes overlapped inside of her.

However, if S chooses to sail above close-hauled and protest, it will be the **protest committee** who decides whether S was "caused" by P to sail above close-hauled, and my guess is they will give S the benefit of the doubt. So *port-tack* boats will want to be very conservative with where they choose to tack in the *zone* near opposite-*tack* boats!

P passes head to wind in the *zone* of a port-hand windward *mark* and S sails in to *leeward* or her telling P to *keep clear* and to give her *mark-room*:

Note that when S becomes *overlapped* with P she instantly gets the right of way under rule 11 (On the Same Tack, Overlapped), so rule 15 (Acquiring Right of Way) requires her to initially give P *room* to *keep clear*. But under rule 18.3 she is entitled to *mark-room*. Therefore S is exonerated (freed from penalty) if she happens to break rule 15 (see rule 43.1(b), Exoneration). Note also that if S needs to luff slightly to get up and around the *mark*, or bear away to round the mark, that too is part of her rounding or passing maneuver, and if she happens to break rule 16.1 (Changing Course), she is also exonerated by rule 43.1(b). And if P is unable to give S *mark-room*, tough luck on P. Rule 18.2(f) (about

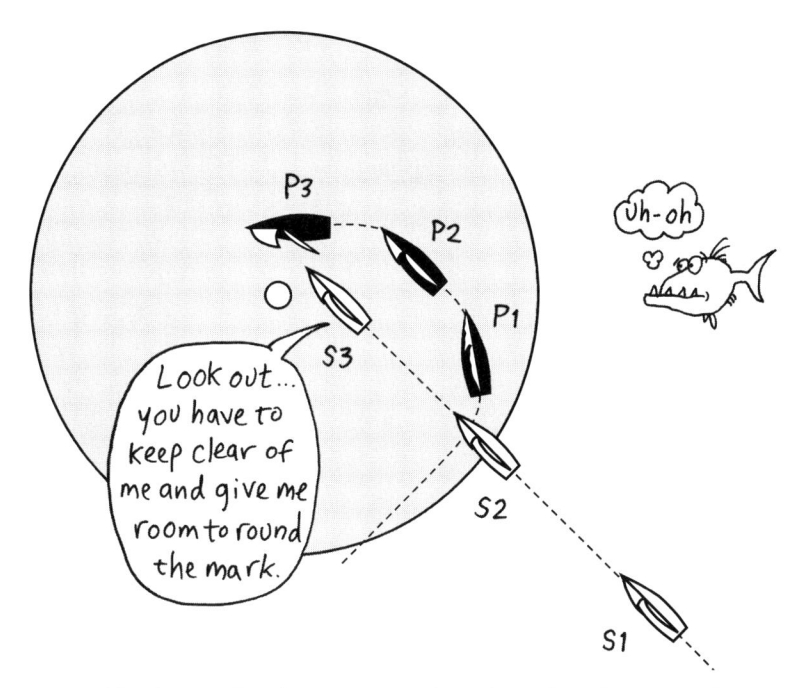

PART 2, SECTION C, RULE 18: TACKING, GYBING & OTHER EXCEPTIONS **207**

Because P passed head to wind in the zone, P must keep clear of S and give S mark-room if S gets an inside overlap. Furthermore, S can change course in either direction necessary to round the mark, and if she breaks rules 15 or 16, she is exonerated (see rule 43.1(b)).

not having to give *mark-room* if unable to do so) does not apply because none of rule 18.2 applies when rule 18.3 applies. The only "limit" on S is that, because she became *overlapped* from *clear astern*, she cannot sail above her *proper course* under rule 17 (On the Same Tack; Proper Course), which means she must bear away to follow her *proper course* around the windward *mark*. And if the boats collide, remember that both boats are subject to rule 14 (Avoiding Contact). Note, once P has tacked within the *zone*, then for the duration of her rounding or passing maneuver, which could take several seconds, a boat *clear astern* (S) is allowed to obtain a *leeward*/inside *overlap* on P, and P must *keep clear* of her and give her *mark-room* (i.e., *room* to round or pass the *mark*)!

P passes head to wind in the *zone* of a port-hand windward *mark* directly ahead of S, and S is unable to round or pass the *mark* due to the disturbed air off of P:

If P tacks sufficiently far ahead of S such that S is not required to take any action to avoid hitting P after the tack and remains *clear astern* of her, and then S fails to make the *mark* due to the disturbed air and water caused by P, P has not broken rule 18.3.

Two *overlapped* *port-tack* boats (PL to *leeward* and PW to *windward*) are approaching a port-hand windward *mark* with S approaching as well, and both PL and PW pass head to wind in the *zone*:

When PL and PW complete their tacks, S is *overlapped* to *windward* of PL. PW, now on the inside of the three boats, luffs above close-hauled to make the *mark*. PL responds and is able to *keep clear*, but her luff causes S to also luff above close-hauled to avoid contact with PL. Both PW and PL have broken rule 18.3 because both of them passed head to wind in the *zone* and both caused S to sail above close-hauled to avoid contact. PL directly caused S to sail above close-hauled; and it was PW's luff that caused PL to luff that caused S to sail above close-hauled to avoid contact with PL.

When PW changed course, rule 16.1 (Changing Course) required her to give PL *room* to *keep clear*. "Room" includes the space needed to not break any rules in Part 2 (see definition *Room*). In this case, when she luffed, PW compelled PL to break rule 18.3, so PL is exonerated by rule 43.1(b) (Exoneration).

Note that between PW and PL, PW was entitled to *mark-room* from PL under rule 18.2(a) (Giving Mark-Room); and though PW broke rule 16.1 (Changing Course) by changing course and forcing PL to break rule 18.3, PW is exonerated for breaking rule 16.1 by rule 43.1(b) (Exoneration) because she was sailing within the *mark-room* to which she was entitled. PW would remain penalized, however, for breaking rule 18.3. PL on the other hand failed to give PW *room* to sail to and around the *mark* without breaking rule 18.3. Therefore PL broke rule 18.2(a).

"It sounds like this rule eliminates the port-tack layline and a port-tacker's tactic of lee-bowing a starboard tacker right at the mark!"

I don't think the rule dramatically changes the way the top of the beat is sailed. If you are doing well in the race, the windward *mark* rounding won't be that congested, and you will probably approach it as close to the layline as you want. If you are farther down in the pack (out of the top 10, let's say), coming in right on the *port-tack* layline isn't a great look anyway. For at least some of the time, you are sailing more slowly in the disturbed air and water of the boats going downwind, or trying to pick your way through the *starboard-tack* boats as they turn and go downwind. So for tactical reasons, as well as because of rule

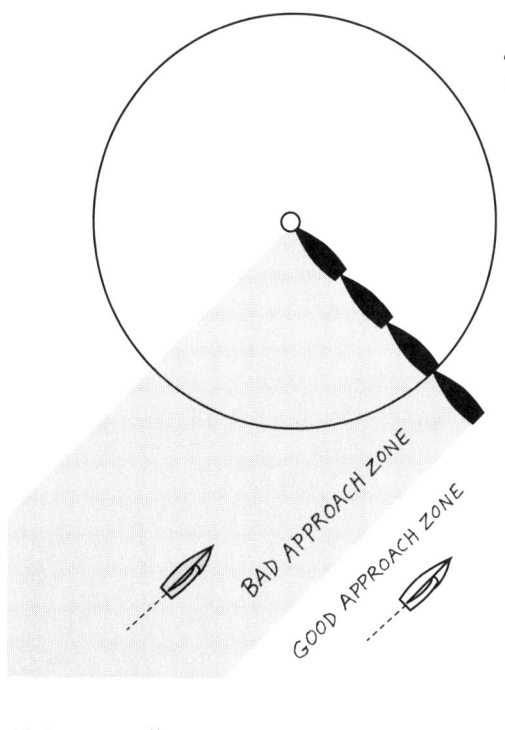

PART 2, SECTION C, RULE 18: TACKING, GYBING & OTHER EXCEPTIONS **209**

Rule 18.3 encourages port-tackers approaching a congested port-hand windward mark to approach about four hull lengths below the port-tack layline so that they can pass head to wind during their tack when clearly outside the zone.

18.3, you will want to approach a port-hand windward *mark* at least four lengths below the *port-tack* layline so you can tack outside of the *zone*.

To me, the most significant effect of this rule is on the decision the *port-tacker* makes on whether to duck the nearby *starboard-tackers* and tack safely up to windward of them or to lee-bow them (i.e., tack just to leeward of them) and hope to make the *mark* from there. My personal experience (and I've been there myself!) is that too often sailors choose the (dare I say) "greedier" choice (lee-bowing), and end up not only not making the *mark*, but causing a real mess for others at the *mark*. I think the net effect of rule 18.3 is that fewer *port-tackers* tack right at the *mark* in crowds, which is a welcome situation for all.

WHEN AN INSIDE RIGHT-OF-WAY BOAT NEEDS TO GYBE TO SAIL HER PROPER COURSE AROUND A MARK

RULE 18.4 — GYBING

When an inside *overlapped* right-of-way boat must gybe at a *mark* to sail her *proper course,* until she gybes she shall sail no farther from the *mark* than needed to sail that course. Rule 18.4 does not apply at a gate *mark*.

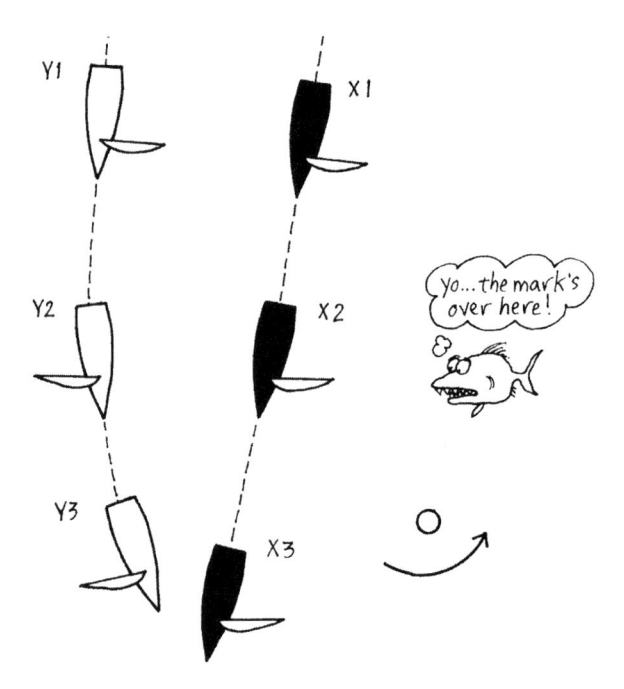

When boats are sailing below ninety degrees to the true wind or when rule 18 applies, the term "overlap" applies to boats on opposite tacks. Therefore, X and Y are "overlapped" at the mark. When the inside boat has the right of way and when she must gybe to sail her proper course, rule 18.4 requires her not to sail any farther from the mark than needed to sail her proper course until she gybes. By sailing past where her proper course was to gybe, X breaks rule 18.4.

First of all, rule 18.4 puts a "limit" on inside right-of-way boats; i.e., *leeward* boats and *starboard-tack* boats. Essentially, that "limit" is that whenever their *proper course* is to gybe at a *mark*, they must do so. Actually, the instruction in the rule is that up until she actually gybes, the right-of-way boat "shall sail no farther from the mark than needed to sail [her *proper course*]." This means that not only does she have to gybe when it is her *proper course* to do so, but she can't luff (turn) away from the *mark* prior to gybing if that takes her farther from it than necessary to sail her *proper course*. This applies even when the outside/*windward* boat initially obtained the *overlap* to *windward* such that L would otherwise have the right to sail above her *proper course*. (See Case 75.)

Note that rule 18.4 has a clear "shut off" time built in. The rule no longer applies once the inside boat gybes (i.e., the boom crosses the centerline). After that, the inside boat is not limited by rule 18.4, though she will continue to be entitled to *mark-room* under rule 18.2(b) (Giving Mark-Room).

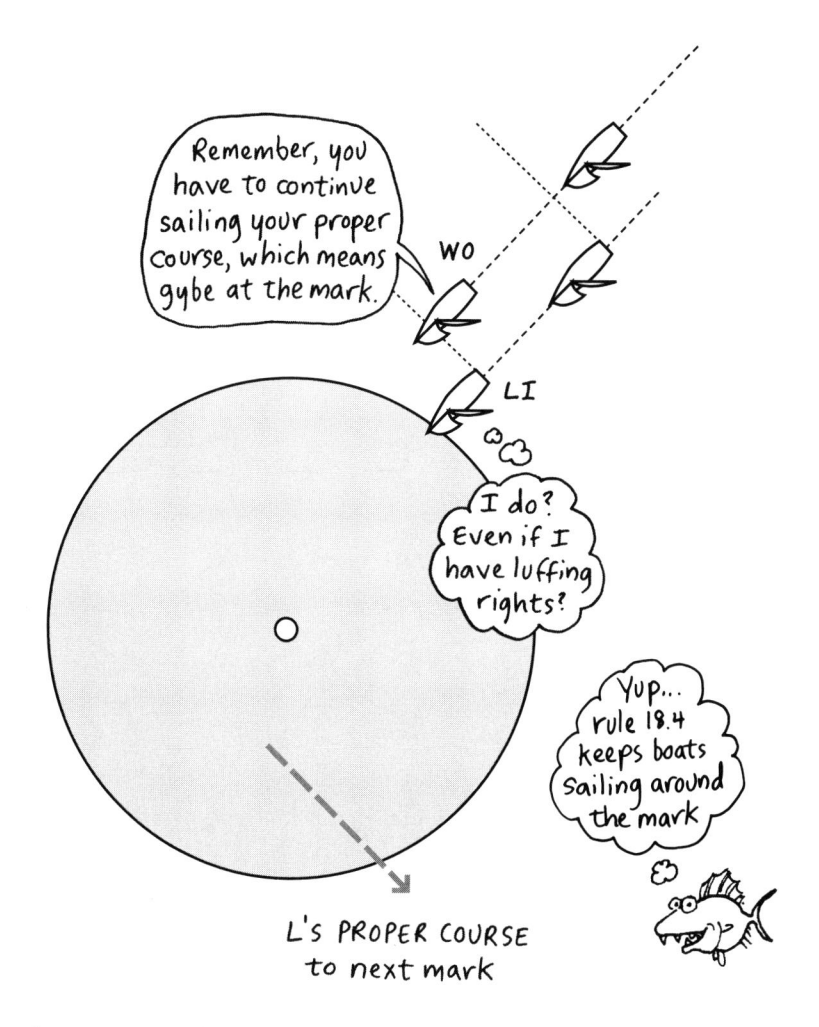

PART 2, SECTION C, RULE 18: TACKING, GYBING & OTHER EXCEPTIONS 211

Remember, you have to continue sailing your proper course, which means gybe at the mark.

WO

LI

I do? Even if I have luffing rights?

Yup... rule 18.4 keeps boats sailing around the mark

L's PROPER COURSE to next mark

The situation will commonly arise at gybe *marks* and leeward *marks* to be left to port when the *leeward/inside* boat or the *starboard-tack/inside* boat will be required to gybe in order to round the *mark*. Notice that a boat's *proper course* is the course she thinks will get her to the finishing line as quickly as possible. Therefore, especially if there are boats just ahead of her, she can certainly swing wide to set up for a "tactical" cut-close rounding.

Note that rule 18.4 applies any time boats are *overlapped*. Therefore, if the boats are not *overlapped* when the boat ahead enters the *zone*, but the boat astern obtains an outside *overlap* later, rule 18.4 applies. Similarly, if the boats are *overlapped* as the boats enter the *zone* and then the *overlap* is broken at any time during the rounding, rule 18.4 does not apply.

"Does this apply at a gate mark as well?"

Good question! Rule 18.4 does **not** apply at a gate *mark*. A "gate" is two *marks* set close to each other, typically at the end of the downwind leg. The boats are required to sail between the *marks*, and then can choose to exit the gate around one *mark* or the other (see rule 28.1, Sailing the Race, and the definition *Sail the Course (c)*).

When inside right-of-way boats are sailing to round a gate *mark*, rule 18.4 does not apply, meaning an inside right-of-way boat is not "limited" to sailing no farther from the *mark* than her *proper course*. She can sail as far as she pleases from the *mark*, force a *windward*/outside boat outside the *zone* if she pleases, then gybe and round the *mark*. Outside keep-clear boats are well advised to not remain *overlapped* with inside right-of-way boats when approaching gate *marks*.

However, if the inside right-of-way boat became *overlapped* from *clear astern*, then she is subject to rule 17 (On the Same Tack; Proper Course), and she is not allowed to sail above her *proper course* for as long as the boats remain *overlapped*. Therefore, at a gate *mark*, even though rule 18.4 does not apply, the inside boat is required by rule 17 to gybe at the *mark* if that is her *proper course* at the time. If she goes farther from the *mark*, she is sailing **above** her *proper course* and is breaking rule 17. Note that the outside keep-clear boat must still *keep clear* and protest.

EXCEPTIONS TO RULE 18

"I notice there seem to be some exceptions to rule 18 listed in the preamble to Section C and in rule 18.1; could you go over those please?"

You bet. There are very narrow situations when boats are rounding or passing *marks* when rule 18 does not apply at all. When rule 18 does not apply at a *mark*, the rules in Section A (Right of Way) and Section B (General Limitations) apply.

PREAMBLE TO SECTION C

Section C rules do not apply at a starting *mark* surrounded by navigable water or at its anchor line from the time boats are approaching them to *start* until they have passed them.

The preamble makes it clear that none of the rules in Section C (18, 19 and 20) apply when boats are approaching a starting *mark* that is surrounded by navigable water or its anchor line to *start* until they have passed them.

"So does this having something to do with barging?"

Yes. I will explain what "barging" is. The preamble to Section C "shuts off" the "mark-room" rules at the starting *marks*. The reason is that it would lead to chaotic starts if *windward*/inside boats were entitled to *room* to pass between the committee boat and *leeward*/outside boats at the start (it's often chaotic enough without them having that right!). When two boats are about to *start* and a *windward* boat tries to sail in between a *leeward* boat and a starting *mark* (often a race committee boat), and hits the *leeward* boat or causes her to bear away to avoid being hit, we say the *windward* boat is "Barging." In fact, she is breaking rule 11 (On the Same Tack, Overlapped). (For more discussion on "barging" see the discussion in Chapter 7 entitled "Section A and B Rules in Action.")

To accurately apply this rule, be sure you understand that an object large enough to satisfy the definition *Obstruction* is **always** an *obstruction*, even when it is used as a *mark*; i.e., it does not cease being one when it becomes the other. Therefore a race committee boat used as one end of the starting line is **both** a starting *mark* and an *obstruction* at the same time.

Now, having said that the preamble "shuts off" rule 18 (Mark-Room) and rule 19 (Room to Pass an Obstruction), there are in fact two narrow situations when, for reasons of safety, the rules **do** entitle a *windward*/inside boat to *room* at a starting *mark* from a *leeward*/outside boat.

Let's look at those first.

1) **At a starting *mark* not surrounded by navigable water:**
   Though this situation is not common, it will arise when one end of the starting line is the end of a long dock or breakwater, or is a bell buoy that marks some shallow rocks or sandbars. "Not surrounded by navigable water" means there isn't enough water for the inside boat to sail around the *mark* without running aground or hitting a dock or other object. At such a *mark*, an inside *overlapped* boat is entitled to *mark-room* under rule 18.2 (Giving Mark-Room) from an outside boat. And if the starting *mark* is a "continuing" *obstruction* (such as the end of a long dock), then the inside boat is entitled to *room* under rule 19.2(b) if there was space to pass between the outside boat and the *obstruction* in safety at the moment the *overlap* began (see rules 18.1(d) and 19.2(c)).

2) **At a starting *mark* that is also an *obstruction* when the boats are not approaching it to *start*:**
   Again, when the starting *mark* is large enough to be an *obstruction* (such as most committee boats), rule 19 (Room to Pass an Obstruction) applies **before** boats are "approaching it to *start*." Therefore, an inside *overlapped* boat is entitled to *room* at such a *mark* under rule 19.2(b) (Giving Room at an Obstruction) from an outside boat, provided the outside boat has been able to give the *room* since the *overlap* began. If the starting *mark* is a "continuing" *obstruction*, then the inside boat is entitled to *room* if there was space to pass between the outside boat and the *obstruction* in safety at the moment the *overlap* began (rule 19.2(c)). This is for safety purposes while boats are sailing past the *marks* well before *starting*.

So, if say at three minutes before the starting signal you were sailing along to leeward of W and were about to sail to leeward of the race committee boat, and for whatever reason W wanted to pass to leeward of it also, you would have to give her *room* to do so under rule 19.2(b), unless you were unable to do so from the moment the *overlap* began. Now to play this out, because boats aren't required to pass the starting *mark* on its "required" side yet (rule 28.1, Sailing the Race, and the definition *Sail the Course*), you can choose to pass it

PART 2, SECTION C, RULE 18: TACKING, GYBING & OTHER EXCEPTIONS **215**

> STARTING LINE
>
> "No I'm not... This starting mark isn't surrounded by navigable water, so you must let me in!"
>
> "Don't go in there... You're BARGING!!"

on either side (see rule 19.2(a)). You, as the *leeward* boat, have the right to sail where you please provided you make no sudden, fast course changes (rule 11, On the Same Tack, Overlapped and rule 16.1, Changing Course); therefore, you can choose to luff and pass to windward of the committee boat. If, however, you choose to pass to leeward of the committee boat and fail to provide enough *room* for W to do likewise if she wishes to, you have broken rule 19.2(b).

Note that when you break a *rule*, even before the starting signal, you must take your Two-Turns Penalty immediately; you do not have to wait until the starting signal to do so (rule 44, Penalties at the Time of an Incident). If W happens to hit the *mark* (i.e., break rule 31, Touching a Mark) because you didn't give her enough *room*, she is exonerated by rule 43.1(b) (Exoneration).

"When is a boat considered to be 'approaching a starting mark to start'?"

Though this question has never been discussed in a case or appeal, I would develop my opinion as follows. What is the purpose of the rule? Clearly it is preventing the situation where *windward*/inside (WI) boats can reach in and demand *room* at starting *marks* from *leeward*/outside boats (LO) that are trying to *start* there. And "when approaching the starting *mark* to *start*" is establishing the period of time during which these *windward*/inside boats know that they are not entitled to any *room*. Before LO is "approaching the starting *mark* to *start*," WI is entitled to *room* at the *mark* (provided it is also an *obstruction*); and the rules are consistently clear in providing predictable and specific times when a boat's rights change. To me, this is no exception. When LO is clearly on her final approach toward the line with the intention of *starting*, i.e., crossing the line after the gun, it will be obvious to WI and she will know to *keep clear*. Furthermore, a boat that is "approaching the starting *mark* to *start*" and is close enough to the starting *mark* to shut out a *windward* boat will clearly be *starting* in close proximity distance-wise to the starting *mark*.

Therefore, in my opinion, a boat that in 15 knots of breeze goes reaching full-speed by the committee boat with one-and-a-half minutes to go before the starting signal, and ends up *starting* halfway down the starting line, was in no way "approaching the starting *mark* to *start*" at the moment she went by the starting *mark*. But a boat that is passing the starting *mark* with ten seconds to go certainly is on her final approach to *start* very near to the starting *mark*. In addition, I feel that a boat that in light air sits nearly wayless behind the race committee boat may be approaching the line to *start* at one minute to go, and it will be more obvious and predictable that she plans to *start* near the *mark*, and the *windward*/inside boats can see this and *keep clear* accordingly.

This is a distinction that in general has caused very few problems, and in general has been very liberally interpreted in the *leeward*/outside boat's favor. But until it is officially interpreted, the safe move on LO's part would be to allow WI *room* up to one minute before the starting signal; and the safe move for WI would be not to try to force *room* with much less than two minutes to go. Both boats have the option to protest, and the protest committee can then decide whether LO was "approaching the starting *mark* to *start*" in the particular circumstances.

PART 2, SECTION C, RULE 18: TACKING, GYBING & OTHER EXCEPTIONS   217

"OK, any other exceptions?"

Yes, a couple more. They are listed in rule 18.1 (When Rule 18 Applies).

RULE 18.1 — WHEN RULE 18 APPLIES

Rule 18 applies between boats when they are required to leave a *mark* on the same side and at least one of them is in the *zone*. However, it does not apply

(a) **between boats on opposite *tacks* on a beat to windward,**
(b) **between boats on opposite *tacks* when the *proper course* at the *mark* for one but not both of them is to tack,**
(c) **between a boat approaching a *mark* and one leaving it, or**
(d) **if the *mark* is a continuing *obstruction*, in which case rule 19 applies.**

"Does rule 18.1(a) mean that 'mark-room' doesn't apply at the windward mark?"

No; rule 18.1(a) means that if two boats are coming into a windward *mark* on **opposite** *tacks* (including a finishing *mark* when the finish is at the end of a beat), rule 18 (Mark-Room) doesn't apply. But if the boats are coming into a windward *mark* on the same *tack*, then rule 18 applies just like at any other *mark*.

Case 132 says in effect that "two boats on opposite tacks are considered to be 'on a beat to windward' (1) when the proper course for each of them is close-hauled or above, or (2) when one or both of them have overstood the close-hauled layline to the mark and are sailing below close-hauled."

Picture a windward *mark* to be left to port or the left end of an upwind finishing line, looking upwind. It would be chaos if suddenly a *port-tack* boat could come in and call for *mark-room* from a *starboard-tack* boat while still on *port tack*. While the boats are on opposite *tacks*, rule 10 (*port/starboard*) applies; and if the *port-tack* boat (PI) tacks to *leeward* of the *starboard-tack* boat (SO) within the *zone*, she is subject to rule 13 (While Tacking) and rule 18.3 (Passing Head to Wind in the Zone).

Notice that the exception in rule 18.1(a) applies only when opposite-*tack* boats are approaching a *mark* on a beat to windward. The reasoning is that at all the other *marks* (offwind *marks*), even though the boats may be on opposite *tacks*, they are going in more or less the same direction, or at least generally converging at much smaller angles. Therefore, at leeward *marks*, inside/*port*-

tack boats **are** entitled to *room* under rule 18.2 (Giving Mark-Room) from outside/*starboard-tack* boats.

"What does rule 18.1(b) refer to?"

This is a bit of a "loophole closer." It covers situations that rarely arise, but can. For instance, on a windward leg the wind shifts 60 degrees to the right. Boats that were near the starboard-tack layline are now reaching on the leg. They are no longer "beating" to windward or "on a beat to windward." However, the boats on the left are beating up to the *mark*, so they are still "on a beat to windward." When a *port-tack* boat (P) from the left meets a *starboard-tack* boat (S) from the right at the *mark*, the exception in 18.1(a) doesn't apply because **both** boats are not "on a beat to windward." But because P's *proper course* is to tack at the *mark*, and because S does not have to tack, the exception in rule 18.1(b) applies, meaning that rule 18 does not apply, P is not entitled to *mark-room*, and she needs to *keep clear* of S under rule 10 (Opposite Tacks).

The same is true when two boats are sailing to a gybe *mark* and a boat finds herself below the *mark* (due to current or a windshift or strong wind carrying her lower than she wanted to be), and she has to tack to get up to the gybe *mark*. Now she will be on the opposite *tack* from boats approaching the *mark*, and because she will have to tack to sail her *proper course* around the *mark*, she is not entitled to *mark-room*.

"Can you explain what the terms "approaching" and "leaving" mean in rule 18.1(c)?"

Sure. The rule writers wanted to make it clear that rule 18 does not apply to boats that aren't rounding the *mark* at essentially the same time. The rule clarifies that if one boat is just completing her rounding maneuver and is "leaving" the *mark* and she meets a boat that is just "approaching" the *mark* to begin her rounding maneuver, neither boat needs to give each other *mark-room*. The rules in Section A and B apply, including rule 16 (Changing Course) which requires a right-of-way boat to give the keep-clear boat *room* to *keep clear* when she changes course. This commonly comes up at port-hand windward *mark* roundings when the boat rounding the *mark* will be on *starboard-tack*. She must watch for nearby *port-tackers* when she bears away around the *mark*. Note that the exoneration from breaking rule 16 in rule 43.1(b) (Exoneration) does not apply, because rule 18 does not apply due to the exception in rule 18.1(c). (See Case 60.)

Finally, the exception in rule 18.1(d) clarifies that if the *mark* is a "continuing *obstruction,*" such as an island while the boats are passing it on a required side, rule 18 does not apply and rule 19 (Room to Pass an Obstruction) applies. This is primarily because it is an undesirable situation to require a boat that was astern or *overlapped* on the outside when first arriving at the island or long *obstruction* to continue to give the other boat(s) *mark-room* even if she gets ahead of them while passing the *obstruction.*

We've discussed thoroughly how rule 18 applies slightly differently in certain situations, primarily at windward *marks* (including windward **finishing marks**), leeward *marks* where inside boats need to gybe to sail their *proper* course, starting *marks* and continuing *obstructions*. These are its only exceptions. Otherwise, the rules for "mark-room" are exactly the same at every other *mark* on the course, including the finishing *marks.*

220

10

Part 2, Section C
When Boats Meet— Room to Pass and Tack at an Obstruction

Rules 19 and 20 are the rules that apply when you are sailing near *obstructions*. Remember, an *obstruction* is an object large enough to require you to make a substantial course change to miss it **if** you were one of your lengths away and aiming directly at the largest part of it, whether or not you are **actually** aiming right at it on the water. In other words, it is a hypothetical test to determine if the **physical size** of the object qualifies it as an *obstruction*. For instance, imagine a 50-foot barge. If you were in a 20-foot boat aiming at the middle of its side, you would obviously have to make a large course change to avoid hitting the forward or aft 25 feet of it. So it ranks as an *obstruction* even if during the race you were only aiming at the last foot of its transom. (See discussion of the definition *Obstruction*.)

Also remember that a boat *racing* is an *obstruction* to you only when she has the right-of-way over **both** you and the boat(s) near you that are about to pass her (see the definition *Obstruction*), or if you and the other boat(s) have to avoid her under rule 22 (Capsized, Anchored or Aground; Rescuing). But note that no vessel under way, including a boat that is *racing*, is ever considered a "continuing" *obstruction*.

Finally note that an object that can be safely passed on only one side, such as a buoy that marks rocks, is an *obstruction*. So is an object, line or area so designated as an *obstruction* in the sailing instructions (see the definition *Obstruction*). But note that the object, line or area must be specifically designated as an "*obstruction*" in the sailing instructions. If the sailing instructions merely say "boats shall not pass between buoy X and the shore," or "shall not cross the starting/finishing line on the downwind leg," these areas are **not** "*obstructions*."

Rules 19 and 20 are rules of safety. If two boats are passing an *obstruction* (such as a seawall, moored boat or *starboard-tacker* that is *racing*), it is reasonable to require the outside boat to give the inside boat *room* to pass in safety between her and the *obstruction*. Just as it is sensible to allow a boat sailing upwind that is about to hit an *obstruction* to call for *room* to tack to avoid the *obstruction*.

RULE 19 — ROOM TO PASS AN OBSTRUCTION

RULE 19.1 — WHEN RULE 19 APPLIES

Rule 19 applies between two boats at an *obstruction* except

(a) when the *obstruction* is a *mark* the boats are required to leave on the same side, or

(b) when rule 18 applies between the boats and the *obstruction* is another boat *overlapped* with each of them.

However, at a continuing *obstruction*, rule 19 always applies and rule 18 does not.

"What is the purpose of rule 19.1(b)?"

This closes a loophole that is scarcely known to most sailors. Between three boats, the one boat that has the right of way over the other two is an "*obstruction*" (see definition *Obstruction*). Consider three *overlapped* boats on *port tack* rounding a port-hand leeward *mark* (L being the outside-most *leeward* boat, M being the middle boat, and W being the inside-most *windward* boat). W is entitled to *mark-room* from L and M under rule 18.2(b) (Giving Mark-Room). But without rule 19.1(b), M would be entitled to *room* under rule 19.2(b) to pass the *obstruction* (L) from W (the "outside boat" at the *obstruction*). This clearly would be a potential problem at tight leeward mark roundings. Rule 19.1(b) removes this issue.

PART 2: WHEN BOATS MEET — ROOM TO PASS & TACK AT AN OBSTRUCTION **223**

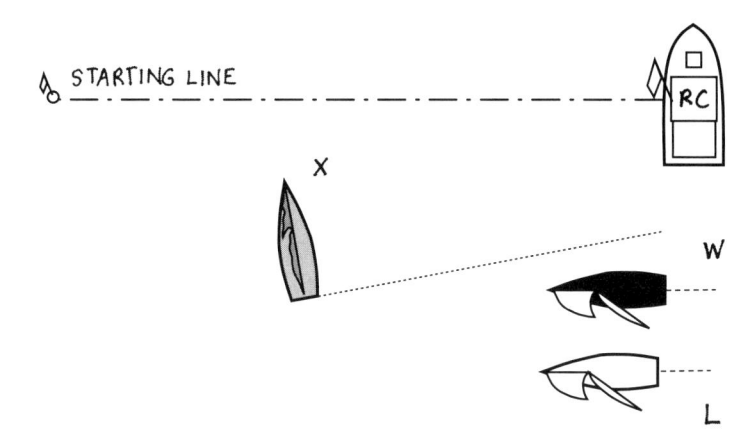

X is clear ahead of both L and W; therefore, as the right-of-way boat over both L and W, she is an obstruction to both. As L and W approach X, L, as the right-of-way boat over W, gets to choose on which side of X she will pass. If she chooses to pass to leeward of X, rule 19.2(b) requires her to give W room to do likewise if W also wants to pass to leeward of X.

Rule 19.1 is a clear statement of when rule 19 applies. Note it does not apply at *marks* that boats are required to leave on the same side unless the *mark* is a "continuing" *obstruction*. At all other marks rule 18 (Mark-Room) applies (see Chapter 8).

"So when does rule 19 begin to apply; is there a 'zone' around obstructions as there is around marks?"

No, there is no "*zone*" around *obstructions*! Rule 19 applies when boats are "at" the *obstruction*. Question 123 says, *"Boats are "at" an obstruction when the obstruction is influencing the course of one of them."* In other words, boats are "at" an obstruction when one of them reaches the point where she must commit to passing on one side or the other of the *obstruction* and will need space from the other boat(s) to do so.

RULE 19.2 — GIVING ROOM AT AN OBSTRUCTION

(a) **A right-of-way boat may choose to pass an *obstruction* on either side.**

"Which boat gets to choose which side of the obstruction the boats will pass on?"

Before one of the boats needs to commit to passing on one side or the other, the rules of Section A and B apply and the right-of-way boat can sail where she pleases, subject to rules 16 (Changing Course) and 17 (On the Same Tack; Proper Course). Rule 19.2(a) reminds of this by saying "*A right-of-way boat may choose to pass an **obstruction** on either side.*" So, approaching an *obstruction*, the right-of-way boat (*leeward* boat or *starboard-tack* boat) gets to choose on which side she wants to pass the *obstruction*, and the other boat(s) must *keep clear*.

"OK, so when does the outside boat have to begin giving room to the inside boat?"

RULE 19.2(b) — GIVING ROOM AT AN OBSTRUCTION

When boats are *overlapped*, the outside boat shall give the inside boat *room* between her and the *obstruction*, unless she has been unable to do so from the time the *overlap* began.

The outside boat, whether the right-of-way boat or not, must give the inside boat *room* to pass between her and the *obstruction* when she needs it, which will be when she needs to commit to sailing on one side or the other of the *obstruction* and needs *room* to do so.

A common example is two *overlapped* boats sailing upwind on *port-tack* (PL and PW) approaching a *starboard-tack* boat (S). As the boats near each other, PL bears away to pass astern of S. When PW gets to the point where she must commit to either bearing away also or tacking, rule 19.2(b) requires PL to give PW *room* to pass astern of S if PW chooses to do so (Case 11).

Another common example is on the starting line. Two *overlapped starboard-tack* boats (SL and SW) are reaching down the line and approaching another *starboard-tack* boat *clear ahead* (A). If SL wants to pass or stop on the *windward* side of A, she may do so by luffing, subject to rule 16.1 (Changing Course), and SW must *keep clear*. If SL chooses to pass astern of A, then she must give SW *room* to do so if SW chooses to pass astern as well. This is true even if SW's bow is ahead of SL's such that she will reach A before SL. (See Case 117 and Appeal 36.)

"What happens if it is not clear on which side the right of way boat will pass the obstruction?"

Good question! Rule 19.2(b) is premised on there being an "inside" and an "outside" boat. If neither boat is clearly the "outside" boat, then it is not possible

PART 2: WHEN BOATS MEET — ROOM TO PASS & TACK AT AN OBSTRUCTION   **225**

to apply rule 19.2(b). It will be up to the protest committee to decide, based on the facts, whether there was an "outside" boat. If, in the starting line example above, SL is aiming at the aft portion of A when SW needs to commit to passing A on one side or the other, I would say it is reasonable for her to assume that SL will pass astern of A; i.e., on the "outside."

However, consider the situation where two *overlapped port-tack* boats (PL and PW) are sailing downwind and approaching a boat ahead on the same *tack* (PA), with PW half a length ahead of PL. As both PL and PW are required to *keep* clear of PA under rule 12 (On the Same Tack, Not Overlapped), PA is an *obstruction*. If PL is clearly sailing a course to pass to *leeward* of PA, then PW is entitled to *room* to do likewise when she arrives at PA.

If PL is clearly sailing a course to pass to *windward* of PA, then PW must *keep clear* under rule 11 (On the Same Tack, Overlapped); and when PL must commit to passing PA to *windward*, she is also entitled to *room* from PW to do so. However, if PL is aiming directly **at** PA's transom, such that it is not possible to determine by the positions of the boats on which side of the *obstruction* PL will pass, there is no clear "outside" boat. As PW will arrive at PA before PL does, she should *keep clear* under rule 11 and should not anticipate receiving *room* under rule 19.2(b). She may end up *overlapping* PA to *windward* as a result of *keeping clear* of PL. If when PL arrives at PA she chooses to pass PA to *leeward*, she must give *room* to PW (assuming the boats are still *overlapped*), but that may be a moot point as PW may not be able to take advantage of that space if she is *overlapped* close to *windward* of PA. Hails between PW and PL regarding PL's intentions as the boats approach PA may be helpful, but are not mandatory under the *rules*. (See Question 123.)

"If I am the outside boat, remind me how much space I need to give the inside boat?"

You have to give her "*room*," which is enough space for her to sail between you and the *obstruction* in the prevailing conditions in a "seamanlike way;" i.e., sailing her boat in its normal way without risk of touching either you or the *obstruction*.

"Does the inside boat have to call for room in order to get it?"

There is no requirement in the *rules* that an inside boat has to call for *room* in order to get it, though I recommend hailing in advance to avoid problems

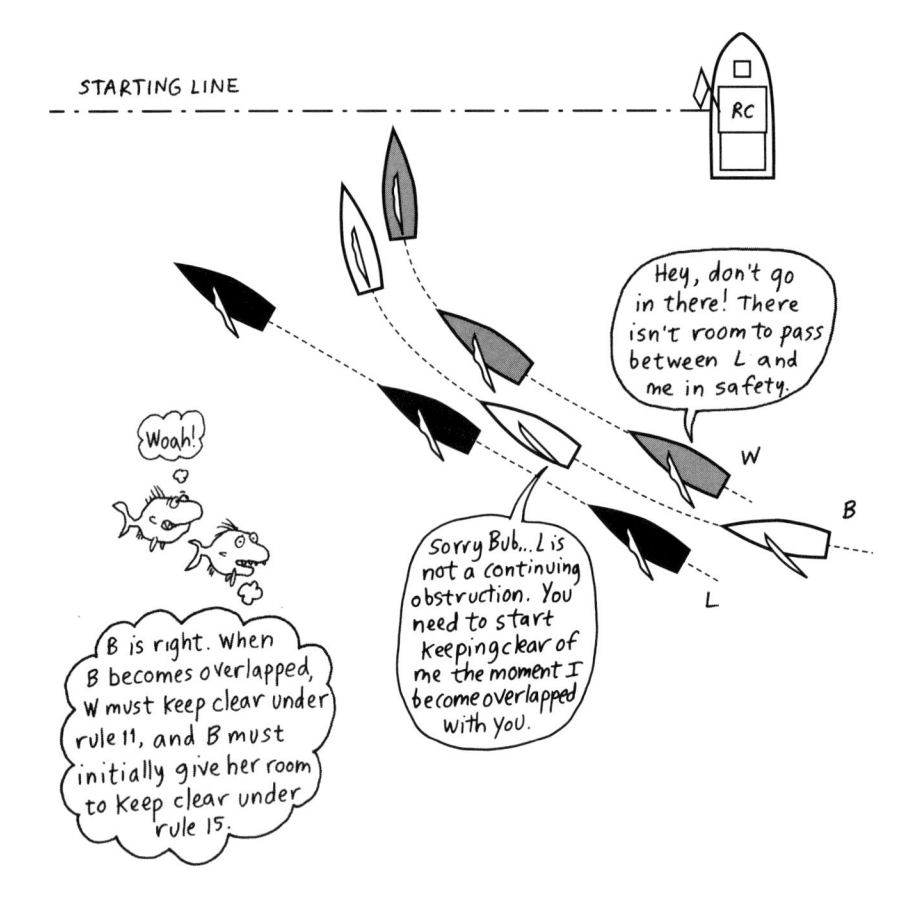

226 UNDERSTANDING THE RACING RULES OF SAILING THROUGH 2024

[Diagram: Starting line scenario showing boats L, W, and B approaching the starting line near the RC boat. Speech bubbles read:

W: "Hey, don't go in there! There isn't room to pass between L and me in safety."

L: "Sorry Bub... L is not a continuing obstruction. You need to start keeping clear of me the moment I become overlapped with you."

Fish: "Woah!"

Thought bubble: "B is right. When B becomes overlapped, W must keep clear under rule 11, and B must initially give her room to keep clear under rule 15."]

later. Boats are expected to know their obligations under the rules, which includes outside boats at *obstructions*. Case 41 reads, "QUESTION 2: Does BW have to hail for room to pass to leeward of A? If not, would BL risk disqualification by not giving room? ANSWER 2: BW is not required to hail for room, although that is a prudent thing to do to avoid misunderstandings. Rule 19.2(b) requires BL to give room to BW if they both pass to leeward of the obstruction, whether or not BW hails for room."

"How does it work when I want to establish an overlap between two boats on the starting line?"

Let's say you were on *starboard tack* approaching two other *starboard-tack* boats (L and W) sitting side-by-side near the starting line. You need to *keep clear* of L under rule 12 (On the Same Tack, Not Overlapped), and W needs to *keep clear* of L under rule 11 (On the Same Tack, Overlapped). Because

PART 2: WHEN BOATS MEET — ROOM TO PASS & TACK AT AN OBSTRUCTION 227

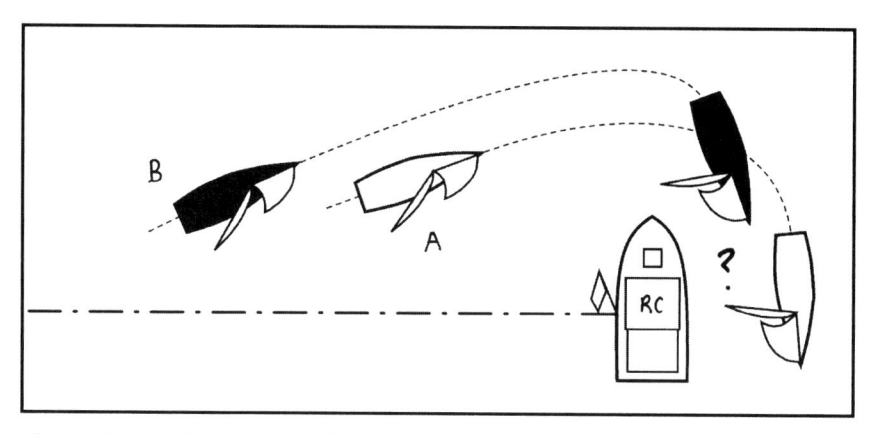

If A and B are only passing the obstruction (race committee boat) for a very short time, it is not a "continuing obstruction." B is permitted to establish an inside overlap and become entitled to room only if A can initially keep clear under rule 11 when B becomes overlapped to leeward of her (see rule 15), and is able to give B room from the time the overlap is established (see rule 19.2(b)).

If A and B are sailing alongside the obstruction for more than a few seconds, the obstruction is a "continuing obstruction" and B is not permitted to establish an inside overlap and become entitled to room because there is not room for her to pass between A and the race committee boat (see rule 19.2(c)).

you **both** need to *keep clear* of L, she is an *obstruction*; but as a vessel under way, she is not a "continuing" *obstruction* (see the definition *Obstruction*). Therefore, rule 19.2(b) applies, meaning that you can establish an *overlap* between L and W even if there is not *room* at that moment to sail all the way between them in safety.

If you become *overlapped* to *leeward* of W, she needs to *keep clear* of you under rule 11; and you need to initially give her *room* to *keep clear* of you under rule 15 (Acquiring Right of Way). W also needs to give you *room* to pass the *obstruction* (L) if she is able to do so from the moment you became *overlapped* with her (rule 19.2(b)). If she is able to *keep clear* of you and give you *room* to pass L, then she must. However, if despite her best effort she is unable to do so, then you break rule 15 if you hit W, or rule 11 if you hit L or force L to avoid you.

"So if the inside boat gets her overlap so close to the obstruction that I physically can't give her room, I don't have to?"

That's right. Rule 19.2(b) says that if an outside boat is "unable" to give *room* from the time the *overlap* begins, she doesn't have to do so. This is a safety feature intended to discourage boats from creating last-minute inside *overlaps* near *obstructions*. Note also that if the boat astern is acquiring the right-of-way when it establishes an inside *overlap*, it also has to comply with rule 15 (Acquiring Right of Way). So again, if the outside keep-clear boat is unable to respond promptly and *keep clear* (which would likely result in them also giving *room*), the inside boat breaks rule 15 and the outside boat does not break rule 19.2(b).

"OK, but what do I do if I'm entitled to room but the outside boat doesn't give me room; can I get exonerated if I am forced to break a rule?"

Yes. Let's say you (PW) and a *leeward* boat (PL) are on *port tack* approaching a *starboard-tack* boat (S). It looks clear to you that PL is going to duck S, i.e., pass astern of her, and you begin to duck S as well. At the point in time that it becomes clear to you that PL is not going to give you *room*, it is not possible for you to tack without hitting S. You continue ducking S and your boom touches PL. You both protest. First, at the point in time that it becomes clear to you that PL is not going to give you *room*, it is not possible for you to avoid contact with either S or PL; therefore you did not break rule 14 (Avoiding Contact). Second, PL failed to give you *room* to pass the *obstruction* (S) and therefore broke rule 19.2(b). Third, though you failed to *keep clear* of the *leeward* boat (PL) and broke rule 11 (On the Same Tack, Overlapped), you are exonerated (freed from penalty) by rule 43.1(b) (Exoneration) because you were sailing within the *room* you were entitled to.

"When does rule 19 cease to apply such that I no longer have to give the inside boat room?"

Once the inside boat no longer needs *room* to sail between the outside boat and the *obstruction*, the boats are no longer "at" the *obstruction* and rule 19 ceases to apply. For instance, take the upwind situation where PL and PW are passing astern of S. Once PW has passed S such that she no longer needs space from PL to avoid S, PL may assert her rights under rule 11 (On the Same Tack, Overlapped) and can luff subject to rule 16.1 (Changing Course) and rule 17 (On the Same Tack; Proper Course).

"If I'm on port tack sailing as close to a shoreline or dock as I can, can I call for 'sea-room' from a starboard-tacker?"

Absolutely not! First, there's no such thing as "sea-room" in the rules. "Sea-

PART 2: WHEN BOATS MEET — ROOM TO PASS & TACK AT AN OBSTRUCTION 229

room" is just a term for "*room.*" Rule 19.2(b) applies only to boats that are "*overlapped.*" Boats sailing upwind on opposite *tacks* are not *overlapped* (see the definition *Clear Astern* and *Clear Ahead*; *Overlap*). Therefore, if you are sailing close-hauled on *port tack* as close to the shore or a dock as you can get, you cannot call for *room* from a converging close-hauled *starboard-tack* boat. Rule 10 (On Opposite Tacks) applies and you must slow down or bear off and take their stern. (See Cases 9 and 43.)

WHEN PASSING A CONTINUING OBSTRUCTION

RULE 19.2(c) — GIVING ROOM AT AN OBSTRUCTION

(c) While boats are passing a continuing *obstruction*, if a boat that was *clear astern* and required to *keep clear* becomes *overlapped* between the other boat and the *obstruction* and, at the moment the *overlap* begins, there is not *room* for her to pass between them,

    (1) she is not entitled to *room* under rule 19.2(b), and

    (2) while the boats remain *overlapped*, she shall *keep clear* and rules 10 and 11 do not apply.

First of all, we need to discuss what a "continuing *obstruction*" is. It is an *obstruction* that a boat "continues" to sail next to for a longer period of time, as opposed to one that is passed in a matter of seconds. For instance, a shoreline or breakwater that a boat is sailing along for more than a few seconds is a "continuing *obstruction*," whereas a small spectator or race committee boat that gets sailed by in just a few seconds is not a "continuing *obstruction*." Note that a vessel under way, **including a boat** *racing*, is never a "continuing *obstruction*" (see the definition *Obstruction*).

"So when can a boat come up from clear astern and obtain an inside overlap between a boat ahead and a continuing obstruction and be entitled to room?"

The answer depends on whether the boat astern has the right of way or not. When boats are passing an *obstruction* and are not *overlapped*, rule 19 places no obligations on the boats, meaning that the rules in Sections A and B apply. For instance, if two boats are running downwind along the shore or a breakwater or dock and the boat astern is on *starboard tack* (SB) and the boat ahead is on *port tack* (PA), PA must *keep clear* of SB under rule 10 (On Opposite Tacks). Of course, PA can defend her position close to the *obstruction* by gybing so that she too is on *starboard tack*. Then SB would need to *keep clear* of her under rule 12 (On the Same Tack, Not Overlapped).

However, if the boat astern is a keep-clear boat, then rule 19.2(c) applies. In that case, the boat *clear astern* (B) can obtain an inside *overlap* between the boat *clear ahead* (A) and a continuing *obstruction* only when, at the moment the *overlap* is obtained, there is enough *room* for B to pass **completely** between A and the *obstruction* at that moment without touching either. In other words, imagine that the moment the *overlap* between A and the *obstruction* is made, you could "freeze" the motion of A and the *obstruction*. If there is enough "room" (physical space) for B to sail through between them in a "seamanlike way" (see the definition *Room*), meaning sailing the boat in its normal way (including boom out in its normal downwind trim, see Case 21) without risk of touching either the *obstruction* or the outside boat, then the *overlap* is legal and A must give B *room* under rule 19.2(b) for as long as they are *overlapped* and B needs the *room* to keep from touching the *obstruction*; i.e., hitting the wall, running aground, etc. If B loses the *overlap* on A, then A ceases to be required to give *room* until B obtains another legal *overlap* and again needs *room*.

One sensitive situation occurs when A is sailing as close as she dares to shore but it's not obvious how close a boat of her class can really go without running aground. Boat B comes up and wants to obtain an inside *overlap*. The question becomes, "How do you determine if there is *room* for her to pass inside of A?" The essence of *room* is whether, under the conditions existing, the inside boat can safely sail between the outside boat and the *obstruction*. If B decides to

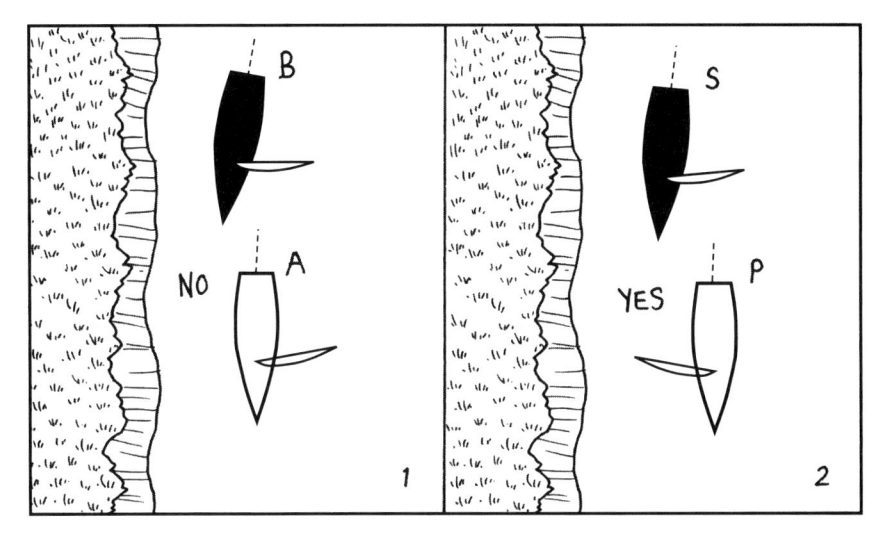

PART 2: WHEN BOATS MEET — ROOM TO PASS & TACK AT AN OBSTRUCTION **231**

In situation 1, B is the keep-clear boat. There is not room for B to sail between A and the shoreline (a continuing obstruction) without hitting one or the other. Therefore, if she did establish an overlap between them, she would not be entitled to room under rule 19.2(b) and she would be required to keep clear of A under rule 19.2(c).

In situation 2, S is the right-of-way boat. P must keep clear of her under rule 10.

risk it and obtains the *overlap*, and then immediately runs aground, she has demonstrated that there was not *room* for her at the time she obtained the *overlap*. But after she has sailed inside for a couple of lengths, she has clearly demonstrated that there was *room* for her to pass safely between the outside boat and the continuing *obstruction* at the moment the *overlap* began, and therefore, having met the criterion in rule 19.2(c), is entitled to *room* for as long as the *overlap* continues to exist.

"If I'm a keep-clear boat and I obtain an overlap when there isn't room to sail between the outside boat and the continuing obstruction, have I broken rule 19.2(c)?"

No. You don't break rule 19.2(c) merely because you obtained an *overlap*. However, if you are not entitled to *room*, then while the boats remain *overlapped*, you are required to *keep clear* of the outside boat under rule 19.2(c) even though you may have subsequently acquired the right of way as a *leeward* or *starboard tack* boat. If the outside boat has to take action to avoid you, now you have broken rule 19.2(c). Note that rules 10 (*port/starboard*) and 11 (*windward/leeward*) do not apply in this situation.

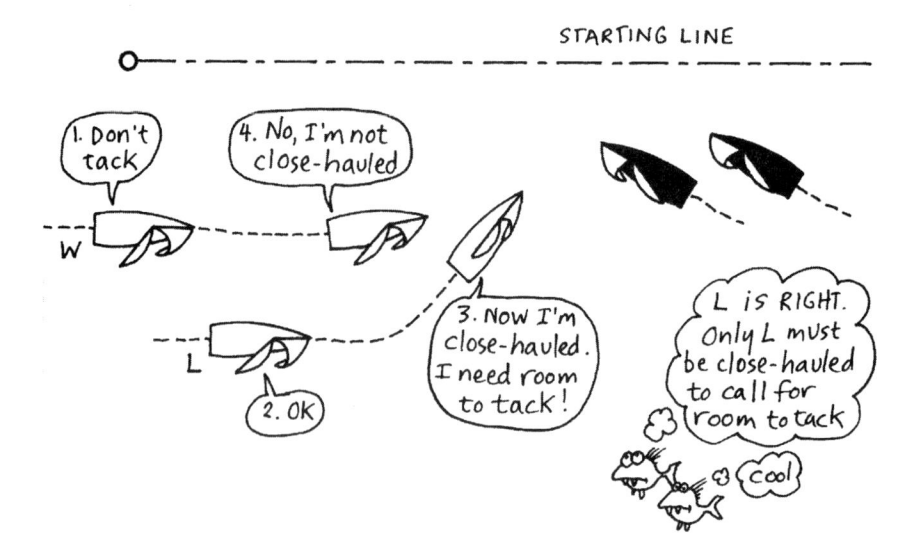

RULE 20 — ROOM TO TACK AT AN OBSTRUCTION

RULE 20.1 — HAILING

A boat may hail for *room* to tack and avoid a boat on the same *tack*. However, she shall not hail unless

(a) she is approaching an *obstruction* and will soon need to make a substantial course change to avoid it safely, and

(b) she is sailing close-hauled or above.

In addition, she shall not hail if the *obstruction* is a *mark* and a boat that is *fetching* it would be required to respond and change course as a result of the hail.

RULE 20.2 — RESPONDING

(a) After a boat hails, she shall give a hailed boat time to respond.
(b) A hailed boat shall respond even if the hail breaks rule 20.1.
(c) A hailed boat shall respond either by tacking as soon as possible, or by immediately replying 'You tack' and then giving the hailing boat *room* to tack and avoid her.
(d) When a hailed boat responds, the hailing boat shall tack as soon as possible.
(e) From the time a boat hails until she has tacked and avoided a hailed boat, rule 18.2 does not apply between them.

RULE 20.3 — PASSING ON A HAIL TO AN ADDITIONAL BOAT

When a boat has been hailed for *room* to tack and she intends to respond by tacking, she may hail another boat on the same *tack* for *room* to tack and avoid her. She may hail even if her hail does not meet the conditions of rule 20.1. Rule 20.2 applies between her and a boat she hails.

RULE 20.4 — ADDITIONAL REQUIREMENTS FOR HAILS

(a) When conditions are such that a hail may not be heard, the boat shall also make a signal that clearly indicates her need for *room* to tack or her response.

(b) The notice of race may specify an alternative communication for a boat to indicate her need for *room* to tack or her response, and require boats to use it.

This is the rule that is used when calling for "sea-room" or *room* at a shore, breakwater or dock. However, it is also commonly used when two *port-tack* boats are sailing side-by-side up a beat and are converging with a *starboard-tacker*. It is a "safety" rule. The purpose of the rule is to permit a close-hauled boat caught between another boat on the same *tack* and an *obstruction* to avoid the *obstruction* without loss of distance when a substantial change of course is required to clear it.

Notice that rule 20.1 does not apply to boats on opposite *tacks*. Case 43 describes a situation where a *port-tack* boat (P) is sailing close-hauled as close to shore as possible. A *port-tack* boat to leeward (S) tacks to *starboard tack* onto a collision course with P. S hails "Starboard" and P hails for "sea-room." In Case 43, the Appeals Committee said, "P is subject to rule 10 and must keep clear… S establishes right of way over P when she tacks onto starboard, but must observe rules 13 and 15. S meets rule 13's requirement by not tacking so close that P has to take avoiding action before S reaches her close-hauled course. After S acquires right of way over P under rule 10, S complies with rule 15 by initially giving P room to keep clear." Therefore, P is not entitled to hail for *room* to tack since rule 20.1 applies to two boats on the "same" *tack*. So, in this situation P must slow down or bear away and pass astern of S.

When all the conditions in rule 20.1 are met, a *leeward* boat or one *clear ahead* will be able to call for "*room* to tack" from a nearby boat that is otherwise preventing her from tacking.

Here is how rule 20 works:

1) For a hail to be a legal hail under rule 20.1, the two boats must be on the **same** *tack* and approaching an *obstruction*, the *leeward* boat (L) or the boat *clear ahead* (A) must be sailing close-hauled or above, and L or A must soon need to make a substantial course change to avoid the *obstruction* safely (rules 20.1(a) and 20.1(b)).

2) Rule 20.1 is intended for the use of L or A when she is about to hit, or be hit by, an *obstruction*, e.g., a sandbar, a dock, a fishing boat, or a *starboard-tack* boat that is *racing*. When there is any doubt as to whether L or A actually is in imminent danger of colliding with an *obstruction*, I would always expect the protest committee to give L or A the benefit of the doubt, and I would encourage sailors on the water to do the same.

3) Rule 20.1 only provides a boat enough *room* to tack without fouling a nearby boat. Let's say the boats are on *starboard tack*. L or A hails for *room* to tack and the windward boat (W) or boat *clear astern* (B) responds, "You tack." If the course of L or A is sufficiently to leeward of W's or B's course such that after tacking onto *port tack* she has *room* to immediately bear away and pass astern of W or B, she is required to do so, since she has the *room* she needs to tack and avoid the other boat. (See Case 35.)

4) Rule 20.1(a) prohibits L or A from hailing the other boat for *room* to tack unless safety requires L or A to make a "substantial change of course" to avoid the *obstruction*. Here, the course change is simply that needed not to hit the *obstruction*. In this case, as my general guideline, a course change of less than 10 degrees is not very "substantial." That's only 3 feet, 6 inches, in a 20-foot boat. Therefore, in a 20-foot boat, if L or A can bear away and miss an *obstruction* that she would otherwise hit only 3 feet from its downwind edge, it is questionable whether she is entitled to hail under rule 20.1. But if she needs to tack to avoid the last 3 feet of its upwind edge, then that's more "substantial." (See Appeal 15 and Case 11.)

"What happens if a boat hails for room to tack, and the boat being hailed doesn't think the hailing boat is approaching an obstruction or needs to make a substantial course change to avoid the obstruction?"

First of all, the boat that was hailed **must respond** to the hail by tacking or replying "You tack" (see the following discussion on rule 20.2(b)), even if the

PART 2: WHEN BOATS MEET — ROOM TO PASS & TACK AT AN OBSTRUCTION   **235**

hailed boat does not see any *obstruction* in front of the hailing boat. This is for safety. Perhaps the hailed boat can't see the rock in front of the other boat; or perhaps the other boat was mistaken that there was a rock. Having responded, the hailed boat (or any boat) can protest the hailing boat for breaking rule 20.1(a). If the protest committee finds that the hailing boat was not approaching an *obstruction* or did not need to make a substantial course change to ensure her safety, or if "safety" was not an issue, the hailing boat will be disqualified. Note the word "shall" in rule 20.1(a), "*However, she shall not hail…*". (See Cases 10 and 33.)

Note, if a sailor tried to take advantage of this situation by intentionally calling for room to tack when there was no *obstruction*, that would be a clear breach of rule 2 (Fair Sailing).

"Is there anything I should know about the hail itself?"

Well, first of all the hail must be **adequate**, which implies that it must be loud enough for the other boat to hear it above the wind and noise of the boats, and it must be absolutely clear as to what the hail means. I personally try to turn my head toward the other boat, use their helmsman's name if I know it, and say to the effect, "I have a dock or a *starboard-tacker* coming up; I need *room* to tack." (See Case 54.)

Secondly, the hailing boat must give the hailed boat **time to respond**; i.e., she cannot hail and tack simultaneously. Appeal 45 reads, "PL was at fault [by] …hailing and tacking simultaneously, contrary to rule 20.2(a)." The purpose of this is to provide time for the specific response called for under rule 20.2(c) (to tack or reply 'You tack'). This requires boats to keep a good lookout so they are not "surprised" by an *obstruction*. Furthermore, it requires boats to be aware of the hailed boat's ability to respond as well. Obviously it will require more time if the hailed boat will have to subsequently hail a boat or boats to windward of them, as permitted in rule 20.3 (see Case 113).

Though the failure of a hailed boat to hear an adequate hail does not relieve her of her obligations under rule 20, before she is hailed a boat is under no obligation to anticipate that another boat is going to hail for room to tack. Appeal 45 reads, "[The finding] that PW should have been prepared to respond is unwarranted." Therefore a boat does not have to anticipate that another boat might be approaching an *obstruction*; and if the other boat does not adequately hail in time and subsequently runs aground or fouls a *star-*

board-tack boat, she cannot blame the hailed boat. Therefore, a boat must not sail into a position, before hailing, where she cannot allow sufficient time for a response.

"I thought that when two port-tack boats were approaching a starboard-tacker, it was whoever hailed first that got to tell the other what to do."

No! Rule 19.2(a) reminds the right-of-way boat that she has the right to choose on which side she will pass the *obstruction*. And if she wants to tack, rule 20.1 gives L or A the right to call for *room* to tack whenever she will have to make a substantial course change to avoid the *obstruction*; and requires W or B to respond to L or A's hail. When two port-tack boats (PW and PL) are approaching a *starboard-tack* boat (S), Appeal 24 says, "PW established an inside overlap on PL when the two boats were several lengths from the obstruction. However, this fact alone did not give PW right to room under rule 19.2(b)…Therefore, PL was under no obligation to give PW room to pass astern of the obstruction if in fact PL desired to tack."

If PL chooses to pass astern of S and PW wants to pass astern of S also, then Case 11 reminds PL that, as an outside boat passing an *obstruction*, "under rule 19.2(b) PW was entitled to room to pass between PL and the stern of S." But if PL chooses to hail for *room* to tack under rule 20.1, PW must comply by tacking or replying "You tack" and giving PL *room* to tack even when PW would rather duck.

When L or A adequately hails, rule 20.2 tells W or B how to respond.

So when L or A adequately hails, W or B is required to respond, even if L or A's hail breaks rule 20.1 (rule 20.2(b)), and she has only two choices for a response: either tack **as soon as possible** or **immediately** reply "You tack" (rule 20.2(c)). W or B does not have the option of disputing L or A's judgment about her need to hail. When W or B feels L or A's hail is not proper (e.g., she is not really near an *obstruction* or she will not soon have to make a substantial course change to avoid an *obstruction*) she nevertheless must respond. She can then protest under rule 20.1 claiming L or A hailed when she was not permitted to do so.

Notice that if you choose to reply "You tack," you must make that hail **immediately**; i.e., without delay. Note also that you must use those **exact two words** in your hail.

However, if you choose to respond by tacking, you need only do that **"as soon as possible."** The reason is that sometimes it will **not** be possible for W or B to respond by tacking "immediately" after hearing a hail. Examples would include: (a) when there are several boats to windward of W or B that need to be hailed; (b) when coming in on *port tack* to a windward *mark* where the boats already going downwind are so close that tacking is impossible; (c) when PW is still ducking one *starboard-tacker* when PL hails for *room* to tack at a second *starboard-tacker*; or (d) when some object in the water such as a log or the windward *mark* momentarily restricts her ability to respond. When it is not possible for W or B to respond by tacking immediately, it is good seamanship for them to inform L or A.

Notice also that it makes no difference whether the hailed boat (W or B) can "fetch" the *obstruction* herself (unless it is also a *mark*; see rule 20.1). If the hailing boat (L or A) cannot clear the *obstruction* without tacking or bearing away sharply, she is entitled to hail and to get a response, regardless of whether the hailed boat can clear the *obstruction*.

Now let's say that you are L and have hailed W for *room* to tack because of a converging *starboard-tacker*. Upon hearing your hail, W tacks. You must begin your tack as soon as you can without hitting W. In other words, you must put your helm down within a couple of seconds after W puts hers down. You break rule 20.2(d) if you continue another couple of boat-lengths before tacking, or if you don't tack at all.

If W responds to your hail with the reply "You tack," again you must put your helm down and tack as soon as it is possible, which normally will be immediately. If you don't, you break rule 20.2(d). Once W hails "You tack" she assumes all the obligation to give you *room* to tack and clear her; so if you hear her reply and immediately put your helm down and hit her, she is wrong under rule 20.2(c) and you are exonerated (freed from penalty) for breaking any Section A rule, or rule 15 or 16, by rule 43.1(b) (Exoneration). And if you have to stop your tack or otherwise change course before completing your tack in order to avoid W, she is wrong as well under 20.2(c).

Note: It is not uncommon, when PL and PW are approaching a *starboard-tacker* (S), for PW to respond "You tack" but then be happy to let PL delay her tack so she can tack close to S (lee-bow tack). This gives PW two good options: tack close to PL (lee-bow tack) or duck S.

"Could you discuss the situation where two port-tackers (PW and PL) are sailing close-hauled side by side on a converging course with a starboard-tacker (S). PL hails PW for 'room to tack,' gets no response, and ultimately S must change course to avoid hitting PL. Who should be penalized?"

The answer will depend on the protest committee's judgment as to whether PL hailed adequately and gave the hailed boat enough time to respond.

Case 3 states, "Having decided to tack and having hailed for room to do so three times, PL was entitled by rule 20.2(c) to expect that PW would respond and give her room to tack. She was not obliged to anticipate PW's failure to comply with rule 20.2(c). PL broke rule 10, but she is exonerated as the innocent victim of another boat's breach of a rule by rule 43.1(a)."

Appeal 19 is another good example of how PL fulfilled her obligation to adequately hail, but then was forced to foul S by PW's failure to respond. "FACTS: [PW and PL] were close-hauled on port tack. S, which was to leeward and ahead of both PW and PL, tacked to starboard. S completed her tack in compliance with rule 15 (Acquiring Right of Way). Twice, PL hailed PW to tack, so that she also could tack and avoid S. By the time it was clear that PW would not respond, it was too late for PL to make any alternative maneuver without interfering with the oncoming S. PL called to S that she could not respond, whereupon S tacked back to port to avoid a collision.

"DECISION: Inasmuch as PL would have had to make a substantial course change to pass astern of S, even if she had borne away instantly when S tacked to starboard, PL's hail did not break rule 20.1 (Room to Tack at an Obstruction: Hailing). PW did not respond to PL's hail as required by rule 20.2(c) and was properly disqualified. However, she did not break rule 10 because at no time was she failing to keep clear of S. By the time it was clear that PW was not giving PL room to tack as required by rule 20.2(c), it was too late for PL to keep clear of S by bearing away. Therefore PL was compelled to break rule 10 as a consequence of PW's breaking rule 20.2(c), so PL is exonerated by rule 43.1(a)."

However, PL must remember that her primary obligation is to *keep clear* of S under rule 10 (On Opposite Tacks). In Appeal 2, the protest committee found that after realizing PW was not responding to her hail, PL could have borne away and passed astern of S. Instead S was required to luff to avoid contact with PL. The Decision reads, "When PW failed to respond to PL's hail

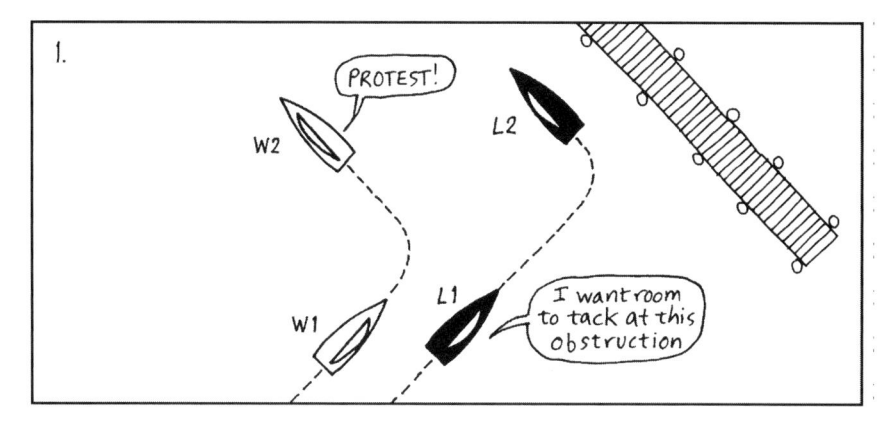

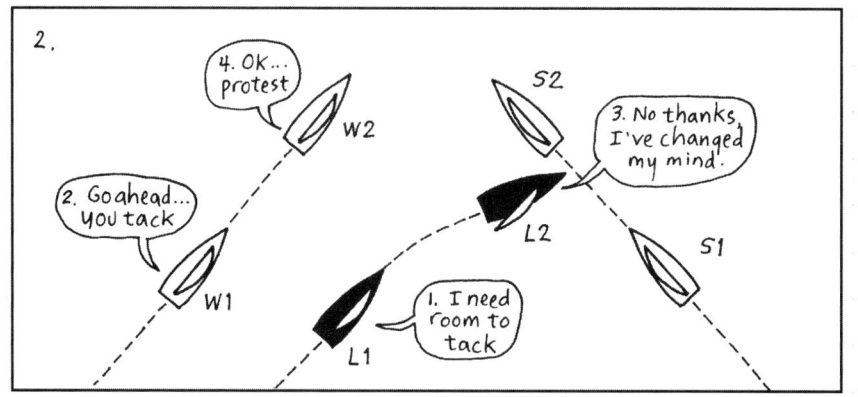

PART 2: WHEN BOATS MEET — ROOM TO PASS & TACK AT AN OBSTRUCTION **239**

In situation 1, L breaks rule 20.2(d) by delaying her tack to starboard. After W tacks in response to L's hail, L must tack as soon as possible.

In situation 2, L breaks rule 20.2(d) by not tacking as soon as possible after W replies "You tack."

for room to tack, PL was faced with the necessity of taking alternative action to avoid S. This raises the question of whether she is exonerated by rule 43.1(a) as the innocent victim of another boat's breach. We think not, since the protest committee found that she could have gone astern of S. A boat breaking a rule is not exonerated by rule 43.1(a) unless she was compelled by another boat to break a rule."

The key to all this is that L or A must keep a good lookout and begin hailing in time for W or B to hear and understand the hail and then respond. If L or A waits until the last second to hail, and then immediately fouls S, she cannot blame W or B. But if after several clear hails W or B does not respond, L or A must make a reasonable effort to *keep clear* of S. If she cannot *keep clear* she is exonerated by rule 43.1(a), and W or B should be penalized for breaking rule 20.2(c). If, however, L or A did have enough time and space to *keep clear* of S after getting no response from W or B but failed to make an effort to use it, she should also be penalized under rule 10 (On Opposite Tacks).

This situation commonly occurs at the windward *mark*. Note that when PW and PL are in the *zone*, PW is entitled to *mark-room* from PL under rule 18.2 (Giving Mark-Room). But from the moment a boat hails for room to tack until she has tacked and avoided the hailed boat, rule 18.2 does not apply between them (see rule 20.2(e)). So if PL wants to tack to avoid a converging S, she can hail PW for "*room* to tack," and as long as it is possible for PW to respond, PW must do so, even if it means sailing to the wrong side of the *mark* (see Appeal 2).

"What about when the obstruction is also a mark; can I still call for room to tack?"

Good question. The answer is in the preamble to Section C and in rule 20.1. Notice that the preamble to Section C says that none of the rules in Section C (which includes rule 20) apply at a "starting" *mark* surrounded by navigable water or at its anchor line once a boat is approaching them to *start* until the boats have passed them. When rule 20 does not apply, none of the hails in rule 20 have any meaning under the rules. Therefore a call for "*room* to tack" at a "starting" *mark* when you are about to *start* or have just *started* places no obligation on other boats. This situation usually develops when there is a race committee boat anchored as the port or "leeward" end of the starting line. A *leeward* boat is truly in "coffin corner" if she sails into a position where she can't clear the race committee boat or its anchor line without tacking, and she can neither tack without fouling the *windward* boat nor bear away and pass astern of the race committee boat.

But if any other *mark* is a boat or other object large enough to qualify as an *obstruction*, then rule 20 applies. However, rule 20.1 says that a boat shall not hail if "*the* **obstruction** *is a* **mark** *and a boat that is* **fetching** *it would be required to respond and change course as a result of the hail.*" Let's say you are approaching a *mark/obstruction* and cannot pass it on its required side without tacking, and that you want to tack but can't without colliding with the boat just to windward of you (W). First you must check to see if W is *fetching* the *mark/obstruction* (able to pass it without passing head to wind). If

PART 2: WHEN BOATS MEET — ROOM TO PASS & TACK AT AN OBSTRUCTION **241**

she is, then you are not allowed to hail for *room* to tack (rule 20.1). In this case you are going to have to gybe or bear away and tack around to try it again. If W cannot *fetch* it herself, then you **can** hail W for "*room* to tack" under rule 20.1.

However, let's say you think you could tack and duck W; i.e., you could tack without making her change course to avoid you. If you choose to call for *room* to tack, and W responds by saying "You tack," and you don't require her to change course to avoid you, then you have not broken rule 20.1. But if W does need to change course to avoid you, you have broken rule 20.1.

Finally, it is important for W or B to remember that even if they are "*fetching the mark*" and would be required to change course to avoid L or A if they hailed, if L or A hails for *room* to tack, W or B **must respond** to the hail by tacking or hailing "You tack" (rule 20.2(b)), and then they can protest L or A for breaking rule 20.1 if they have to change course as a result.

"What if it's so windy or the boats are far enough apart that it is likely the hailed boat will not be able to hear a hail for room to tack or 'You tack'?"

Rule 20.4(a) says, *"When conditions are such that a hail may not be heard, the boat shall also make a signal that clearly indicates her need for room to tack or her response."* Examples of such signals include arm signals, whistle or horn blasts or even a hail on the radio. Note also that the notice of race may specify an alternative communication for a boat to indicate her need for *room to tack* or her response, and require boats to use it (rule 20.4(b)). In that case the alternative communication takes the place of the hail "You tack" in rule 20.2(c). (See Case 54.)

"Now do I know everything there is to know about room at marks and obstructions?"

Yes!

11

Part 2, Section D
When Boats Meet— Other Rules

Section D contains rules that apply in special situations that arise on the race course (rules 21–23). Again, these rules contain times when a right-of-way boat may find herself with a **temporary obligation** to *keep clear* of, or otherwise avoid, a keep-clear boat. An example is if you are on *port tack* shortly after the start and a *starboard-tack* boat is sailing back to the line because she was over early, rule 21.1 (Starting Line Errors; Taking Penalties; Backing a Sail) requires her to *keep clear* of you because you have *started* correctly, even though she is on *starboard tack* and you are on *port tack*. In this case you become the right-of-way boat and she the keep-clear boat for as long as the rule requires her to *keep clear*. Another example is that all boats are required to avoid a boat that is capsized, whether holding right of way over her or not (rule 22, Capsized, Anchored or Aground; Rescuing).

PREAMBLE TO SECTION D

When rule 21 or 22 applies between two boats, Section A rules do not.

This preamble clarifies that whenever rule 21 (Starting Errors; Taking Penalties; Backing a Sail) or rule 22 (Capsized, Anchored or Aground; Rescuing) applies, it takes precedence over the basic right-of-way rules in Section A. Note, however, that the rules of Section B still apply, which most significantly means that rule 16 (Changing Course) applies to a boat given the right of way in rule 21.

RULE 21 — STARTING ERRORS; TAKING PENALTIES; BACKING A SAIL

RULE 21.1

A boat sailing towards the pre-start side of the starting line or one of its extensions after her starting signal to *start* or to comply with rule 30.1 shall *keep clear* of a boat not doing so until her hull is completely on the pre-start side.

RULE 21.2

A boat taking a penalty shall *keep clear* of one that is not.

RULE 21.3

A boat moving astern through the water, or sideways to windward, by backing a sail shall *keep clear* of one that is not.

Rule 21 is actually three rules in one. Let's look at rule 21.1 first. Rule 28.1 (Sailing the Race) reads in part, *"A boat shall start..."*. So, if your hull isn't completely on the pre-start side of the starting line or its extensions at the starting signal, you have to get there before you can *start* the race. However, even when you and everyone else knows you are on the course side of the starting line at the starting signal (OCS), you keep all your right of way until you are sailing **back towards** the pre-start side of the starting line or one of its extensions; i.e., you are converging with it. This means that you continue to have rights even while slowing down or luffing in order to get clear enough to turn back. When it is obvious that you are sailing back towards the starting line, you must then *keep clear* of all boats that have *started* properly or are on the pre-start side of the starting line.

Once your hull is completely on the pre-start side of the starting line or its extensions, you are instantly subject to the Section A rules again; however, remember that if you acquire the right of way over another boat, you have to initially give her *room* to *keep clear* of you under rule 15 (Acquiring Right of Way).

Notice that when rule 30.1 (I Flag Rule), commonly referred to as the "one minute rule" or "round-an-end rule" is in effect, the requirement to *keep clear* in rule 21.1 applies only when you are sailing towards either end of the starting line to comply with rule 30.1 **after** your starting signal. Before your starting signal you have your normal right of way, even when you are over the line and obviously sailing toward an end to comply with rule 30.1.

Between two or more OCS boats sailing towards the pre-start side of the line after the starting signal, the Section A rules apply in the usual way.

"I realize that if another boat fouls me and forces me over the starting line just before the gun I'm OCS, but do I have to go back and restart?"

I'm afraid you do. If you don't, then you haven't *started* the race and have broken rule 28.1 (Sailing the Race). And you are only exonerated for breaking a *rule* when another boat "compels" you to break a *rule* (see rule 43.1(a), Exoneration). In your case, the other boat may have forced you over the line, and you certainly should win your *protest* against her, but she hasn't caused you to not return to the pre-start side and *start*. Therefore no exoneration is available. This is similar to the situation when an outside boat wrongfully fails to give you enough *room* at a *mark* and forces you on the wrong side of it. Though you were clearly fouled, you still must round the *mark* on the correct side.

These are two examples of situations where you can be right under the *rules* but have your finishing place seriously hurt by a keep-clear boat with no way for a protest committee to compensate you. At these times I'm reminded of the old saying, "He was in the right as he sped along; but he's just as dead as though he were wrong!"

Rule 21.2 talks to boats that are doing either a One-Turn Penalty for breaking rule 31 (Touching a Mark) or a Two-Turns Penalty for possibly breaking a rule of Part 2, under rule 44.2 (One-Turn and Two-Turns Penalties). It clearly tells them that, while they are taking their penalties, they have to *keep clear* of other boats, which makes sense.

Notice that when you hit a *mark* or possibly break a rule of Part 2, you still have all your rights as long as you continue sailing the course and while you are sailing well clear of the other boats in preparation to doing your penalty turn(s). But the moment it is obvious to other boats that you are clearly beginning to make a penalty turn, you must then *keep clear* of other boats in the race. You get your rights back when you have completed your last turn; but remember that if you acquire the right of way over another boat, you must initially give her *room* to *keep clear* of you under rule 15 (Acquiring Right of Way).

Note that if you touch a starting *mark* or possibly break a rule of Part 2 before the starting signal, you can make your penalty turn(s) immediately, as opposed to waiting for the starting signal before doing them. And when two boats are making a penalty turn, the Section A rules apply in the usual way, as does rule 23.2 (Interfering with Another Boat).

Rule 21.3 covers the situation where a boat actually backs its sail (i.e., holds the sail against the wind) and thereby causes the boat to move backwards, or sideways to windward (called "crabbing"), through the water. When a boat does this, she must *keep clear* of any other boat that is not doing likewise. Furthermore, she must remember that when she begins moving backwards or sideways, her action gives the right of way to boats astern or to windward of her; therefore they do not have to give her any *room* to *keep clear* of them under rule 15 (Acquiring Right of Way) because they acquired the right of way by the action of the boat moving astern or sideways.

Note that if a boat begins to move backwards or sideways due to the backing of her sail, she continues to be subject to this rule for as long as she is moving astern or sideways, even if she lets her sails come amidships. However, if a boat simply begins to move backwards because she has lost her headway, rule 21.3 does not apply to her.

RULE 22 — CAPSIZED, ANCHORED OR AGROUND; RESCUING

If possible, a boat shall avoid a boat that is capsized or has not regained control after capsizing, is anchored or aground, or is trying to help a person or vessel in danger. A boat is capsized when her masthead is in the water.

Rule 22 is a common sense rule of safety, and as such it complements rule 1 (Safety). These two rules place the safety of sailors and their boats well above the importance of any race they may be in. The rationale for rule 22 is clear: If a boat is anchored, aground or capsized it cannot very well "move" to get out of another boat's way, and it may be in danger; and if one boat is in the act of rescuing another boat or person, no other boat should hinder the rescue in any way.

Note that rule 22 requires you to "avoid" the boats described in the rule. In my opinion, this means not only avoid contact but keep away from them as well. However, the rule's opening phrase ("If possible…") clarifies that if for whatever reasonable reason it is not possible for you to avoid them, you should not be penalized. This further emphasizes the safety principle in that if you are attempting to assist a boat that otherwise has right-of-way over you, you should not be penalized.

SHEMP

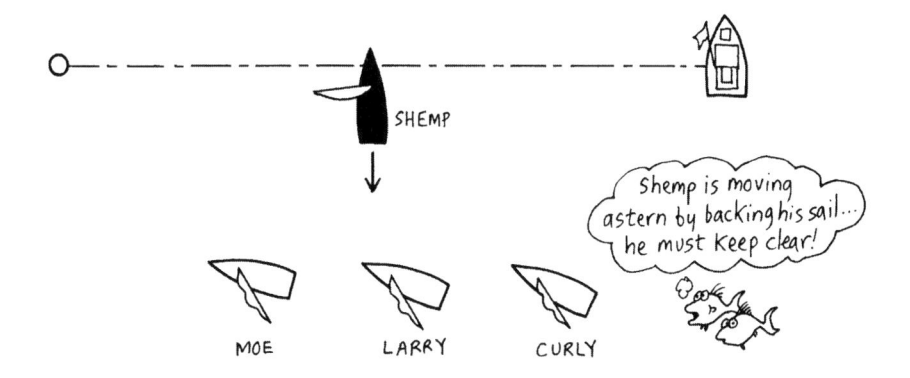

Shemp is moving astern by backing his sail... he must keep clear!

MOE   LARRY   CURLY

Also note that the definition *Obstruction* states that boats which others must "avoid" under rule 22 are considered *"obstructions."* This is a further safety aspect requiring outside boats to give inside boats *room* to avoid these boats in distress under rule 19 (Room to Pass an Obstruction).

Finally, note that a sailboat is considered "capsized" based on the location of its masthead. Given that it is possible to "capsize" a boat without the very top of the mast ever touching the water, I interpret "masthead" to include the top few feet of the mast. Note also that rule 22 offers protection to a sailboat while she is regaining control after capsizing.

RULE 23 — INTERFERING WITH ANOTHER BOAT

Rule 23 states two situations in which a boat cannot interfere with other boats.

RULE 23.1

If reasonably possible, a boat not *racing* shall not interfere with a boat that is *racing*.

Rule 23.1 makes it clear that before you begin *racing* and once you are no longer *racing*, you cannot interfere with boats that are *racing*. "Interfere" means that you have adversely affected a boat's forward progress or maneuverability. Remember, boats begin "racing" at their preparatory signal. The principle of the rule is that a boat that is not *racing* should not adversely affect a boat that is *racing*.

Note that any "interference" will potentially break this rule. Particularly after *finishing*, boats need to be very careful where they sail so that their wind-shadow and physical presence do not hurt boats still *racing*. However, the rule's opening phrase ("If reasonably possible…") means that boats do not need to go to unreasonable measures to avoid interfering. If they are careful, they should have no problems.

Remember, the preamble to Part 2 says, *"a boat not **racing** shall not be penalized for breaking one of these rules…except rule 23.1."* Rule 44.1 (Taking a Penalty) says, *"A boat may take a Two-Turns Penalty when she may have broken one or more rules of Part 2 in an incident **while racing*** (emphasis added)." Therefore, if you break rule 23.1 you cannot take a Two-Turns Penalty. You can be protested and penalized under rule 64.2 (Penalties). Note, rule 64.2 says *"If a boat has broken a rule when not **racing**, her penalty shall apply to the race sailed nearest in time to that of the incident."* (See Appeal 16.)

RULE 23.2

If reasonably possible, a boat shall not interfere with a boat that is taking a penalty, sailing on another leg or subject to rule 21.1. However, after the starting signal this rule does not apply when the boat is sailing her *proper course*.

Rule 23.2 is intended to provide some protection to boats while they are returning to *start* or taking penalties, and to try to stop boats from interfering with a competitor who is a leg or more ahead of them. If, after the starting signal, you are sailing your *proper course* (i.e., the course that will get you to the finishing line the fastest) and you interfere with a boat that is OCS and returning to start, taking a penalty or sailing on another leg, you do not break this rule. But, if you are not sailing your *proper course* and interfere with them, you break this rule. Note that before the starting signal you can never interfere with a boat taking a penalty.

12

Part 3 and Part 4
Conduct of a Race and Other Requirements When Racing

Part 3 contains the rules that govern the conduct of a race (rules 25–37). Part 4 contains other rules that govern us while we are *racing* (rules 40–56). Most of the rules are straightforward and simple to understand. I'll focus on the five for which an explanation might be helpful: rule 31 (Touching a Mark), rule 42 (Propulsion), rule 44 (Penalties at the Time of an Incident), rule 47 (Trash Disposal), and rule 55 (Setting and Sheeting Sails). Note rule 43 (Exoneration) is discussed in chapter 8.

RULE 31 — TOUCHING A MARK

While *racing*, a boat shall not touch a starting *mark* before *starting*, a *mark* that begins, bounds or ends the leg of the course on which she is sailing, or a finishing *mark* after *finishing*.

Prior to the 1969–73 rules, if you touched a *mark* and it was your fault, you had to drop out of the race. In the 1968 Olympics in Mexico, the late Carl Van Duyne, sailing the Finn for the United States, saw the leech of his main touch the windward *mark* as he rounded it in first place. Despite the claims of the race officer at the *mark* who insisted that Carl did not touch the *mark*, Carl withdrew from the race. From this example and others, the rule writers saw the obvious over-severity of this penalty for the infraction, and changed the rule to permit sailors to take a penalty when they accidentally touch a *mark*.

Notice that the rule applies only while you are *racing*, which is the time from your preparatory signal until you have *finished* and cleared the finishing line and finishing *marks*. Also, if the starting line is set to leeward of the leeward *mark* on the first leg or the finishing line is set to windward of the windward *mark* on the last leg, that leeward or windward *mark* does not begin, bound or end that first or last leg so there is no penalty for touching it. Otherwise, when you touch a starting or finishing *mark*, or any *mark* that begins, bounds or ends a leg on which you are sailing, you have broken rule 31.

When you've broken rule 31 and want to take a penalty, rule 44 (Penalties at the Time of an Incident) tells you how to do that. You must first get well clear of other boats as soon as possible after touching the *mark* (not half-way down the leg!). Then, once clear you must **promptly** (i.e., without delay) make "one turn" including one tack and one gybe. Notice that your turn does not need to be a complete 360-degree turn (see Case 108). Nor does it matter whether you do the tack or gybe first. As long as you have completed one tack and one gybe, you are all set. (See rule 44.2 for full discussion). While you are making your turn, you have to *keep clear* of other boats under rule 21.2 (Starting Errors; Taking Penalties; Backing a Sail). Once you have completed your turn, you have completed your penalty and the rules of Section A apply to you again. Remember, if you acquire right of way over another boat after your turn, you have to initially give them *room* to *keep clear* under rule 15 (Acquiring Right of Way).

"If I hit one of the starting marks after the preparatory signal but well before the starting signal, when can I make my penalty turn?"

As soon as possible! In fact you are required to do so under rule 44.2 (One-Turn and Two-Turns Penalties). The rationale is that the penalty should fit the crime. Touching the *mark* three minutes before your start probably has little effect on anyone's race; likewise your penalty turn will be of little adverse consequence to you. However, touching it ten seconds before the start means that you are probably somewhere you shouldn't be and are likely adversely affecting the start for others; by the same token, making a penalty turn while others are *starting* will be of more negative consequence to you.

PART 3 AND PART 4: CONDUCT OF A RACE AND OTHER REQUIREMENTS 251

The penalty for touching a mark is a One-Turn Penalty that includes a tack and a gybe. The turn does not need to be a full 360 degree turn; i.e., after the boat has done a tack and a gybe (in either order) it may continue in the race.

"What do I do if I accidentally hit the finishing mark after I've finished but before I've cleared the mark?"

If you touch a finishing *mark* **before** you have cleared the finishing line and *marks* (i.e., while you are still *racing*), you should take a One-Turn Penalty. You can make your penalty turn anywhere, but you then have to cross the finishing line again from the course side of the line. The second time you cross will be your finishing place or time. (See rule 44.2, the definition *Finish*, and the discussion of the definition *Racing* for a discussion on when you have cleared the finishing *marks*.)

Notice rule 44.1(b), *"However, if the boat…despite taking a penalty, gained a significant advantage in the race or series by her breach her penalty shall be to retire."* This is clearly intended to deter boats from sailing into situations where they calculate that they can hit the *mark*, do a quick penalty turn and still come out well ahead of where they would be had they not done so. One example is at a crowded windward *mark* with a long line of *starboard-tackers*, where there is not enough space for a *port-tacker* (P) to tack in to leeward of the *starboard-tackers* and make it around the *mark* without either fouling the *starboard-tackers* or hitting the *mark*. P could probably come out ahead by hitting the *mark* and doing a quick penalty turn as opposed to ducking the line of *starboard-tackers*, but this wouldn't be fair; hence the rule against it in rule 44.1(b).

"What happens when I'm forced to touch a mark by another boat that was required to keep clear of me or give me room or mark-room?"

Whenever you touch a *mark*, you have three options:

1) If it was your own fault that you touched the *mark*, you can get clear of other boats and take your penalty as described in rule 44.2.

2) If another boat wrongfully compelled you to hit the *mark*, you are exonerated (freed from penalty) by rule 43.1 (Exoneration; see the discussion of rule 43 in chapter 8). Of course, if you are protested, the protest committee will decide if you are exonerated by rule 43.1. That is why it is prudent for you to protest the other boat (by hailing the word "Protest" and, if required, flying your flag at the first reasonable opportunity). If the other boat acknowledges breaking a rule of Part 2 and takes a penalty (Two-Turns or Scoring Penalty, etc. under rule 44) or retires from the race, the protest committee will likely decide you are exonerated by rule 43.1 for breaking rule 31 (Touching a Mark), provided it decides that it was that breach that caused you to touch the *mark*. If the other boat does not take a penalty, you must hope the protest committee decides that in fact it was the other boat's Part 2 rule breach that compelled you to touch the *mark*, in which case it will disqualify the other boat and confirm your exoneration. If it doesn't, you will be disqualified under rule 64.2 (Penalties) for breaking rule 31.

3) If you believe another boat wrongfully compelled you to hit the *mark*, you can do a penalty turn; i.e., take the penalty in rule 44.2 as "insurance." You can then protest the other boat if you choose to. If the protest committee decides the other boat broke a *rule*, she will be disqualified. Note: You cannot be compensated for your loss of time and distance during your voluntary penalty. If the protest committee decides she didn't break a *rule*, you will not be disqualified for breaking rule 31 because you already took a penalty for that (see rule 64.2(a), Penalties).

"Does it count if just my head brushes against the mark?"

Absolutely yes. In the Introduction of *The Racing Rules of Sailing* under 'Terminology' it says, "*'Boat' means a sailboat and the crew on board.*" In fact, if

PART 3 AND PART 4: CONDUCT OF A RACE AND OTHER REQUIREMENTS 253

you have a late spinnaker take-down and your spinnaker sheet trails behind the boat and rubs against the *mark* after you're already around and a boat-length away from it, you still have to take your penalty. Case 77 sums it up, "A boat touches a mark within the meaning of rule 31 when any part of her hull, crew or equipment comes in contact with the mark. The fact that her equipment touches the mark because she has maneuvering or sail-handling difficulties does not excuse her breach of the rule."

"If I get the mark's anchor line caught on my centerboard but quickly raise my board and clear the line before I touch the mark, have I hit the mark? What happens when I'm not so quick and the mark is dragged in and touches my boat?"

Remember that the anchor line of a *mark* is not part of the *mark* (see the definition *Mark*). So, on a race committee boat with a high bow, where 15 feet of anchor line may be above the water, the *mark* begins at the bow of the boat. The same is true when a *mark*'s anchor line is partially or wholly submerged. In both cases, there is no penalty for touching the line. However, if touching its anchor line causes the *mark* to be drawn against your boat, you have touched the *mark* and must do a penalty turn or protest. Appeal 10 reads, "If, however, fouling its anchor line causes the mark to be drawn against the boat, the boat has broken rule 31."

"What if I foul another boat and hit a mark in the same incident?"

Good question. Rule 44.1(a) (Taking a Penalty) says, *"However, when a boat may have broken a rule of Part 2 and rule 31 in the same incident she need not take the penalty for breaking rule 31."* Therefore, when a Two-Turns Penalty or a Scoring Penalty under rule 44 is available, and you choose to take that penalty, you do not have to also do an additional penalty turn for hitting the *mark*.

RULE 42 — PROPULSION

RULE 42.1 — BASIC RULE

Except when permitted in rule 42.3 or rule 45, a boat shall compete by using only the wind and water to increase, maintain or decrease her speed. Her crew may adjust the trim of sails and hull, and perform other acts of seamanship, but shall not otherwise move their bodies to propel the boat.

Rule 42 is the "pumping, rocking, ooching, sculling" rule. The rule specifically tells sailors how they can, and cannot, propel their boats in a sailboat race. The principle behind rule 42 is simple: the rule writers (and most sailors themselves) want people to race their sailboats by sailing them (i.e., using the natural wind) as opposed to by propelling or slowing them in other ways. If you are a bit too early for a start, it is more of a sport if you have to slow down using your sails and rudder than if you could just stick your arms in the water and backpaddle; just as it's more challenging and fun to try to ride the waves on a windy reach as opposed to handing all the sheets to Igor and telling him to "pump" nonstop to the leeward *mark*.

"It seems that there could be a variety of interpretations and applications of rule 42 by competitors and judges. Are there any official interpretations of rule 42 that helps get all the competitors and officials reading and applying the rule the same way?"

In fact there is. World Sailing has published a comprehensive document entitled *Interpretations of Rule 42, Propulsion* and specific interpretations for many international classes. These are available on the World Sailing website (sailing.org/raceofficials/rule42/index). The intention of these documents is to provide a clear and consistent interpretation of rule 42 as it applies to specific commonly-used actions while sailing a boat. This permits sailors and judges alike to prepare for events with confidence that they will be sailing and officiating properly under rule 42. I strongly encourage all who race or officiate boats that can be propelled by kinetic actions to read and study these documents carefully.

Compliance with rule 42 continues to be a major issue facing the sport. In my opinion, the rule and the *Interpretations* clearly state what is permitted and what is prohibited. After an explanation of the rule, I will discuss the more central issue of competitor self-control and self-policing vs. the growing reliance on putting judges on the race course to police the kinetics.

Rule 42.1 clearly states the basic premise: *"A boat shall compete by using only the wind and water to increase, maintain or decrease her speed. Her crew may adjust the trim of sails and hull, and perform other acts of seamanship, but shall not otherwise move their bodies to propel the boat."* This is the way sailboats are to be raced; i.e., they can be powered only by the natural action of the wind and water. The last phrase in the rule serves to prohibit any crew action that **in and of itself** propels the boat. Paddling is an obvious example.

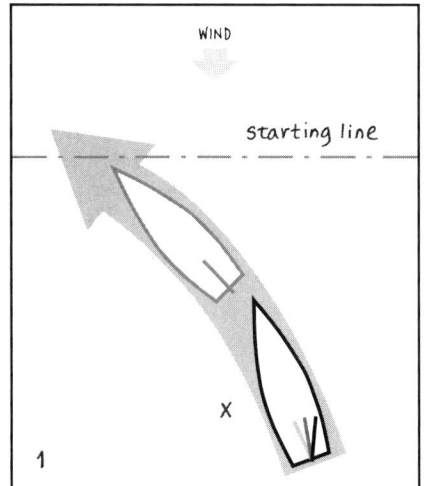

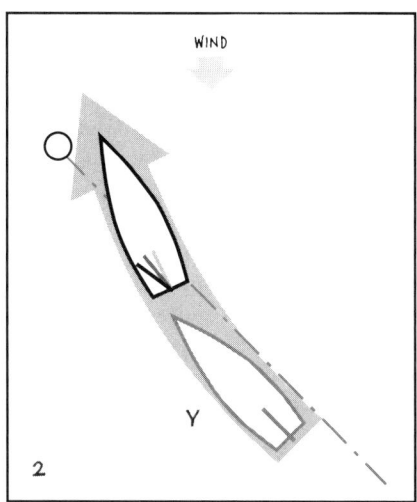

PART 3 AND PART 4: CONDUCT OF A RACE AND OTHER REQUIREMENTS   255

In diagram 1, Boat Y is moving slowly and is repeatedly forcefully moving her tiller to turn the boat down from almost head to wind to a close-hauled course. Though this action is "sculling" it is permitted under rule 42.3(d), as an exception to rule 42.2(d).

In diagram 2, as long as Boat X was above a close-hauled course and moving slowly when she began repeatedly forcefully moving her tiller ("sculling"), she is not breaking rule 42.2(d) because she is turning towards a close-hauled course on port tack. However, once she has sculled in one direction, she breaks rule 42.2(d) if she then sculls in the other direction before getting to a close-hauled course.

But even one good hard roll of the boat that propels the boat would be illegal as well. Note that the term "crew" refers to **all** sailors on board, including the helmsman.

Notice that it is just as illegal to slow yourself down ("decrease speed") unnaturally as it is to propel yourself. So if you're early for a start or trapped on the outside of a crowd at a *mark*, you can't stick your leg in the water to slow down. Likewise, if you luff a boat before the start and hit them, you can't hang on to them to slow yourself down so you're not early. However, there are legal ways to slow yourself down using the natural action of the wind and water. One is to physically hold the boom out so the wind pushes against the sail; another is to turn the rudder hard over against the flow of the water provided it is not done repeatedly back and forth (see discussion of "sculling" in rule 42.2(d)). (See Appeal 25.)

Note also that a boat can be penalized for breaking rule 42 only while she is *racing* (see preamble to Part 4). Case 69 says, "During the period in which the boat was racing she was using wind as a source of power as required by rule 42.1. Her motion also resulted from momentum created by engine power that propelled her before she began racing. Nothing in the rule requires that a boat be in any particular state of motion or non-motion when she begins racing." Likewise, in light air and adverse current, a boat can just get its bow across the finish line (thereby *finishing*), drift backwards, and, when clear of the finishing line and finishing *marks* (i.e., no longer *racing*), turn on her engine and power out of the course area.

THERE ARE SOME COMMON-SENSE EXCEPTIONS built into rule 42 for safety reasons.

RULE 42.3(g)

Any means of propulsion may be used to help a person or another vessel in danger.

RULE 42.3(h)

To get clear after grounding or colliding with another boat or object, a boat may use force applied by the crew of either boat and any equipment other than a propulsion engine.

These reinforce the overriding safety principle that you should get to a boat or person's rescue as fast as you can using any means available, including paddling, rocking, or an engine when you have one. Obviously, this is not intended to be misused as a deceitful way to advance along the race course. Case 20 and the discussion of rule 1.1 (Safety, Helping Those in Danger) are clear as to the responsibility all racing sailors have, and when and how a boat that renders assistance should be compensated.

Also, when you go aground or hit another boat, you may use whatever means of force is necessary to clear yourself, except that you can't use your engine to propel yourself. Note that you can use the power from your engine to run a winch or windlass, etc. if necessary.

"Can I anchor?"

Yes. Rule 45 (Hauling Out; Making Fast; Anchoring) states, *"[A boat] may anchor or the crew may stand on the bottom."* Rule 42.1 specifically permits the actions described in rule 45. Generally boats anchor either as a safety measure or to decrease the speed at which they are moving away from their destina-

PART 3 AND PART 4: CONDUCT OF A RACE AND OTHER REQUIREMENTS 257

tion (as in adverse current). Note that a means of anchoring is the crew standing on the bottom. Of course if that crew starts walking the boat around, rule 42.1 is broken.

Note, recovering an anchor, whether it was lowered or thrown forward, so as to gather way over the ground, breaks rule 42.1. Anchoring should be a means of keeping you where you are, and not a means of advancing yourself along the race course. Clearly, if you throw your anchor forward and then recover the anchor, you will be "pulling yourself" forward past where you were when you threw out the anchor. Therefore, when *racing*, the anchor should be **dropped straight down**. Likewise, when you pull the anchor back up, you can't generate momentum that will cause the boat to move **past** the point where the anchor was on the ground; i.e., where it was dropped. (See Case 5.)

"Now what about the actions listed in rule 42.2; are they always prohibited, or only when they are actually capable of propelling the boat?"

Rule 42.2 lists five specific types of actions which are **always** prohibited, regardless of whether they are capable of propelling the boat or not. This makes it easier for sailors to know what they can't do, and for judges to administer the rule on the water and in protest hearings. The five are the major "offenses."

RULE 42.2 — PROHIBITED ACTIONS

Without limiting the application of rule 42.1, these actions are prohibited:

(a) pumping: repeated fanning of any sail either by pulling in and releasing the sail or by vertical or athwartships body movement;

(b) rocking: repeated rolling of the boat, induced by
  (1) body movement,
  (2) repeated adjustment of the sails or centreboard, or
  (3) steering;

(c) ooching: sudden forward body movement, stopped abruptly;

(d) sculling: repeated movement of the helm that is either forceful or that propels the boat forward or prevents her from moving astern;

(e) repeated tacks or gybes unrelated to changes in the wind or to tactical considerations.

Let me reemphasize: If you do any of these above-listed actions, you have broken rule 42.2. It does not matter whether the action actually propelled the boat, or even if it was capable of propelling the boat! Therefore, it applies to boats of all sizes. Note that class rules (but not the notice or race or the sailing instructions!) can change rule 42, including some of the prohibitions in rule 42.2 (see rule 86.1(c), Changes to the Racing Rules).

To understand these descriptions, notice the use of the word "repeated" throughout. The World Sailing *Interpretations of Rule 42* define "repeated" as "more than once in the same area on a leg." "Ooching" is the only action prohibited by rule 42.2 that involves a singular movement.

(a) **Pumping**: the World Sailing *Interpretations of Rule 42* define "fanning" as "moving a sail in and out not in response to wind shifts, gusts or waves." So for a sail to be "pumped," it must be repeatedly pulled in and then released with no apparent connection with wind shifts or gusts, and this is illegal. This can be done using the sheets, or by using body motions. Bouncing up and down on the rail is an example of "vertical" movement; and crossing the boat quickly from side to side is "athwartships" movement. In a small boat with a flexible mast, bouncing can "pump" the top of the sail. Likewise, movement side to side will commonly cause the angle of heel to change, which in turn can act to "pump" the sail. These means of "pumping" are also illegal. Rule 42.3(c) allows you to pump in certain conditions.

Note, this rule is not designed to inhibit good sailing techniques. On a puffy or shifty day, the mainsail can be trimmed in and out constantly to keep the boat flat or the sails well trimmed, provided it doesn't become a "fanning" action. Similarly, downwind, the spinnaker sheet can be constantly played in response to changes in apparent wind.

(b) **Rocking**: Your boat is "rocking" when it is repeatedly rolling back and forth. You may be intentionally doing it with your body, or you may have simply encouraged it by pulling your centerboard up, letting your boom way out, and then starting the action like a pendulum with one lean back of your shoulders. It doesn't matter whether your body continues to move; if you started your boat rhythmically rolling back and forth, it's "rocking," and that is illegal at all times. Obviously, waves themselves will cause the boat to toss about. You do not have to run all over the boat counteracting every wave action. If you watch a fleet of boats on a broad reach or run, you will see that they all are being tossed in a similar way. If one boat is being intentionally "rocked," she will stand out instantly as being different from the others.

(c) **Ooching**: "Ooching" is a "sudden forward body movement, stopped abruptly." The key to "ooching" is that it is forward motion, it is sudden, and it is stopped abruptly. Even just one "ooch" is illegal. Pushing or pulling on the mast or shrouds (forward hand movements), slamming forward on the front of the cockpit, mast shrouds or forestay, and subtle abrupt forward motions with the rear or feet are all examples of "ooching" and are illegal at all times.

(d) **Sculling**: First of all, any "repeated forceful movement" of the helm is "sculling" and is illegal, with two exceptions (see below). Second of all, repeated movement of the helm that is turning the boat is not movement that is propelling the boat forward; therefore, it is legal to repeatedly move your tiller back and forth to turn your boat as long as you don't do it "forcefully." In that situation, typically your tiller won't cross centerline and your bow will be clearly moving to one side or the other. Finally, note that if you are stopped, you can't wiggle your tiller to keep from moving backward.

One exception is that you are allowed to "scull" if you are trying to turn to a close-hauled course after getting very slow or stopped above close-hauled (rule 42.3(d)). This will often happen on the starting line or when shooting head to wind to try to get around a windward *mark*. Also, it is legal to slow yourself down by repeatedly moving your helm (rule 42.3(e)).

(e) **Repeated tacks or gybes unrelated to changes in the wind or to tactical considerations**: You cannot repeatedly tack or gybe back and forth in quick succession unless you can justify your maneuvers based on changes in the wind (windshifts, etc.) or tactical considerations (covering another boat, etc.). Notice, you can tack or gybe for any reason you want; you just can't do it "repeatedly" without the specific reasons listed in this rule.

"Are there any exceptions to the prohibitions in rule 42.2?"
Yes. They are in rule 42.3, Exceptions.

RULE 42.3 — EXCEPTIONS

(a) A boat may be rolled to facilitate steering.

(b) A boat's crew may move their bodies to exaggerate the rolling that facilitates steering the boat through a tack or a gybe, provided that, just after the tack or gybe is completed, the boat's speed is not greater than it would have been in the absence of the tack or gybe.

(c) When surfing (rapidly accelerating down the front of a wave), planing or foiling is possible
   (1) to initiate surfing or planing, each sail may be pulled in only once for each wave or gust of wind, or
   (2) to initiate foiling, each sail may be pulled in any number of times.

(d) When a boat is above a close-hauled course and either stationary or moving slowly, she may scull to turn to a close-hauled course.

(e) If a batten is inverted, the boat's crew may pump the sail until the batten is no longer inverted. This action is not permitted if it clearly propels the boat.

(f) A boat may reduce speed by repeatedly moving her helm.

(g) Any means of propulsion may be used to help a person or another vessel in danger.

(h) To get clear after grounding or colliding with a vessel or object, a boat may use force applied by her crew or the crew of the other vessel and any equipment other than a propulsion engine. However, the use of an engine may be permitted by rule 42.3(i).

(i) Sailing instructions may, in stated circumstances, permit propulsion using an engine or any other method, provided the boat does not gain a significant advantage in the race.

"Can I change the angle of my boat's heel to steer the boat more efficiently than using the rudder?"

Yes. Rule 42.3(a) permits "rolling" the boat to facilitate steering. For instance, sailing downwind in waves it is legal to heel the boat to leeward to head up over a wave, then heel it to windward to steer down the backside, etc. Notice

PART 3 AND PART 4: CONDUCT OF A RACE AND OTHER REQUIREMENTS **261**

also that on a run most boats sail faster when heeled to windward, and the crew can position their weight to do this, provided the boat doesn't start "rocking" back and forth as a result.

"So it is legal to roll-tack and roll-gybe?"

Absolutely yes! Rule 42.3(b) specifically permits you to exaggerate the rolling provided it helps you steer the boat onto the new *tack*, and provided you don't come out of your tack or gybe going faster than just before you began it. Therefore, you can begin your tack with a slight heel to leeward to begin the boat heading up. Then, as the boat is at or near head to wind, you can roll the boat hard to the new leeward side to help "pivot" the boat onto its new close-hauled course. Finally, you can bring the boat upright or even past upright as it gets to its close-hauled course.

The most important thing is that once the boat is brought up from its roll, the mast cannot make a major dip to leeward and back up again. This second "pump," which serves to accelerate the boat rather than steer it, is illegal.

"Does rule 42.3(c) permit one pump of each sail per wave?"

Yes, unless you are attempting to foil in which case you can pump as much as you want to. Rule 42.3(c) permits "pumping," but only to initiate surfing, planing or foiling. The rule permits one "pump" for each sail (main, spinnaker and jib if desired, though pumping the jib is generally slow unless you are winging it) to attempt to surf or plane, and as many pumps as you'd like to foil. However, if the "pump" on the main gets the boat surfing, planing or foiling, a subsequent "pump" on any sheet would not be legal. If the main and spinnaker were "pumped" simultaneously, there would be no problem.

Notice that for surfing you must be trying to launch down the front of the wave (the "downhill side"), meaning you cannot ordinarily pump upwind unless there is a wave coming from behind you (such as a motorboat wake or after a large windshift). You can't "pump" up the backside of the wave claiming it will get you over the top and down the front side faster. A "surfing" boat will shoot through the water faster than boats around it that are not surfing. A "planing" boat will be lifted partly out of the water by its own bow wave, and its stern wave will disappear. Visually it will look like the boat is skimming across the surface of the water. A "foiling" boat will be lifted completely out of the water and will be riding on its foils.

Also you can "pump" using anything controlling the sail, including the vang or a special "pumping" line unless prohibited by class rules.

"What if after a tack or gybe my compression batten is inverted; can I repeatedly pull in on the main to 'pop' it?"

Yes. But you break rule 42.2(a), pumping, if you clearly propel the boat as a result (see rule 42.3(e)).

"Is it true I can never ooch?"

That's basically right. Rule 42.3 makes no exception for ooching. However class rules can permit ooching (see next paragraph); and the Intercollegiate Sailing Association (ICSA), which governs college racing in the U.S., permits it in its Procedural Rules.

"Why is rule 42.2 so restrictive, and can the rule ever be made more permissive other than the exceptions in rule 42.3?"

The rule writers have taken this step to reduce the strength factor required to race sailboats successfully, and to ensure that the sport remains a sailing contest. Notice that sailing instructions cannot change rule 42 (rule 86.1, Changes to the Racing Rules). Only **class rules** can make rule 42 more permissive by modifying it with a specific reference to it (rule 86.1(c), Changes to the Racing Rules). Therefore a class can permit more than one pump per wave or ooching or more liberal rules about roll tacking and gybing, etc. Additionally a class can permit pumping, rocking and ooching when the wind speed exceeds a specified limit (see Appendix P5, Flags O and R). This is an issue the members of each class should thoroughly discuss, and sailors should be proficient in those skills if permitted.

"I heard that a protest committee can throw me out under rule 42 without a hearing, and that a DSQ under rule 42 can't be used as a 'throwout' race; is this true?"

Absolutely not! Under previous editions of *The Racing Rules of Sailing* this was permitted, but no longer. If a judge sees an apparent infringement of rule 42 on the water and Appendix P (Special Procedures for Rule 42) is in effect, he or she can act as permitted (see next paragraph). Otherwise, the judge must protest the boat; and if the protest committee decides the boat broke rule 42, it will disqualify her under rule 64.2 (Penalties), just as with any other rules breach.

PART 3 AND PART 4: CONDUCT OF A RACE AND OTHER REQUIREMENTS

"So how does Appendix P (Special Procedures for Rule 42) work?"

The system, found in Appendix P (Special Procedures for Rule 42), gives judges on the water the authority to penalize boats for alleged breaches of rule 42. Note that Appendix P is in effect **only** if the notice of race or sailing instructions state that it is. It has been used successfully at the international level, including the Olympics and World Sailing class world championships for many years now. Many sailors and judges feel that competitors break rule 42 far less when they know the judges are watching for potential breaches of the rule and have the authority to penalize them on the spot, and as a result the racing is cleaner and fairer. Of course this requires knowledgeable judges to ensure correct interpretations and applications of rule 42.

"Now I understand what rule 42 allows and doesn't allow; but what do I do when another competitor starts to rock or pump by me?"

Most active racers believe that the rule itself is clear enough and is not the cause of the problem. The real problem is the enforcement of the rule. There are several extreme positions, and there have been many creative attempts made at resolving this issue. Some say the enforcement should be left completely up to judges around the course; i.e., flood the course with referees. Others argue that it is impractical to put that many judges on the course; and that because competitors will never police themselves, the rule itself should be abolished altogether and the race committees given the authority to proclaim before or during a race that either "anything" or "nothing" goes.

Fortunately, the majority of us believe that the racing is best when the sailors themselves have the responsibility to sail within the *rules*. We have seen too many regattas with either too few judges or poorly qualified ones. More to the point, we like the concept of competitor-enforced *rules* which makes the sport unique from almost all others.

But it takes only a few people in each fleet to ruin it for the rest. If some decide that doing well in the race by cheating is okay, and they start pumping and sculling off the starting line and rocking downwind, it puts the other sailors in a very awkward position. Either they can join in, or warn and then protest the other boat, or do nothing. To join in, they have to admit that the problem is not worth their effort to fight it. To do nothing is frustrating because those sailors will feel that not only are they being left behind, but that nothing is being done to enforce the rule.

I strongly recommend sailors take these three steps: 1) first warn the other boat; 2) then get the attention of some other boats nearby with the hopes that they'll say something too; and 3) then protest if the illegal actions continue. You are not being the "bad guy" for simply doing what you'd do if a *port-tacker* hit you when you were on *starboard-tack*. It is destructive to the racing when people feel they can get away with cheating; and they will continue to only get worse if no one calls them on it.

In the hearing the protest committee should (a) find out exactly what the wind and wave conditions were; (b) discuss what the sailing characteristics of the boat are from their shared experiences, competitors' testimony and expert witnesses when useful; and (c) determine what the exact actions of the protestee were. Witnesses are useful to everyone and are desired. Keep in mind that when judges see an apparent infringement, the US Sailing prescription to rule 63.1 (Hearings: Requirements for a Hearing) precludes them from being on the protest committee if they will also be the protestor or will give evidence in the hearing. Note also that rule 63.6 (Taking Evidence and Finding Facts) says, "*A member of the protest committee who saw the incident shall, while the parties are present, state that fact and may give evidence.*" Even if the protest committee member does not offer evidence, a *party* or the protest committee can call them as a witness, in which case they can no longer be on the protest committee for that hearing (see the US Sailing prescription to rule 63.1). Furthermore, when the sailing instructions state that the US Sailing prescription to rule 63.1 is not in effect, it is permissible for members of the protest committee to also be the protestor, but they must be sure to give their entire testimony while all the *parties* to the hearing are present and able to ask questions and otherwise respond. (See rule 60, Right to Protest; Right to Request Redress or Rule 69 Action; rule 63.3, Right to be Present; and rule 63.6, Taking Evidence and Finding Facts.)

The bottom line to the rule 42 issue is that everyone who races should make the effort to understand exactly what the rule does and does not allow, and then sail within the rule's limits. The rule is not that complex to understand, and my guess is that most sailors who have studied it have a good sense of what is right and wrong. Where it breaks down is when sailors intentionally ignore the rule for their own personal gain. All fleets of sailors should talk about this issue.

The Two-Turns Penalty is two turns in the same direction (in either direction) that include two tacks and two gybes. The second turn does not need to be a full 360-degree turn; i.e., after the last tack and gybe, the boat may continue in the race.

RULE 44 — PENALTIES AT THE TIME OF AN INCIDENT

RULE 44.1 — TAKING A PENALTY

A boat may take a Two-Turns Penalty when she may have broken one or more rules of Part 2 in an incident while *racing*. She may take a One-Turn Penalty when she may have broken rule 31. Alternatively, the notice of race or sailing instructions may specify the use of the Scoring Penalty or some other penalty, in which case the specified penalty shall replace the One-Turn and the Two-Turns Penalty. However,

(a) when a boat may have broken a rule of Part 2 and rule 31 in the same incident she need not take the penalty for breaking rule 31;

(b) if the boat caused injury or serious damage or, despite taking a penalty, gained a significant advantage in the race or series by her breach her penalty shall be to retire.

Rule 44.1 states that if you think you may have broken one or more rules of Part 2 or rule 31 (Touching a Mark) in an incident while *racing*, you can

always take a voluntary penalty at the time of the incident. This is sensible. Mistakes happen, and there should be a consequence for breaking a rule; but forcing sailors to retire and sail in for a minor infraction is not in balance with the great effort, time and expense that goes into participating in a race.

Rule 44.1 states that the penalty is the One or Two-Turns Penalty (see the discussion of rule 44.2) unless the notice of race or sailing instructions specify the use of some other penalty. Another common penalty is the Scoring Penalty, often known as the "percentage penalty." When the Scoring Penalty is in effect, it replaces the One- or Two-Turns Penalty as the penalty. This is clearly described in rule 44.3 (Scoring Penalty) and won't be discussed in this book.

Note that even a right-of-way boat can need to take a penalty. If a right-of-way boat fails to avoid contact with another boat when it was reasonably possible for her to do so, she breaks rule 14 (Avoiding Contact). If damage results from the contact, she is liable to being penalized and can do a Two-Turns Penalty to absolve herself.

"Can I ever take a penalty on shore?"

Check the sailing instructions for your race or event to see if Appendix T (Arbitration) or US Sailing Appendix V (Alternative Penalties) is in effect. The rules in these appendices are intended to improve compliance with the Basic Principles: Sportsmanship and the Rules, and to encourage boats to enforce the rules by protesting. Appendix V provides for a lesser alternative penalty on the water, and both appendices provide an alternative penalty (30%) that encourages competitors to take a penalty on shore when they realize they may have broken a rule of Part 2 or rule 31.

"Is there a situation where the only penalty a boat can take is to retire from the race?"

Yes. If a boat has broken a rule of Part 2 (including rule 14) and has caused "injury" or "serious damage" or has gained a "significant advantage" in the race or series by her breach despite taking a penalty, **she must retire**; i.e., she cannot take a turns or scoring penalty on the water (rule 44.1(b)). This is a clear reminder to all competitors, whether holding the right of way or not, to be careful and sportsmanlike.

"Before going on, could you discuss the terms 'injury' and 'serious damage'?"

Sure. Understand, however, that these terms are difficult to define precisely.

I will discuss what, in my opinion, are the important considerations based on the rule, the appeals and cases, the dictionary and my interpretation. In a *protest*, protest committees will need to exercise their best judgment in these situations. Notice that the judgment that "injury" or "serious damage" occurred is not a "fact found;" it is a conclusion based on the "facts found" and therefore subject to appeal.

An "injury" is something that physically hurts a **person**, and more than just briefly, and in a way that ordinarily affects the person's ability to function normally and/or requires the person to be attended to at some point. The reason the rule does not refer to "serious" injury is that "injury" implies that the hurt is "serious." "Damage" refers to physical damage to a **boat or its equipment**. (See Cases 19 and 110.)

Case 141 discusses "serious damage." "**Question:** Is there a special meaning in the racing rules of the term 'serious' when it is used in the phrase 'serious damage'? **Answer:** No. The term 'serious' is not defined in *The Racing Rules of Sailing* (RRS). The Terminology section of the Introduction states that 'other words and terms are used in the sense ordinarily understood in nautical or general use.' As understood in general use, when 'serious' is used in the phrase 'serious damage', the term means: important because of possible danger or risk; having potentially undesired consequences; giving cause for concern; or of significant degree or amount.

This suggests that when a protest committee has concluded from the facts found that damage occurred in an incident, it must then consider whether any of the four criteria implied by the definition above apply, and if so it should conclude that the damage is 'serious.' Questions to consider may include:

(1) Did the damage reduce the safety of the crew?

(2) Did the damage adversely impact the boat's sailing performance in a significant way?

(3) Will the cost of repairing the damage be a significant amount relative to the market value of the boat?

(4) Will the value of the boat after repairing the damage be significantly diminished?

Certainly, if the damage causes the boat to discontinue the race, it is "serious." If the boat can safely continue in the race and loses no finishing places as a direct result of the damage, and the nature and cost of any necessary repair isn't too high, the damage is not "serious." (Note that it is impossible to put a price tag on "serious;" that will have to be decided by the protest committee after considering all the relevant factors.)

If the damage is a deep scratch that penetrates the fiberglass, thereby requiring immediate repair after the race so that further damage doesn't result or so that the future speed, performance or maneuverability of the boat isn't affected, that damage would begin to fall into the "serious" category. And if the repair required more professional work and became a more costly and time-consuming affair, I would be more inclined to rule it "serious." But if the extent of the repair were such that it could be handled that evening by the sailors involved with a minimum of hassle and expense, and the damage does not affect the overall speed, performance or maneuverability of the boat, I would be inclined to rule it not "serious."

If the damage is a broken boom near the finish and the boat loses no places but cannot repair or replace the boom before the second race of that day, I'd consider the damage to be "serious;" but if the damage was to something that could normally be repaired or replaced on the water, such as a bent guy hook, the damage would not be "serious." (See Case 19.)

"Thanks! Now how do I take a One- or Two-Turns Penalty?"

RULE 44.2 — ONE-TURN OR TWO-TURNS PENALTIES

After getting well clear of other boats as soon after the incident as possible, a boat takes a One-Turn or Two-Turns Penalty by promptly making the required number of turns in the same direction, each turn including one tack and one gybe. When a boat takes the penalty at or near the finishing line, her hull she be completely on the course side of the line before she *finishes*.

When you want to do a One- or Two-Turns Penalty you must first get well clear of other boats as soon **as possible** after the incident (not half-way down the leg!). Remember that while you are getting clear you still have all your Section A rights; i.e., you are not taking a penalty until you clearly begin making your turns (rule 21.2, Starting Errors; Taking Penalties; Backing a Sail).

Once you are clear of other boats, you must **promptly** (i.e., without delay) make one or two turns in the same direction, each turn including a tack and

PART 3 AND PART 4: CONDUCT OF A RACE AND OTHER REQUIREMENTS 269

a gybe. Notice that the turn does not need to be a complete 360-degree turn. Once you complete your final tack or gybe, your penalty is complete and you may continue in the race. This is why it is not called a "360" or "720." Note that you have to do one turn immediately after the other, though it is generally acceptable to build enough speed after the first turn to be able to sail efficiently through the second one. While you are making your turns, you have to *keep clear* of other boats (see rule 21.2 and Case 108).

"What if I am not sure I have broken a rule; do I get some time to think about it before deciding to take a penalty?"

Unfortunately No! Appeal 60 says "Rule 44.1 permits a boat to take a penalty at the time of the incident. Rule 44.2 requires the boat to sail well clear of other boats as soon as possible after the incident and promptly make two turns as described in the rule. Together, these rules require a boat that decides to take a penalty to do so as soon as possible after the incident. The rule does not provide for time for a boat to deliberate whether she has broken a rule. If she delays in doing her penalty turns, she is still liable to be disqualified."

Once you have completed your turns, i.e., your final tack or gybe, you have completed your penalty and the rules of Section A apply to you again. Remember, if you acquire right of way over another boat after your second turn, you have to initially give them *room* to *keep clear* under rule 15 (Acquiring Right of Way).

Note that if you break a rule before the starting signal, you can do your Two-Turns Penalty immediately; i.e., you don't have to wait until after the starting signal. As in touching a *mark*, the rationale is that the penalty should fit the crime. Breaking a rule three minutes before your start probably has little effect on anyone's race; likewise your turns penalty will be of little adverse consequence to you. However, breaking a rule ten seconds before the start means that you are probably somewhere you shouldn't be and are likely adversely affecting the start for others; by the same token, doing a Two-Turns Penalty while others are *starting* will be of more negative consequence to you.

If you break a *rule* near the finishing line, including while or just after you have *finished* but are still *racing*, you can do your Two-Turns Penalty anywhere, but you then have to cross the finishing line again from the course side of the line. The second time you cross the finishing line will be your actual *finish* (see the definition *Finish*).

"How many penalty turns do I have to take if I break more than one rule in the incident; and if I take a penalty on the water, can I still be disqualified for that incident?"

You only need to take one penalty per "incident," regardless of how many rules you may have broken in that incident (first sentence of rule 44.1). Therefore, when a keep-clear boat breaks rule 10 (On Opposite Tacks) and fails to avoid a collision, thereby breaking rule 14 (Avoiding Contact), she need only do one Two-Turns Penalty. The same is true if you break a rule of Part 2 and rule 31 (Touching a Mark) in the same incident. Rule 44.1(a) is in effect saying that you know you got yourself in trouble; do your two turns for fouling the other boat but there's no need to do a third turn for touching the *mark*!

Appeal 65 discusses the question of when two occurrences are considered one or two incidents, saying in essence that the test is whether the second occurrence was the "inevitable result" of the first.

If you have taken an applicable penalty on the water, you cannot be further penalized on shore unless the protest committee decides a turns or scoring penalty was not available to you or that you took it incorrectly, in which case it can disqualify you for the Part 2 rule(s) you broke (see rule 64.2(a)).

"If I'm not sure who's right, can I do a One- or Two-Turns Penalty and still protest the other boat, or am I admitting guilt by taking a penalty?"

Excellent question. You can definitely protest the other boat and your penalty turns are not an admission of guilt. Rule 44.1 carefully says, *"A boat may take a…Penalty when she **may*** (emphasis added) *have broken one or more rules…"*. Furthermore, the US Sailing prescription to rule 67 (Damages) says, *"A boat that retires from a race or accepts a penalty does not, by that action alone, admit liability for damages."*

Let's say you do a Two-Turns Penalty and protest, and that the other boat did neither. If the protest committee finds that the other boat was wrong in your incident, she will be disqualified; but you cannot be compensated for anything you lost by taking your penalty. However, if the protest committee decides that you actually were wrong, you can't be further penalized because you already took a penalty (rule 64.2(a)). Therefore, you can view your Two-Turns Penalty as "insurance" against further penalty in an incident where you're not 100% certain how the protest committee will decide it.

PART 3 AND PART 4: CONDUCT OF A RACE AND OTHER REQUIREMENTS **271**

BASIC PRINCIPLES: ENVIRONMENTAL RESPONSIBILITY

Participants are encouraged to minimize any adverse environmental impact of the sport of sailing.

RULE 47 — TRASH DISPOSAL

Competitors and *support persons* shall not intentionally put trash in the water. This rule applies at all times while afloat. The penalty for a breach of this rule may be less than disqualification.

Rule 47 is the teeth in the Basic Principle which states that participants in the sport of sailing should take an active role in protecting the environment. There are many actions that all participants can and should take in that direction, including using refillable instead of disposable water bottles. But most are difficult or impossible to enforce or are not practical for all events. A ban on putting trash in the water, however, is enforceable and easily implemented. Notice that this rule applies to both competitors and their *support persons*.

"If a boat uses yarn or rubber bands to "stop" their spinnaker, does the boat break rule 47 if those stops fall in the water when the spinnaker is set?"

Yes! Appeal 110 states, "**Assumed Facts:** Boat A stops a sail using commercially available biodegradable yarn or rubber bands. When the sail is hoisted and the stops are broken, some of them fall into the water. Boat B protests A, alleging that she broke rule 47. In the hearing, A argues that the stops are not trash because they are biodegradable. **Question:** Did Boat A break rule 47? **Answer:** Yes. The broken sail stops that fall into the water, although biodegradable, are trash that the competitor intentionally put in the water; therefore Boat A broke rule 47. This applies at all times while afloat during an event; however the penalty for breaking rule 47 may be less than disqualification." Note that many sailmakers now have alternative "stops" that do not fall in the water when opened.

And if rule 47 is broken when not *racing*, rule 64.2 says, *"If a boat has broken a rule when not racing, her penalty shall apply to the race sailed nearest in time to that of the incident."* So you can be disqualified from a race already sailed or not yet sailed for breaking this rule. Note that the rule permits the protest committee to apply a less harsh penalty than disqualification for a breach of the rule.

Also note that the rule requires that the act of putting trash in the water be **intentional**, to prevent a boat from being penalized, for example, for capsizing and not being able to retrieve objects that might be categorized as trash.

There are many excellent programs now that support this concept. One that is commonly used at US Sailing championships and other regattas is "Clean Regattas" run by Sailors for the Sea.

> **Sailors for the Sea Clean Regattas program**
>
> Sailors for the Sea
> 449 Thames Street, 300D
> Newport, RI 02840
>
> phone: (401) 846-8900
>
> info@sailorsforthesea.org
> sailorsforthesea.org

RULE 55 — SETTING AND SHEETING SAILS

RULE 55.1 — CHANGING SAILS

When headsails or spinnakers are being changed, a replacing sail may be fully set and trimmed before the replaced sail is lowered. However, only one mainsail and, except when changing, only one spinnaker shall be carried set at a time.

PART 3 AND PART 4: CONDUCT OF A RACE AND OTHER REQUIREMENTS 273

RULE 55.2 — SPINNAKER POLES; WHISKER POLES

Only one spinnaker pole or whisker pole shall be used at a time except when gybing. When in use, it shall be attached to the foremost mast.

RULE 55.3 — SHEETING SAILS

No sail shall be sheeted over or through any device that exerts outward pressure on a sheet or clew of a sail at a point from which, with the boat upright, a vertical line would fall outside the hull or deck, except:

(a) a headsail clew may be connected (as defined in *The Equipment Rules of Sailing*) to a whisker pole, provided that a spinnaker is not set;

(b) any sail may be sheeted to or led above a boom that is regularly used for a sail and is permanently attached to the mast from which the head of the sail is set;

(c) a headsail may be sheeted to its own boom that requires no adjustment when tacking; and

(d) the boom of a sail may be sheeted to a bumkin.

RULE 55.4 — HEADSAILS AND SPINNAKERS

For the purposes of rules 54 and 55 and Appendix G, the definitions of 'headsail' and 'spinnaker' in *The Equipment Rules of Sailing* shall be used.

Note that this rule does not require that a spinnaker pole be used at all when flying a spinnaker! The only pole requirements are in rule 55.2. In other words, you can only use one pole at a time; and when it is "in use," i.e., projecting the spinnaker or headsail outboard, it must be attached to the mast.

With no requirement to use a pole, boats are free to do "gybe-sets" and "floater-drops." In both of these maneuvers, the spinnaker is set and drawing with no pole attached. In other words, a boat can legally gybe around the windward *mark*, set her spinnaker, fill it, and sail on down the leg with no pole. And likewise, when coming into a leeward *mark*, a boat can legally remove her pole and sail for as long as she chooses before lowering her spinnaker.

"So can a crew member lean out over a boat's lifelines to hold the spinnaker guy after the pole has been removed?"

Yes, but only "briefly." Rule 49.2 (Crew Position; Lifelines) forbids competitors from leaning their torsos out over the lifelines "except briefly to perform a necessary task." Appeal 72 reads, "Without a spinnaker pole, a spinnaker is less efficient and more unstable. As a boat prepares to round a leeward mark, removing the pole is one of the first necessary steps. From that time until the spinnaker is lowered, holding the guy by hand is a less effective but nonetheless useful means of controlling the spinnaker, which remains a "necessary task" even without the pole. The interval of time is normally a brief one, since generally there is no advantage in flying a spinnaker without a pole."

Also note that there is no requirement that the tack of the spinnaker be in "close proximity" to the outboard end of the spinnaker pole. The rationale is that it is generally faster to have the tack close to the outboard end, such that there is no reason to penalize a boat if she chooses not to do so.

Note that rule 86.1(c) (Changes to the Racing Rules) permits class rules to change this rule.

"I see a lot of boats flying asymmetrical spinnakers from bowsprits; I assume this is legal?"

Yes. Rule 55.3 specifically states, *"No sail shall be sheeted over or through any device that exerts outward pressure on a sheet or clew of a sail at a point from which, with the boat upright, a vertical line would fall outside the hull or deck."* Rule 55.3 is not broken provided that the bowsprit is used to attach the tack (the windward corner) of the spinnaker or as a lead for a line attached to the tack.

13

Part 5
Protests, Redress, Hearings, Misconduct and Appeals

Part 5 (Protests, Redress, Hearings, Misconduct and Appeals) contains all the rules governing who can protest, how to protest, how to ask for redress, how and when a protest or redress hearing should be run, what penalties can be applied, the rules about misconduct, and how to appeal (rules 60–71). It is divided into four sections: Section A, Protests; Redress; Rule 69 Action; Section B, Hearings and Decisions; Section C, Misconduct; and Section D, Appeals. I will focus on the Section A and B rules governing protests and requests for redress.

Remember that a *protest* is defined as "*An allegation made under rule 61.2 by a boat, a race committee, a technical committee or a protest committee that a boat has broken a **rule***" (see the definition *Protest*). A *protest*, therefore, is merely a means of bringing a *rules* issue to a hearing after the race where the sailors involved and the members of the protest committee can review the incident and decide how the *rules* apply.

Our sport is premised on competitors doing just that when there is an incident in which neither boat acknowledges being in the wrong. In fact, at the very beginning of the rule book the section entitled Basic Principles: Sportsmanship and the Rules, says, "*Competitors in the sport of sailing are governed by a* body of **rules** *that they are expected to follow* **and enforce** (emphasis added)." *Protests* that are the result of honest differences of opinions on the *rules* or observations of the incident should never have a negative taint to them.

Competitor enforcement of the *rules* is the tradition of our sport, and when the *rules* are not followed, or their application is in question, we owe it to our fellow competitors and ourselves, for the quality and fairness of the racing, to protest.

Note: To file a protest, or to request redress or that a hearing be reopened, you should use the standard hearing request form (see preamble to Part 5).

SECTION A — PROTESTS; REDRESS; RULE 69 ACTION

RULE 60 — RIGHT TO PROTEST; REQUEST REDRESS OR RULE 69 ACTION

RULE 60.1

A boat may

(a) protest another boat, but not for an alleged breach of a rule of Part 2 or rule 31 unless she was involved in or saw the incident;

(b) request redress; or

(c) report to the protest committee requesting action under rule 60.3(d) or 69.2(b).

Any boat that thinks another boat may have broken a *rule* can protest. This can occur during a race, or before or after a race; and it can involve a boat in the same race or one in a different race (see Appeal 116). Note, however, that the use of the word "may" in rule 60.1 clarifies that it is a boat's choice as to whether or not she protests. A boat cannot be penalized for choosing not to protest.

If you want to protest another boat for breaking a rule of Part 2 (When Boats Meet) or rule 31 (Touching a Mark), you must have been directly involved in the incident or have seen it happen yourself. A *protest* involving a Part 2 rule or rule 31 cannot be initiated by you when you learn about the incident from a "report" by a competitor from another boat in the race, or some other person such as a spectator.

PART 5: PROTESTS, REDRESS, HEARINGS, MISCONDUCT AND APPEALS 277

"What is a 'third-party protest,' and are they allowed?"

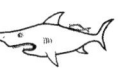

If you witness an incident in which you are not involved, and in which you think that at least one of the boats has broken a rule of Part 2 or rule 31, you can protest. It doesn't matter if they have contact or not. In this case you are the "third party." The protest committee will simply call a hearing based on your *protest*, find the facts about what happened in the incident, and penalize any boat that broke a *rule*.

RULE 60.2

A race committee may

(a) protest a boat, but not as a result of information arising from a request for redress or an invalid *protest*, or from a report from a person with a *conflict of interest* other than the representative of the boat herself;

(b) request redress for a boat; or

(c) report to the protest committee requesting action under rule 60.3(d) or 69.2(b).

If the race committee thinks a boat may have broken a *rule*, it may also protest (again, the word "may" is permissive meaning the race committee is under no obligation to protest). Note that it can't protest if it learned of the possible breach from someone who has a close personal interest in the outcome of the protest, may reasonably appear to have a personal or financial interest which could affect his ability to be impartial, or who stands to benefit from the protest committee's decision (see the definition *Conflict of Interest*). And it can't protest based on information it learned either in a *protest* that is found to be invalid or in any request for redress.

If the race committee feels a boat may be entitled to redress, it can request redress on behalf of that boat. And if it feels the actions of a boat or competitor or *support person* should be reviewed under rule 60.3(d) (for *support persons*) or rule 69 (Misconduct), it can report that to the protest committee.

"Can the race committee score me DSQ if it thinks it saw me foul a boat or hit a mark?"

No. A boat cannot be penalized without a protest hearing, with a couple of limited exceptions (rule 63.1, Requirement for a Hearing). If the race committee thinks a boat has broken a *rule*, and it thinks the boat should have a hearing to consider being penalized, all it can do is **protest** the boat. The protest committee will then call a hearing, find the facts, decide if the boat broke a *rule*, and penalize her if she did.

"Can the race committee penalize me without a hearing if it thinks I did not sail the course correctly?"

Yes! If a boat fails to *start*, *sail the course*, or *finish* correctly, the race committee can score her DNS (Did not *start*), OCS (on the course side), DNF (Did not *finish*) or NSC (Did not *sail the course*) without a hearing (rule A5.1, Scores Determined by the Race Committee). Similarly, the race committee can also score a boat worse than her actual finish position when the Z Flag Rule (rule 30.2), U Flag Rule (rule 30.3) or Black Flag Rule (rule 30.4) apply, or when the boat takes a Scoring Penalty (rule 44.3). If a boat feels the race committee has scored her incorrectly, the boat can speak directly with the race committee and/or request redress under rule 62.1(a) (Redress). Rule 90.3(c) says, *"When the race committee determines from its own records or observations that it has scored a boat incorrectly, it shall correct the error and make the corrected scores available to competitors."*

RULE 60.3

A protest committee may

(a) protest a boat, but not as a result of information arising from a request for redress or an invalid *protest*, or from a report from a person with a *conflict of interest* other than the representative of the boat herself. However, it may protest a boat
  (1) if it learns of an incident involving her that may have resulted in injury or serious damage, or
  (2) if during the hearing of a valid *protest* it learns that the boat, although not a *party* to the hearing, was involved in the incident and may have broken a *rule*;

(b) call a hearing to consider redress;

(c) act under rule 69.2(b); or

(d) call a hearing to consider whether a *support person* has broken a *rule*, based on its own observation or information received from any source, including evidence taken during a hearing.

Similar to the race committee, the protest committee may also protest a boat that may have broken a *rule*. Again, it can't protest if it learned of the possible breach from a person with a *conflict of interest* (see definition *Conflict of Interest*), nor based on information it learned either in a *protest* that is found to be invalid, or in any request for redress. If the protest committee feels a boat may be entitled to redress, it can call a hearing to consider redress; and if it believes the actions of a boat or competitor should be reviewed under rule 69 (Misconduct), it can call a hearing under rule 69.2(b).

The protest committee can also protest a boat in two other situations. One is when it learns of an incident that may have resulted in injury to a person or serious damage to a boat from **any** source, including from an invalid *protest* or overhearing competitors discussing an incident in the parking lot. See the discussion of rule 44.1 for a discussion of the terms "injury" and "serious damage."

The other situation is when the protest committee is hearing a valid *protest* and in the course of the hearing it learns that another boat involved in the incident, but not currently a *party* to that hearing, may have broken a *rule* in that incident. If the protest committee wishes to protest that boat, rule 61.1(c) says, "*If the protest committee decides to protest a boat under rule 60.3(a)(2), it shall inform her as soon as reasonably possible, close the current hearing, proceed as required by rules 61.2 and 63, and hear the original and the new protests together.*" In other words, the protest committee must stop the current hearing, inform the boat it is being protested **in writing** clearly identifying the reason for the *protest* (rule 61.2, Protest Contents), inform all the boats involved of the time and place of the new hearing, and give the boat time to prepare for the hearing (rule 63.2, Time and Place of the Hearing; Time for Parties to Prepare).

The protest committee may also call a hearing under rule 60.3(d) to consider whether a *support person* has broken a rule, which includes a parent or coach (see the definition *Support Person)*. Rules *support persons* might break include sailing instructions regarding where support boats are confined to, or rule 69.1(a) (Obligation not to Commit Misconduct; Resolution). *Support persons* and the competitors they are supporting may be penalized under rule 64.5 (Decisions Concerning Support Persons).

An explanation of the US Sailing prescriptions to rule 60.3 occurs at the end of this chapter.

Rules 60.4 and 60.5 will not be discussed in this book.

RULE 61 — PROTEST REQUIREMENTS

RULE 61.1 — INFORMING THE PROTESTEE

(a) The protesting boat shall inform the other boat at the first reasonable opportunity. When her *protest* will concern an incident in the racing area, she shall hail 'Protest' and conspicuously display a red flag at the first reasonable opportunity for each. She shall display the flag until she is no longer *racing*. However,

  (1) if the other boat is beyond hailing distance, the protesting boat need not hail but she shall inform the other boat at the first reasonable opportunity;

  (2) if the hull length of the protesting boat is less than 6 metres, she need not display a red flag;

  (3) if the incident was an error by the other boat in *sailing the course*, she need not hail or display a red flag but she shall inform the other boat either before or at the first reasonable opportunity after the other boat *finishes*;

  (4) if at the time of the incident it is obvious to the protesting boat that a member of either crew is in danger, or that injury or serious damage resulted, the requirements of this rule do not apply to her, but she shall attempt to inform the other boat within the time limit of rule 61.3.

(b) If the race committee, technical committee or protest committee intends to protest a boat concerning an incident the committee observed in the racing area, it shall inform her after the race within the time limit of rule 61.3. In other cases the committee shall inform the boat of its intention to protest as soon as reasonably possible. A notice posted on the official notice board within the appropriate time limit satisfies this requirement.

When you are involved in or see an incident in the racing area and you want to protest, you have to:

1) hail the word "Protest" at the first reasonable opportunity (unless the other boat wouldn't be able to hear your hail in which case you have to tell the other boat at the first reasonable chance you have that you intend to protest them); and

PART 5: PROTESTS, REDRESS, HEARINGS, MISCONDUCT AND APPEALS   281

2) if you are sailing a boat whose hull is 6 meters (19.68 feet) or longer, conspicuously display a red flag at the first reasonable opportunity.

Notice that rule 61.1(a) says you "shall" do these things. "Shall" means it is mandatory. If you do not correctly do these two things, your *protest* will not be valid and no hearing on the incident should occur. Rule 63.5 (Validity of the Protest or Request for Redress) states clearly, "*At the beginning of the hearing the protest committee shall take any evidence it considers necessary to decide whether all requirements for the **protest** or request for redress have been met. If they have been met, the **protest** or request is valid and the hearing shall be continued. If not, the committee shall declare the **protest** or request invalid and close the hearing.*" (See Appeal 66.)

There are two exceptions to the hail and flag requirements. If at the time of the incident it is obvious to the protesting boat that a member of either crew is in danger or that injury or serious damage resulted from the incident, then she does not need to hail "Protest" or fly a flag (rule 61.1(a)(4)). However, she must still try to inform the boat(s) being protested within the time limit for lodging protests that a *protest* will be lodged. The idea is that when there is an incident where someone is in danger or that clearly results in serious damage or injury, the boats are clearly aware of it and should be aware that one or more boats involved may have broken a *rule*. Often the focus of the situation is on separating the boats, checking the extent of the damage or injury, and getting on with the race if possible, etc. To require competitors to also make mandatory hails and fly flags in order to have the incident go to a protest hearing seemed unnecessary and undesirable. However, to be on the safe side, I would recommend that all boats considering protesting make the required hail and fly the flag if required to ensure that their *protest* will be heard.

The other exception is when you see a boat skip a *mark* or go around a *mark* the wrong way. Rule 61.1(a)(3) says, "*if the incident was an error by the other boat in sailing the course, [a boat intending to protest] need not hail or display a red flag but she shall inform the other boat either before or at the first reasonable opportunity after the other boat finishes.*"

THE HAIL

Note that you must use the actual word "Protest." Telling another boat to "do your penalty turns!" does not satisfy this rule. The purpose of the requirement is to be sure that the other boat(s) in and near the incident clearly know you intend to protest. As with other mandatory hails in the *rules*, the hail should be loud and clear, and it should be unambiguous as to which boat is being protested. When there could be confusion, I strongly suggest including in the hail the boat's number or name, or the person's name if you know it. Note that if the protest committee decides that you did not hail as required by rule 61.1(a), it is required to declare the protest invalid and close the hearing (rule 63.5, Validity of the Protest or Request for Redress).

The hail must be made at "the first reasonable opportunity" after you become aware of the incident, whether you are involved in the incident or merely saw it ("third party protest"). Though some may exist, it is very difficult to imagine a situation in which the first reasonable opportunity to say the word "Protest" isn't **immediately** after the incident. Remember that you can always decide not to go through with a *protest*, including for the reason that you just aren't sure who it was that fouled you. But if you don't say the word "Protest" at the time of the incident, you lose the opportunity to protest that incident. Therefore, it is always prudent to simply say "Protest" immediately. (See Appeals 61 and 122.)

Note that rule 61.1(a)(1) anticipates that there may be an instance where the boat you intend to protest is so far away at the time of the incident that there is no way the sailor(s) on that boat could possibly hear a hail. This would depend of course on factors such as the distance between the boats, the amount of wind, and the relationship of the boats to the wind (sound travels farther downwind than upwind). In this case, the rule simply requires you to tell the other boat at the first reasonable chance you have that you intend to protest them. I expect that this exception will typically apply to "third-party" *protests*; i.e., situations where the protestor is not directly involved in the incident but, for instance, sees a boat hit another boat or cut a *mark*.

If you intend to protest based on an incident that either occurred in the racing area without you being aware of it, or did not occur in the racing area, you do not need to say the word "Protest," but you do need to inform the other boat of your intent to protest as soon as is reasonably possible after becoming aware of the incident. The purpose of this rule is to be sure that boats intending to protest make every prompt and reasonable effort to go tell the other boat that a *protest* will be lodged, so that all the boats involved can be prepared and present for the hearing.

PART 5: PROTESTS, REDRESS, HEARINGS, MISCONDUCT AND APPEALS 283

"So is it correct that if I am racing a dinghy I don't need to fly a protest flag to protest; and if that's correct, won't sailors try to get out of protests by saying that they didn't know they were being protested?"

It is correct that if you are racing on a boat less than 20 feet long (6 meters or 19.68 feet to be exact), you do not have to fly a protest flag to protest (unless of course the notice of race or sailing instructions change rule 61.1(a)). The length refers to the hull length; i.e., from the bow to the stern, and does not include protrusions such as bowsprits, rudders, etc. This will encompass most dinghies, sailboards, catamarans and even some small keel boats.

My opinion is that with no flag requirement, more *protests* will be heard than fewer. Many *protests* get bogged down, and many get disallowed, on the issue of whether the flag was flown quickly enough or was big enough, leaving the actual *rules* issue unresolved. Not having to endure this frustrating situation should be a welcome relief to competitors and protest committees. Furthermore, often a dinghy was forced to sail a little more slowly or with a little less control while one of its sailors put up the flag, which was both unfair and a reason that often dinghy sailors chose not to protest.

In an incident, the boats are typically near each other such that a quick and audible hail of the word "Protest" should clearly inform the other boat that it is being protested. In college racing, where thousands of races a year have been run successfully for over fifty years with no protest flag requirement, when protestors say they hailed "Protest," the protest committees take them at their word unless the protestee can satisfy the protest committees otherwise. This puts an end to the nefarious claims that the "protestor did not hail." But sailors who say they hailed "Protest" when they know full well that they did not, do themselves and the sport a great disservice, and typically that lack of integrity catches up with them.

THE FLAG

Now, in the event you are required to fly a flag to protest, let's look at the flag requirements (rule 61.1(a), Informing the Protestee). When you are aware of an incident as it occurs in the racing area and want to protest because of it, you must conspicuously display a red flag at the first reasonable opportunity, whether you were involved in the incident or merely saw it ("third party protest"). Again, the purpose of the requirement is to provide a visual signal to the other boat that you intend to protest her. The Appeals are loud and clear throughout that if you are required to fly a flag and do not, then the protest committee cannot hear your *protest*.

Notice that even if the incident involves a breach of a class rule or sailing instructions, etc., you must display your flag. (See rule 63.5, Validity of the Protest or Request for Redress, Case 39 and Appeal 67.)

On the other hand, if you intend to protest because of an incident that either occurred in the racing area without you being aware of it, or did not occur in the racing area, you do not need to display a flag. Remember that you do need to inform the competitor that you intend to protest at the first reasonable opportunity after becoming aware of the incident.

"Just how quickly do I need to get my flag up?"

Rule 61.1(a) requires that it be displayed "at the first reasonable opportunity" after the incident. My best advice is that the "first reasonable opportunity" is normally **immediately**. Remember that the purpose of the rule is to provide a visual signal to the other boat, and to any other boats in the incident or vicinity, that you intend to protest because of **that** incident. Any delay at all only raises the likelihood that the boat being protested won't be aware of that fact, or that it won't be clear for which incident your flag is being displayed.

The timeliness of the flag issue is the cause of some acrimony in our sport, generally arising when a boat's protest is refused because the protest committee decides that her flag was not displayed soon enough after the incident. Often it is suggested that the flag requirement is less important when the other boat is fully aware of the protesting boat's intent to protest; e.g., after a collision and an immediate hail of "Protest." I agree that it is frustrating when a *protest* is refused on a validity issue rather than resolving the rules issue contained in the *protest*. But the *rules* are carefully worded to provide safe and fair racing, and that would be undermined if protest and appeals committees were permitted to overlook the requirements in *rules* when they decide that the "intent" of the *rule* was satisfied (see rule 63.5).

With a little attention and preparation, each boat can prepare a flag that can be easily displayed (Velcro is wonderful), and find a reasonable and convenient place to store their flag during a race so that members of the crew know where it is and so it can be displayed very quickly after an incident with a minimum of hassle (when all else fails put it in your windsuit pocket or rolled up around

PART 5: PROTESTS, REDRESS, HEARINGS, MISCONDUCT AND APPEALS **285**

your backstay). You may never use it, but if you do and you put it up immediately after an incident, you will not have your *protest* refused for that reason.

As for examples of when it might be reasonable to delay the display of the flag for a brief time, in my opinion it would be reasonable to delay the display of the flag after a big collision until just after you and your crew finish checking to be sure things were OK; or could stop hiking without risk of capsizing, or when setting the spinnaker, when all hands were no longer involved putting it up. However, if after the collision or during the spinnaker set, at least one crew member is not doing anything, it is reasonable to expect that he or she can display the flag. Delaying because the flag is in the ditty bag, which is up in the bow under the anchor, is not reasonable to me. (See Appeals 67, 82 and 124.)

"Can I just fly anything red and call it a protest flag?"

Absolutely not. Case 72 reads, "QUESTION: What is the test of whether an object is a flag within the meaning of rule 61.1(a)? ANSWER: In the context of rule 61.1(a), a flag is used as a signal to communicate the message 'I intend to protest.' Only if the object used as a flag communicates that message, with little or no possibility of causing confusion on the part of those on competing boats, will the object qualify as a flag. A flag must be seen primarily to be a flag." The bottom line is that whatever you display must be RED, and it must be obvious that it's a flag, and not a telltale, baseball-type cap or piece of clothing.

"Does the flag have to be flown on the starboard shroud or anywhere else in particular?"

No. The flag must simply be "conspicuously displayed." There is no requirement in the rule that the flag need be put anywhere in particular. The test of "conspicuous" is whether the flag is initially highly visible to the protested boat. In many cases the starboard side of the boat may be the worst (least conspicuous) place to display it. Notice also, that the flag can be displayed simply by holding it up and waving it at the other boat, which you can do as you head for the location where you will attach it.

Note that "conspicuous" applies not only to the location of the display but to the actual size of the flag. In Appeal 66, the Appeals Committee decided that a 2-inch by 8-inch flag on a 40-foot boat was not of sufficient size or of suitable proportions to be "conspicuously displayed."

Also notice that you must keep your flag displayed until you are no longer *racing*; i.e., until you have *finished* and cleared the finishing line and *marks* or retired. If your flag blows off your shroud while you are still *racing*, **you can't protest**. My advice is to devise a good system and carry a spare. If your incident occurs so close to the finishing line that the first reasonable opportunity to display the flag doesn't occur until after you are no longer *racing*, you still need to display your flag because the incident occurred "in the racing area." Though often not required, it is prudent to ensure that the race committee sees that you have displayed your flag.

"If the race or protest committee is going to protest me, do they have to hail 'Protest' at the time of the incident as well?"

No. If the incident they observe occurs in the racing area, they need to inform you of their intention to protest you after the race and within the time limit for lodging protests, and they need to deliver their written *protest* to the race office within that time limit as well. If the incident does not occur in the racing area, then they need to inform you as soon as reasonably possible, and deliver their *protest* within two hours of learning of the possible *rules* breach (see rules 61.1(b) and 61.3, Protest Time Limit).

RULE 61.2 — PROTEST CONTENTS

A *protest* shall be in writing and identify

(a) the protestor and protestee;

(b) the incident;

(c) where and when the incident occurred;

(d) any *rule* the protestor believes was broken; and

(e) the name of the protestor's representative.

However, if requirement (b) is met, requirement (a) may be met at any time before the hearing, and requirements (d) and (e) may be met before or during the hearing. Requirement (c) may also be met before or during the hearing, provided the protestee is allowed reasonable time to prepare for the hearing.

Rule 61.2 clearly lists the details about the *protest*. Notice that the *protest* must be **in writing**. Also notice that the only detail that cannot be corrected once the time limit for lodging *protests* is past is an omission of a description of the incident itself. Therefore, be sure you clearly identify the incident in your *protest*.

PART 5: PROTESTS, REDRESS, HEARINGS, MISCONDUCT AND APPEALS   287

RULE 61.3 — PROTEST TIME LIMIT

A *protest* by a boat, or by the race committee, technical committee or protest committee about an incident observed in the racing area, shall be delivered to the race office within the protest time limit stated in the sailing instructions. If none is stated, the time limit is two hours after the last boat in the race *finishes*. Other *protests* shall be delivered to the race office no later than two hours after the protestor receives the relevant information. The protest committee shall extend the time if there is good reason to do so.

Notice that the first place to look for the time limit for lodging a *protest* is the sailing instructions. If the sailing instructions are silent, then the default time limit in rule 61.3 is "two hours after the last boat in the race *finishes*." Also notice that the protest committee **must** extend the time limit is there is a good reason to do so. This may be useful to you if you have made every reasonable effort to deliver your *protest* in time but were unable to do so for good reason.

RULE 62 — REDRESS

RULE 62.1

A request for redress or a protest committee's decision to consider redress shall be based on a claim or possibility that a boat's score or place in a race or series has been or may be, through no fault of her own, made significantly worse by

(a) an improper action or omission of the race committee, protest committee, organizing authority or technical committee for the event, but not by a protest committee decision when the boat was a *party* to the hearing;

(b) injury or physical damage because of the action of a boat that was breaking a rule of Part 2 and took an appropriate penalty or was penalized, or of a vessel not *racing* that was required to keep clear or is determined to be at fault under the *IRPCAS* or a government right-of-way rule;

(c) giving help (except to herself or her crew) in compliance with rule 1.1; or

(d) an action of another boat, or a crew member or *support person* of that boat, that resulted in a penalty under rule 2 or a penalty or warning under rule 69.

"Redress" is a form of compensation the protest committee can give boats when they have lost finishing places or time as a result of certain circumstances that were out of their control. Rule 62.1 lists the four specific circumstances under which a boat can request redress. If something else makes a boat's finishing score or place worse, it is tough luck. Three examples of "tough luck" are: (1) when a boat fouls you and the boats get locked together for a time but there is no physical damage or injury, (2) you get fouled and forced over the starting line as a result, and (3) when a boat fails to give you *mark-room* and you are forced to the wrong side of the *mark* in order not to hit them. These unfortunate situations always remind me of the old saying, "he was in the right as he sped along; but he's just as dead as though he were wrong."

Note that in order to be entitled to redress, your score or place in the race or series has to have been, or will possibly be, made significantly worse. In other words, if the sailing instructions specify that marks will be yellow and the race committee uses orange marks instead, this is an "improper action;" but if you sailed the course with no confusion, your finishing score or place wasn't made worse by the "improper action" of the race committee; therefore, you are not entitled to redress.

Finally note that your finishing score or place has to be worsened by one of the four circumstances in rule 62.1 **and** "through no fault of your own." For instance, if you know you are over the starting line early (OCS) but the race committee fails to signal your OCS properly, and you don't come back and *start*, the race committee made an "improper action," but you also contributed to your OCS score because you knew you had not *started* the race and chose to break rule 28.1 (Sailing the Race) (see Cases 31 and 71).

Another example is when the leeward *mark* is drifting downwind, but instead of rounding it and *finishing*, you drop out of the race and request redress. You caused your finishing score to be DNF, so you cannot get redress for the *mark* being out of position.

"OK, so *what do I have to do to request redress?*"

RULE 62.2

A request shall be in writing and identify the reason for making it. If the request is based on an incident in the racing area, it shall be delivered to the race office within the protest time limit or two hours after the incident, whichever is later. Other requests shall be delivered as soon as reasonably possible after learning of the reasons for making the request. The protest committee shall extend the time if there is good reason to do so. No red flag is required.

PART 5: PROTESTS, REDRESS, HEARINGS, MISCONDUCT AND APPEALS **289**

(a) However, on the last scheduled day of racing a request for redress based on a protest committee decision shall be delivered no later than 30 minutes after the decision was posted.

Rule 62.2 says that you have to make a **written** request for redress which clearly identifies the incident you think justifies you receiving redress. You can use the standard hearing request form available at most regattas, which has a box to check indicating you are requesting redress. Keep in mind, if your request is based on a claim that the race committee did something wrong, you are not "protesting" the race committee; you are simply requesting redress based on their action (see Case 44). You do not need to fly a red flag or do anything special on the water to request redress. If the incident happened in the racing area, you need to file your request within the protest time limit or two hours after the incident, whichever is later. For other requests, file them as soon as reasonably possible after learning of the reasons for making the request. (See Case 102 and Appeal 90.)

"Can you walk me through the four circumstances that might entitle me to redress?"

Sure.

- **RULE 62.1(a)**: These are circumstances where a committee does something it is not supposed to do, or fails to do something it is supposed to do. Note that if the sailing instructions say the race committee "will" do something and it fails to, or does something else instead, that is an "improper action or omission" of the race committee. If the protest committee fails to follow the procedures for a hearing in Part 5, Section B of *The Racing Rules of Sailing*, that too is an "improper action." And if the organizing authority for an event for instance supplies the boats, and one of them is defective, that is an "improper action" of the organizing authority. Note that if you are a *party* in a hearing and you do not agree with the protest committee decision (as opposed to its procedures), you cannot request redress. Your only two options are to request that the hearing be reopened (see rule 66, Reopening a Hearing), or appeal (see rule 70.1, Appeals and Requests to a National Authority, and Appendix R, Procedures for Appeals and Requests). (See also Cases 31 and 71.)

- **RULE 62.1(b)**: This is the circumstance where your boat has been physically damaged or someone on your boat has been injured by a boat that was required to *keep clear* of you under Part 2 of the racing rules (When Boats Meet) or a non-racing boat required to keep clear under the government right-of-way rules for the area in which you are sailing.

  Note that this does not apply in the circumstance where a keep-clear boat has made you lose time or places by forcing you off course or forcing you on the wrong side of a *mark* or even capsizing you. This applies only when something on the boat was physically broken ("damaged") as a direct result of a rules breach by keep-clear boat, and that damage directly caused the boat to finish worse than she would have had there been no damage (see Case 110). Note, in order to be entitled to redress under rule 62.1(b), the other boat, if it were also *racing*, must have taken a penalty or have been penalized, which means you should always protest the boat that caused the physical damage or injury.

- **RULE 62.1(c)**: This is the circumstance where you give help to someone in trouble. Remember, Rule 1.1 (Helping Those in Danger) says, *"A boat, competitor or **support person** shall give all possible help to any person or vessel in danger."* When you lose finishing places or time as a result of giving help, you are entitled to compensation ("redress") for that. (See the discussion of rule 1.1 and Case 20.)

- **RULE 62.1(d)**: This is the circumstance where someone has done something bad enough to break rule 2 (Fair Sailing) or receive a warning or penalty under rule 69.2(h) (Misconduct; Action by a Protest Committee) and their action adversely affected you. An example is a boat cuts a *mark* and sits on your wind causing you to lose ten places. You would need to protest them for breaking rule 28.1 (Sailing the Race) and rule 2, claiming it was an intentional infringement. You could suggest that it also warranted a hearing under rule 69 (see rule 60.1(c)), but that would ultimately be up to the protest committee to decide. Assuming the boat was found to have broken rule 2, and/or received a warning or penalty under rule 69.2(h), and assuming the protest committee decided that the boat's action directly caused your score to be significantly worse through no fault of your own, you are entitled to redress. (See Case 34.)

PART 5: PROTESTS, REDRESS, HEARINGS, MISCONDUCT AND APPEALS 291

"Thanks. So when the protest committee decides I am entitled to redress, what do they do?"

Once the protest committee decides that a boat is entitled to redress, they turn to rule 64.3 (Decisions on Redress).

RULE 64.3 — DECISIONS ON REDRESS

When the protest committee decides that a boat is entitled to redress under rule 62, it shall make as fair an arrangement as possible for all boats affected, whether or not they asked for redress. This may be to adjust the scoring (see rule A9 for some examples) or finishing times of boats, to *abandon* the race, to let the results stand or to make some other arrangement. When in doubt about the facts or probable results of any arrangement for the race or series, especially before *abandoning* the race, the protest committee shall take evidence from appropriate sources.

Case 31 says, "When it is decided that a boat is entitled to redress, rule 64.3 requires the protest committee to 'make as fair an arrangement as possible for all boats affected.' This might be to adjust a boat's finishing time, add some number of places to her actual or average finishing place, reinstate her in her finishing place, or to make some other adjustment that conforms to rule 64.3. Clearly, rule 64.3 gives a protest committee tremendous discretion to do whatever it thinks is fairest for all the boats that will be affected by the arrangement the protest committee decides to make, whether or not they asked for redress. The last sentence of rule 64.3 reminds protest committees to take appropriate evidence before making its decision when it has some questions as to the facts or probable results of any arrangement for the race or series. (See Cases 31 and 71.) Rule A9 (Guidance on Redress) gives protest committees some suggestions.

RULE A9 — GUIDANCE ON REDRESS

If the protest committee decides to give redress by adjusting a boat's score for a race, it is advised to consider scoring her

(a) points equal to the average, to the nearest tenth of a point (0.05 to be rounded upward), of her points in all the races in the series except the race in question;

(b) points equal to the average, to the nearest tenth of a point (0.05 to be rounded upward), of her points in all the races before the race in question; or

(c) points based on the position of the boat in the race at the time of the incident that justified redress.

"If a boat is requesting redress, am I entitled to be in that hearing and give evidence?"

If the US Sailing prescriptions to rules 60 (Right to Protest; Right to Request Redress or Rule 69 Action) and rule 63.2 (Time and Place of the Hearing; Time for Parties to Prepare) are in effect (and they are in effect in the U.S. unless the notice of race or sailing instructions specifically say they are not; see rule 88.2, National Prescriptions), then you are allowed to participate in the hearing and the protest committee is required to request redress for you, making you a *party*.

The prescription to rule 63.2 says, "*US Sailing prescribes that when redress has been requested or is to be considered for one or more boats:*

(a) *Any other boat may participate in the hearing.*

(b) *The protest committee shall make a reasonable attempt to notify all boats of the time and place of the hearing and the reason for the request or for considering redress, and boats shall be allowed reasonable time to prepare for the hearing.*

(c) *The protest committee shall request redress for boats*
   (1) *that participate in the hearing, or*
   (2) *that request in writing to do so before the hearing begins,*

making them parties *to the hearing. It need not state a reason for such a request; this changes rule 62.2."*

And the prescription to rule 60.3 says, "*US Sailing prescribes that rule 60.3(b) is changed to: (b) request redress for a boat or call a hearing to consider redress.*"

So when the prescriptions are in effect and the protest committee receives a request for redress, the norm is for it to post a copy of the request on the official notice board with the time and place of the hearing, leaving a reasonable amount of time for sailors to prepare for the hearing or to make a written request to participate if they are unable to be there in person but wish to become a *party* to the hearing. All sailors who participate in the hearing, or make a written request to do so before the hearing begins, must be made *parties* to the hearing by the protest committee, with the full right to give evidence, ask questions, call witnesses and appeal.

The Finishing Line

"There is no finishing line."

— said by many a wise person

Well done for getting across the finishing line by completing this book! The sport provides many combinations and permutations for ways the boats can interact, and in trying to clearly and fairly provide the rights and obligations of each boat in each situation, the rules can appear to be complex when approached in their entirety.

Rules knowledge grows with experience, and is a never-ending journey. The more you race or hear protests or write sailing instructions or attend seminars or teach the rules to others, the deeper your own rules knowledge will get. My advice is to focus in on an aspect of the rules that interests or is important to you at any given time and study it hard. Return to the pertinent sections in this book and re-read them as you may get something additional out of what is written. Be sure to read each referenced Case or Appeal.

In this chapter I have listed additional rules resources to help you continue to grow your rules knowledge and confidence. And there are many more in addition to these. As I have said, becoming clear and confident with the rules will make you a better game player and/or a more effective race official, both of which help make the sport more fun to play and are satisfying personal goals to work towards.

Good luck!
Dave Perry

294

Rules Resources

From the US Sailing store

ussailing.org > Shop > Racing > Racing Rules

- *The Racing Rules of Sailing*
  This is the rule book for sailing and includes the US Sailing prescriptions to the rules.

- *Dave Perry's 100 Best Racing Rules Quizzes*
  This is Dave's other book on the rules. Each page has a quiz which is a protest situation with a set of facts and often a diagram. The readers decide how they would decide the protest, and then Dave supplies the answer. Included is an invaluable paper by Bill Ficker on how to prepare for a protest hearing.

- The US Sailing *Appeals Book*
  This is a compilation of all the US Sailing Appeals Committee's published decisions. An extremely helpful feature of the *Appeals Book* is the Index of Abstracts. Each appeal begins with a short summary of the decision, called an "abstract," and these abstracts are sorted by rule number in the Index, making it easy to find an appeal pertaining to a particular rule.

From the US Sailing website

ussailing.org > Competition > Race Officials

- Hearing request and decision forms
- US Sailing *Judges* and *Race Management Manuals*

From the World Sailing website

sailing.org > Technical > Race Officials

- *Judges Manual*
- *Race Management Manual*
- Question & Answer (Q&A) service

sailing.org > Technical > Documents & Rules

- *The Racing Rules of Sailing*
- *Case Book*
- *Match Racing and Team Racing Call Books*
- *Equipment Rules of Sailing*

Independent Rules Sites

- **Learn the Racing Rules 2024**

  speedandsmarts.com

  Learn The Racing Rules 2024 is a step-by-step interactive online program. Written and narrated by David Dellenbaugh, it is filled with live sailing demos, 3D animations and quizzes to check your understanding.

- **The Racing Rules of Sailing Forum**

  racingrulesofsailing.org

  This is an independent international forum for sailors and race officials to discuss the rules in an informal online setting. The website also has forums and event documents that are helpful to race committee members and judges when running events and protest hearings, etc.

- **UK Sailmakers Racing Rules Quiz**

  uksailmakers.com/rules-quiz

  This is an independent animated Rules Quiz program created and maintained by UK Sailmakers.

- **Play the Rules**

  game.finckh.net/indexe.htm

  This is an independent animated Rules Quiz program, sorted as easy, medium and difficult; and translated into 16 different languages.

Other Rules Resources and Useful Addresses

- **ussailing.org/competition/rules-officiating/appeals**

  For lists of regional and national appeals committees, FAQs about filing an appeal, the *US Sailing Appeals and Requests Information Form*, a link to the World Sailing *Case Book*, and *The Appeals Book for 2021-2024*.

- **ussailing.org/competition/rules-officiating/racing-rules**

  For instructions on downloading US Sailing's mobile rulebook app, changes to the *rules* or US Sailing prescriptions made after 1 January 2021, as well as information on scoring a long series, writing sailing instructions, personal flotation devices, indemnification, experimental rules, how to find (or become) a certified race official, judge, umpire or classifier, and more.

- **shop.ussailing.org**

  For printed editions of *The Racing Rules of Sailing*, rules in-brief cards, race signal flag stickers, as well as books and DVDs on racing tactics, strategies and the *rules*.

- **ussailing.org**

  For more information on one-design and offshore sailing, race management and safety-at-sea seminars, learn-to-sail, adaptive and community sailing programs, and much more.

- **sailing.org**

  For changes to the *rules*, World Sailing Codes regarding eligibility, advertising, anti-doping, categorization and misconduct; World Sailing *Case Book*, *Call Books for Match and Team Racing*, *Equipment Rules of Sailing* and *Offshore Special Regulations*; guidance on discretionary penalties, conflicts of interest, misconduct, Rule 42 (Propulsion), notices of race and sailing instructions, as well as other rules-related documents published by World Sailing.

  The Notice of Race and Sailing Instructions Guides (formerly Appendix K and Appendix L) are available, in various formats, at the World Sailing website at sailing.org/racingrules/documents.

About the Author

DAVE PERRY grew up sailing on Long Island Sound. Learning to sail in Sunfish, Blue Jays and Lightnings from his parents and in the junior program at the Pequot Yacht Club in Southport, Connecticut, he won the Clinton M. Bell Trophy for the best junior record on L.I.S. in 1971. While at Yale (1973–1977) he was captain of the National Championship Team in 1975, and was voted All-American in 1975 and 1977.

Other racing accomplishments include: 1st, 1978 Tasar North Americans; 5th, 1979 Laser Worlds; 1st, 1979 Soling Olympic Pre-Trials (crew); 10th overall, 1981 SORC (crew); 3rd, 1982 Soling Worlds; 1st, 1982, 2006, 2008, 2011 and 2015 U.S. Match Racing Championship (POW); 1st, 1983 Star South American Championship (crew); 1st, 1983 and 1984 Congressional Cup; 2nd, 1984 Soling Olympic Trials; 6th, 1985 Transpac Race (crew); 1st, 1988 and 1992 Knickerbocker Match Race Cup; 1st, 1994, 1999 and 2003 Ideal 18 North American Championship; 1st, 2007 South American Match Racing Championship and 1st, 2010 Detroit Cup (Match Racing).

Dave has been actively working for the sport since 1977. He has led hundreds of US Sailing instructional seminars in over 50 one-design classes; directed U.S. Olympic Yachting Committee Talent Development Clinics; coached the 1981 World Champion U.S. Youth Team; and given seminars in Japan, Australia, Sweden, Argentina, Brazil and Canada. He has been the Youth Representative on the US Sailing Board of Directors and the Chairman of the U.S. Youth Championship Committee, and has served on the following other US Sailing committees: Match Racing, Olympic, Training, Class Racing and O'Day Championship. He is currently a member of the US Sailing Appeals Committee and a US Sailing National Judge.

In 1992 Dave was voted into the *Sailing World* Hall of Fame; in 1994 he received an honorary Doctorate of Education from Piedmont College; in 1995 he became the first recipient of US Sailing's Captain Joe Prosser Award for exceptional contribution to sailing education; in March 2001 Dave received the W. Van Alan Clarke, Jr. Trophy, US Sailing's national award for sportsmanship; and in 2020 Dave received the Nathanael G. Herreshoff Award for outstanding contribution to the sport, and was voted into the National Sailing Hall of Fame.

He was the Director of Athletics at Greens Farms Academy, a K–12 coed independent day school in Westport, Connecticut from 1986–2006; and has served as the Rules Advisor to *Victory Challenge* (the Swedish 2007 America's Cup challenger) and *Artemis Racing* (the Swedish 2013 and 2017 America's Cup challenger), Coach for women's match racing for the 2009–2012 U.S. Sailing Team, and Rules Advisor for the U.S. Olympic Sailing Team in 2008, 2012 and 2021.

Dave has authored two other books on racing: *Dave Perry's 100 Best Racing Rules Quizzes* and *Winning in One-Designs*.

About the Illustrator

BRAD DELLENBAUGH grew up in Fairfield, Connecticut, where he learned to sail at the Pequot Yacht Club and raced Lightnings with Dave Perry. He has been coaching and teaching sailing for over 40 years. Recently retired as the Sailing Director at the New York Yacht Club based in Newport, Rhode Island, Brad previously coached the offshore sailing team at the U.S. Naval Academy in Annapolis from 1992–2005, the intercollegiate team at Brown University from 1980–1990, as well as the U.S. Women's Team from 1984–1987. From 1977–1980 he coached the sailing team at the Hotchkiss School in addition to teaching in the art department, and taught junior sailing from 1973 through 1982 on Long Island Sound. He continues to lecture on racing tactics and the rules, and is an active sailing umpire and soccer referee.

In addition to many national and international regattas serving as an International Judge and Umpire, Brad has been on the America's Cup umpire team in 2002–2003 (Auckland), 2004–2007 (Valencia), 2011–2012 (San Francisco), 2014–2017 (Bermuda), and 2020–2021 (Auckland). He also served as the Rules Advisor to Young America and the U.S. Olympic Sailing Team in 2000.

An avid racer, Brad has been involved in three Olympic campaigns in the Soling class (including one with Dave in 1981–1984), as well as serving as tactician or helmsman in numerous national, continental and world championships in a wide variety of one-designs and offshore boats. He won the 1987 and 1988 US Sailing Team Racing Championship, the 1989 J/24 World Championship, the 1990 and 1991 J/22 World Championships and the 1997 US Sailing Prince of Wales Match Racing Championship.

Brad graduated from Brown University with a major in fine arts and has pursued this interest as a freelance artist, illustrating for a number of sailing magazines and books.

NOTES